Advances in Digital and Cultural Tourism Management

Series Editors

Marinos Ioannides⬮, Cyprus University of Technology, Limassol, Cyprus

Bart Neuts, Department of Earth and Environmental Sciences, Katholieke Universiteit Leuven, Leuven, Belgium

João Martins, CTS-UNINOVA and FCT/UNL, Monte de Caparica, Portugal

This series highlights works dealing with the economic and social impact of cultural tourism in Europe, with a focus on digital and cultural heritage tourism. It targets policymakers, researchers, and industry professionals interested in sustainable development and innovative approaches to cultural tourism. Books cover topics such as Digital/eTourism, Cultural and Heritage Management, and Tourism Technologies. Each book follows a structured editorial process including review by key experts in the related topics, ensuring high quality and relevance. With an emphasis on successful policies, emerging trends, visitor management systems, and the integration of digital technologies, the series aims to enhance understanding and promote smart, sustainable, and inclusive growth in the cultural tourism sector.

Bart Neuts · João Martins · Marinos Ioannides
Editors

Advances in Cultural Tourism Research

Proceedings of the International Conference on Cultural Tourism Advances, June 2023, Belgium

 Springer

Editors
Bart Neuts
Department of Earth and Environmental
Sciences
Katholieke Universiteit Leuven
Leuven, Belgium

João Martins
NOVA School of Science and Technology
UNINOVA-CTS and LASI, NOVA
University Lisbon
Monte de Caparica, Portugal

Marinos Ioannides
UNESCO Chair on Digital Cultural
Heritage at the Cyprus University
of Technology
Limassol, Cyprus

Advances in Digital and Cultural Tourism Management
ISBN 978-3-031-65536-4   ISBN 978-3-031-65537-1   (eBook)
https://doi.org/10.1007/978-3-031-65537-1

This Springer imprint is published by the registered company Springer Nature Switzerland AG
The registered company address is: Gewerbestrasse 11, 6330 Cham, Switzerland

If disposing of this product, please recycle the paper.

Foreword

Anyone who has worked in the field of cultural heritage knows the importance of its preservation. The cultural heritage lover does not need explanations. However, they are confronted sometimes with the need to explain to others why we should preserve our European thousands of years old legacy. Often, the love we feel for this magnificent cultural richness standing on European soil does not seem to be enough to convince some people. When this occurs, we have to turn to too well-known arguments to persuade those who are not at all interested in history and culture: the economy.

Nowadays no one is discussing the economic benefits that culture brings to a given area having a rich cultural heritage. "There we have an argument", think those who love history and heritage for their own sake, and, more important, a valid argument that everybody understands.

Cultural tourism is gaining more and more adepts, this creates markets and economic flows and brings benefits. But we are starting to experience in Europe also the problems of over-dimensioned touristic flows in some areas.

Cultural heritage is fragile. Flows of thousands of tourists, without the necessary protection measures, can kill the hen with the golden eggs. Once heritage is destroyed, there is no way back, the damage is irreversible.

Therefore, it is paramount to carry on multidisciplinary research bringing together specialists from a large variety of fields that analyse the problems from a wide diversity of angles.

This is what the six projects funded by the Horizon Europe programme have done, to bring a constellation of European Researchers to work together, each researcher within the frame of their project, and each project cooperating with the others.

This book is the result of their work, and we hope it will be a landmark in the research on the field of cultural tourism.

Brussels, Belgium

Dr. Rodrigo Martín Galán
Research Programme Officer
Research Executive Agency
European Commission
Unit C.1—Inclusive, Innovative
and Reflective Societies

Disclaimer The opinions expressed in this foreword are strictly those of the author and, as such, they do not reflect the opinion or policies of the European Research Executive Agency.

Preface

This book presents new roads, perspectives, and approaches in cultural tourism, consolidating insights from six European-funded projects and presented during the International Conference on Cultural Tourism Advances, organized in Brussels on 27–28 June 2023. The European Union has long recognized the importance of culture as part of a qualitative and unique tourist experience and as an element to enhance the profile and values of Europe. While exact estimates are difficult to make due to incomplete arrival and motivation-based statistics, it is estimated that approximately 40% of all European tourists base their destination choice on tangible and intangible cultural offerings, ranging from museums, historical cities, and archaeological sites, to music, and gastronomy. Similarly, at local levels, national and regional destination management organizations have typically leveraged local cultures as main attractors for the regional and international market.

Furthermore, cultural tourism is often juxtaposed to less sustainable forms of mass tourism and identified as a potential driver and enabler of sustainable development, supporting regional and macro-regional development strategies and potentially inviting visitors with genuine interests in local values, experiences and products. This leads to significant economic effects and has further strengthened the view of cultural heritage as a strategic resource for its economic impact but also for its role in creating and enhancing social capital and achieving the goals of smart, sustainable and inclusive growth. Notwithstanding the potential beneficial effects of cultural tourism, its development also introduces important challenges to destinations, related to potential issues such as overcrowding—or rather an uneven tourist spread leading to both over and under exploitation—cultural appropriation, gentrification, the loss of authenticity, and an unequal distribution of economic effects, often being more prevalent in urbanized areas.

The goal of the Conference on Cultural Tourism Advances—and thus also of this book—is to further the understanding of the sustainable development potential of cultural tourism by focusing on successful policy interventions and participatory approaches for community-based development, providing assessment frameworks for responsible and human-centred tourism, and introducing new digital and analytical applications to advance cultural tourism management and planning. This book is organized as follows:

Participatory Approaches to Cultural Tourism Management

The first part of the book highlights the importance of an integrated local community and stakeholder involvement as an essential building block for sustainable development through cultural tourism. In the first chapter of this part, Hanna Szemző, Eszter Turai, and Gergö Berta (Chap. Challenges in Developing Sustainable Tourism Locally: Viewpoints from the Ground) discuss the challenges and perspectives of bottom-up driven cultural tourism development in light of communities as multifaceted entities with diverging interests and understandings about local heritage. Elena Bussolati, Serena Cecere, Roberta De Bonis Patrignani, and Matteo Tabasso (Chap. How Cultural Tourism Management Initiatives Come to Light Starting from Local Needs: The Case of the Crespi D'Adda Company Town) focus on the case of Crespi d'Adda company town, and particularly the integration of a bottom-up approach with local stakeholder and resident involvement within the process of defining a UNESCO Management Plan, explaining both the participatory processes themselves as well as the way the actions were identified and customized.

Subsequently, Shabnam Pasandideh, João Martins, Pedro Pereira, Alessandra Gandini, Mikel Zubiaga De La Cal, Tarmo Kalvet, Tatjana Koor, Amaia Sopelana, and Amaia Lopez de Aguileta (Chap. Co-Creation Method for Fostering Cultural Tourism Impact) present a novel method to enhance the impact of cultural tourism through collecting and analysing data from diverse sources, including stakeholders and local communities and recreating a comprehensive decision-making system. Furthering local community involvement strategies, Małgorzata Ćwikła, Cristina Garzillo, Martina Bosone, and Antonia Gravagnuolo (Chap. Stakeholders Engagement Processes for Co-Creation of Strategic Action Plans for Circular and Human–Centred Cultural Tourism in European Heritage Sites) describe co-creative processes conducted with various types of stakeholders in six European regions, with the specific aim to activate local communities to co-create innovative solutions within the framework of a circular economy-oriented approach.

In the final chapter of the first part, Theano S. Terkenli and Vasilki Georgoula (Chap. Cultural Tourism in the Cyclades Before and After the Pandemic: A Stakeholders' Perspective) discuss the effects of the COVID-19 pandemic on cultural tourism in the Cyclades, from the perspective of local tourism stakeholders and with a particular focus on the problems, pitfalls and potential ensuing from the pandemic, moving towards a more resilient, sustainable, and transformative future.

Responsible, Circular, and Human-Centred Regional Development Potential

The second part of this book introduces a number of management frameworks, development indicators, and key factors to support informed and evidence-driven decision-making and planning. Vanessa Glindmeier and Gary Treacy (Chap. A Framework for Responsible Tourism in Scotland's Historic Environment: Experiences from Transforming Tourism at a Film-Induced Heritage Visitor Attraction) provide an overview of the application of the Responsible Tourism Framework of Historic Environment Scotland on the case study of Doune Castle, aiming to put responsible tourism practices at the heart of decision-making, balancing the needs of local communities, visitors, the environment, and the cultural heritage itself.

Zvonimir Kuliš and Blanka Šimundic (Chap. Heritage and Territory: Tangible and Intangible Cultural Resources as Drivers of Regional Development in Croatia) present an analytical spatial autoregressive approach, investigating the relationship between cultural heritage, tourism demand, and regional development in Croatia, revealing that cultural heritage has a significantly positive effect on regional development at NUTS 3 level, both directly and indirectly.

Ludovica La Rocca, Francesca Buglione, Eugenio Muccio, Martina Bosone, Maria Cerreta, Pasquale De Toro, and Antonia Gravagnuolo (Chap. Towards a Circular Cultural Tourism Impact Assessment Framework for Decision Support in Less-Known and Remote Destinations) highlight a newly developed methodological and operational approach, based on a set of impact criteria and indicators and reconsidering the linearity of the Theory of Change, to guide the evaluation and monitoring process of circular and human-centred cultural tourism strategies in less-known and remote cultural tourism destinations in a dynamic and iterative process. Related to this topic, Milada Šťastná and Antonín Vaishar (Chap. Golden Rules for Sustainable Cultural Tourism Development: Findings of the EU SPOT Project) present the findings of 15 case studies aimed at exploring the use of cultural tourism as a vehicle for improving the social and economic fabric of disadvantaged rural areas. Through stakeholder dialogues and statistical data, key factors are described that need to be addressed for the aim to progress sustainable cultural tourism in new locations or to capitalize on existing examples.

New Data Methods and Digital Tools

In the final part of the book, a number of digital tools and analytical approaches are covered to help better understand and manage destinations, visitor flows, motivations, and inform strategic planning. Marinos Ioannides, Orestis Rizopoulos, Drew Baker, Elena Karittevli, Maria Hadjiathanasiou, Panayiota Samara, Ioannis Panayi, Marina Mateou, Iliana Koulafeti, Marios Koundouris, Kyriakos Efstathiou, George Savva, and Elina Argyridou (Chap. The Holistic, Digital Cultural Heritage Documentation of the Fikardou Traditional Village in Cyprus) present the case study of Fikardou village in Cyprus, a UNESCO World Heritage Tentative List monument, particularly focusing on the adoption of digital technology as a force multiplier to achieve the aims for a sustainable destination management strategy. Continuing with the potential of digital applications, Karima Kourtit, Peter Nijkamp, Henk Scholten, and Yneke van Iersel (Chap. Methodology and Application of 3D Visualization in Sustainable Cultural Tourism Planning) introduce the concept of digital twins which provide 3D visualizations of spatial tourist realities, applied to the Parkstad region in Limburg, the Netherlands, as a potential tool for evidence-based planning.

Bart Neuts (Chap. Identifying Cultural Tourists via Computational Text Analysis and Association Rule Mining) presents an analytical approach to assist in identifying cultural tourist motivations through computational text analysis and association rule mining, as an alternative to traditional visitor surveys. The methodology is tested on scraped user-generated content for the city of Ghent, lending additional information on the relative importance of different cultural travel motives.

Anat Tchetchik, Shilo Shiff, Yaron Michael, Michael Sinclair, Irit Cohen-Amit, Irit Shmuel, and Micheal Sofer (Chap. SPOT-IT: An Advanced Tool for Dynamic Cultural Tourism Management and Regional Development) equally focus on the obstacles on achieving reliable information on the diverse nature of cultural tourism, presenting a decision-supporting platform that includes both traditional and novel concepts and components, reflecting contemporary tourism patterns and trends. Finally, João Martins, Pedro Pereira, Shabnam Pasandideh, Kashyap Raiyani, Tarmo Kalvet, Mikel Zubiaga De la cal, and Alessandra Gandini (Chap. Redefining Cultural Tourism Leadership: Innovative Approach and Tool) continue this discussion on innovative approaches to manage cultural heritage through novel tools and data, offering a forward-looking perspective through assessing the impact of strategic decisions.

We wish to express our thanks to all the contributors to this volume.

Leuven, Belgium   Bart Neuts
Monte de Caparica, Portugal   João Martins
Limassol, Cyprus   Marinos Ioannides

Acknowledgements and Disclaimer

This work was partially supported by the European Commission, grant number 870747 IMPACTOUR and by Portuguese national funds through FCT Fundação para a Ciência e a Tecnologia with reference UIDB/00066/2020 and UIDP/00066/2020, the TExTOUR project, which has received funding from the European Union's Horizon 2020 research and innovation programme under grant agreement number 101004687, the SPOT project, which has received funding from the European Union's Horizon 2020 programme for research and innovation under grant agreement number 870644, the INCULTUM project, which has received funding from the European Union's Horizon 2020 programme research and innovation under Grant Agreement number 101004552, the SmartCulTour project, which has received funding from the European Union's Horizon 2020 research and innovation programme under grant agreement number 870708 and the Be.CULTOUR project, which has received funding from the European Union's Horizon 2020 research and innovation programme under grant agreement number 101004627.

However, the content of this publication reflects only the authors' views and the European Commission, the Research Executive Agency in Brussels, the Cyprus University of Technology, Limassol, Cyprus, KU Leuven in Belgium, the UNINOVA Research Institute, Lisbon, Portugal are not liable for any use that may be made of the information contained herein.

Contents

Participatory Approaches to Cultural Tourism Management

Challenges in Developing Sustainable Tourism Locally: Viewpoints from the Ground

Hanna Szemző, Eszter Turai, and Gergő Berta

Abstract Sustainability has become a key concept for tourism development. Understanding and using local resources, developing an area in a way that is in line with the wishes and aspirations of the local community is essential, however, not without complications. Communities themselves are multi-faceted entities, with diverging interests and understandings about local heritage, its value and its possible social/economic role. Relying on the research carried out in the TExTOUR (Social Innovation and Technologies for sustainable growth through participative cultural TOURism) project the paper explores community attitudes towards local heritage and tourism, and creates a more in-depth picture about the challenges and perspectives of bottom-up driven cultural tourism development, as well as its social context. The paper uses the results of the qualitative interviews and focus groups carried out in 8 pilots in the course of 2021, and relies on deliverables produced in the project.

TExTOUR is an EU-funded project operating for 45 months, which co-designs pioneering and sustainable cultural tourism strategies to improve deprived areas in Europe and beyond. The project has received funding from the European Union's Horizon 2020 research and innovation programme under grant agreement No.101004687. The project started in January 2021 and finishes in September, 2024. More details about the project can be found in its website: https://textour-project.eu/

The two deliverables in question are TExTOUR D1.3 "Data collection methodology" and TExTOUR D1.4 "Results from the data collection phase".

1 Introduction

Recent decades have brought about the complete restructuring of the tourism sector worldwide, generating increasing visitor numbers everywhere, and making tourism the main source of income for a rising number of households (UNWTO, 2021). This process has contributed substantially to pushing the issue of sustainable tourism in the centre of attention both in academic research and policy debates, all with the

---

H. Szemző (✉) · E. Turai · G. Berta
Metropolitan Research Institute, Budapest, Hungary
e-mail: szemzo@mri.hu

© The Author(s) 2025

B. Neuts et al. (eds.), *Advances in Cultural Tourism Research*, Advances in Digital and Cultural Tourism Management, https://doi.org/10.1007/978-3-031-65537-1_1

aim to critically analyse and find solutions to the economic, ecological and social challenges and ensuing inequalities created by the rise of the global tourism sector (for a comprehensive summary see Mowforth & Munt, 2016).

Nevertheless, defining sustainable tourism and narrowing down its content has been a long process, partially because the concept of sustainability has become rather elusive. It emerged with a broad ecological focus in the 1980s (Redclift, 2005), and the ensuing crises—including subsequent political and economic changes—have given increasing attention to the concept in various fields, including the areas of heritage management and tourism (Butler, 1999; Loulanski & Loulanski, 2011; Buckley, 2012; Harvey & Perry, 2015). As a consequence, during the last two decades various aspects of sustainability—mostly social, economic and environmental—have been addressed in tourism literature, with a surging push for the inclusion of culture as its fourth aspect to embrace the multifaceted nature of the term (Sabatini, 2019; Ottaviani et al., 2023). Moreover numerous debates took place about the value and the appropriate application of the concept and the necessity to make it even more comprehensive (Mooney et al., 2022; Rastegar et al., 2023).

In parallel, diverse international bodies—like the World Tourism Organisation (WTO), the United Nations Environmental Body (UNEP) or the European Commission—have started to focus on sustainable tourism from a practical point of view. The former two developed guidelines for sustainable tourism in 2005, targeting governments at various levels, and pledging the need for tourism in general to become sustainable, whereby the sustainability would mean minimizing its negative effects and empowering the local communities. As both the WTO and UNEP stress, the development of sustainable tourism entails the careful use of environmental resources, respect of the local culture and traditions and finally the support of economic and business models that benefit the local community. (UNEP and WTO, 2005). Similarly, the European Commission, when reviewing the uses of cultural heritage, has pledged its support for its innovative and sustainable use, highlighting its ability to *"actively engage people,—thereby helping to secure integration, inclusiveness, social cohesion and sound investment, all necessary ingredients of smart, sustainable and inclusive growth."* (European Commission, 2015, p. 9.)

To complement debates and approaches about sustainable tourism various tools to support the planning and management of touristic destinations as well as to measure tourism's local impact were developed. These have contributed to gaining a more comprehensive overview of the effects of tourism, and have been part of an effort to find ways of achieving a more balanced distribution of revenues, of providing techniques for anti-exploitation measures, of supporting eco-friendly solutions and fighting unequal development in the sector (Gössling, Hall, & Scott, 2015; Jauhari, 2021).

Situated in this context, the TExTOUR project specifically focuses on the issues of sustainability and sustainable tourism development in off beat areas that lay in the shadows of more prominent touristic places and are in need of more investment and attention. The project works to establish methods and ways to support the development of the local communities residing there, allowing them to become the primary developers and the beneficiaries of cultural tourism in their areas. To this

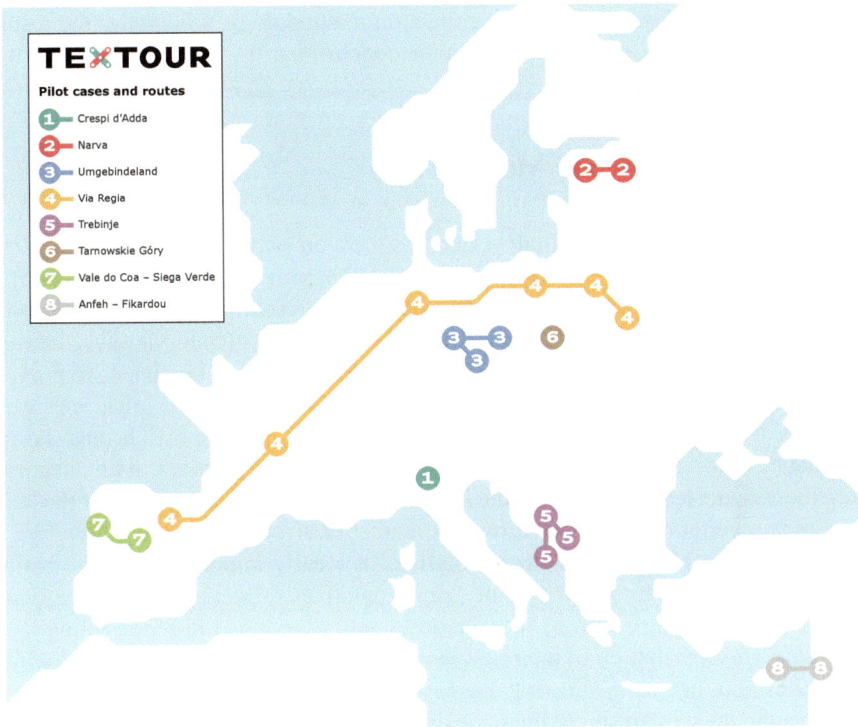

Fig. 1 List of TExTOUR pilots. *Source* TExTOUR website, https://textour-project.eu/

end TExTOUR has worked with 8 pilots[1] (see Fig. 1), collaborating closely with the local communities, local experts and stakeholders and strengthening the local tourism ecosystem. This focus on local empowerment is in line with the policy suggestions of the UNEP and WTO (2005), who foresee the development of sustainable tourism primarily a local task, where national policies only provide the supporting framework.

The current paper focuses on these TExTOUR pilots, and examines community attitudes towards local heritage and tourism development in them, creating a more in-depth picture about the challenges and perspectives of bottom-up driven sustainable tourism development. The point of departure is embedded in the conviction that identity and community building are hard to define and difficult processes, especially in areas undergoing major transitions. Issues like how heritage is perceived and dealt, the role it plays in the life of the communities are highly volatile and strongly interlinked with socio-economic changes (Sadowy & Szemző, 2023). The paper relies on data collected by semi-structured interviews and focus groups in the TExTOUR project, enabling a better understanding of this multi-dimensional phenomena. The

---

[1] The pilots sites are Crespi d'Adda (Italy), Narva (Estonia), Umgebindeland (Germany), Via Regia (the European route's Ukraine section), Trebinje (Bosnia), Tarnowskie Góry (Poland), Vale do Côa (Portugal) and the double sites of Anfeh (Lebanon) and Fikardou (Cyprus).

following section describes the data collection methodology, whereafter the results are explained. The paper then ends with the conclusions.

2 Data Collection and Methodology

The data collection was qualitative and it relied on expert interviews and focus groups. Expert interviews were semi-structured, that provided a base for an in-depth analysis focusing on the unique experiences and perspectives of a single respondent. They also allowed the comparison between different interviewees. In each pilot site four interviews were conducted, largely in the native languages to provide better accessibility to information and evade language barriers. The interviews were recorded, transcribed and then translated into English, reating a rich material for the analysis. To choose the appropriate experts to be interviewed, five categories were identified: representatives of the local municipality, representatives of the local tourism bureau/tourist info centre, owners/employees from local SMEs interested in (cultural/sustainable) tourism, representatives of locally important cultural institution (e.g. museum, library) and finally, representatives of local NGOs active in the field of (cultural) tourism (e.g. heritage preservation or active in representing local interests). The distribution of interviewees among the categories was flexible, which was a conscious decision, allowing the pilots to choose the interviewees according to their specific local interests. At the same time, it was clearly communicated that more categories should be chosen for each pilot to assure the richness of perspectives.

The expert interviews were divided into four main sections: the first enquired after how the potential for sustainable tourism development was viewed, the second focused on the challenges and barriers associated with it, the third zoomed in on the attitudes and opinions about local culture and heritage, and finally, the last one asked about their attitudes and opinions towards Europe and Europeanization. At the end interviewees also had the chance to bring up any other related topics that they felt were important to the pilots.

Unlike the expert interviews, the focus group discussions were targeting local residents. Generally, the focus group technique is an effective tool to discover the scale of opinions and attitudes of a certain target group of people about a specific topic (Vicsek, 2006). In comparison with other qualitative research tools, this method helps to uncover hidden agendas through group dynamics. Interaction between participants may bring to light aspects that would likely remain hidden in a one-to-one situation (Hennink & Leavy, 2015). As a result of the group environment, people tend to be more motivated to elaborate and support their opinion, because they may be confronted by other participants, while during individual interviews the interviewer usually takes a neutral position (Vicsek, 2006). Furthermore, the group dynamic often reveals "collective narratives" of a certain topic, producing data that would not be available during one-on-one situations. On the other hand, some opinions may be distorted or remain hidden as a result of conformity, peer pressure or other group dynamics. Some of these tendencies can be managed or counterbalanced by careful moderation.

Focus group discussions were organized in each pilot involving 8–12 local community members. Still strongly affected by the COVID-19 pandemic, half of the focus group events were held online. Participants were rather diverse, they were chosen from groups that were important from the pilots' perspective. Among others, the panel of invited participants of Crespi d'Adda was composed of people linked to the site and have some knowledge about it. The twelve participants of Narva came from tourism, culture, and sport sectors. In the case of Umgebindeland, all the respondents were residents of the Upper Lusatia region, most of them from the German part, however, representatives from Poland were also present. The respondents of Via Regia all represented non-governmental organizations of the Rivne region, but with diverse backgrounds. The group in Trebinje consisted of young people active in the tourism, cultural and civic sectors. This was in line with their chosen topic about the involvement of young people in recent individual and group initiatives. The background of the participants at Tarnowski Góry was also diverse but everyone is connected to the region, some of them are teachers and students. Target group of Vale de Côa consisted secondary school students from a certain institution related to the region. Through this the data shows an insight to the approach of young people to cultural heritage and tourism. Finally, the focus group of Anfeh involved 3 restaurant owners and 3 guesthouse owners which resulted in a well-balanced discussion. Similarly, residents actively involved in the local community council were present in Fikardou.

Topics to be raised were chosen to deepen and complement the information by then already obtained through the expert interviews, supporting a deeper understanding of the sites in the analysis. All the groups discussed the issues of identity and local culture, which provided particular information from the sites and participants' own relation to the historical sites and culturally significant places of their settlement. Barriers and development trajectories also appeared in most focus group discussions, and often developed into a brainstorming about the future of the region. Finally, the topic of Europeanization and community's relation to European identity was also debated everywhere.

3   Results and Analysis

The mix of institutional as well as occupational backgrounds of the respondents and participants resulted that the interviews and focus groups reflected knowledge from different official levels and fields of local tourism development and heritage protection. The information obtained was multi-layered and pointed to many different directions. This is beneficial as it reflects the complex reality of the local social fabric around the questions of sustainable tourism.

In the following, the results are analysed according to three main topics, all considered necessary for sustainable tourism development. The first topic is 'heritage and identity', which is viewed essential for building a common local understanding of cultural tourism development. The second topic, 'barriers to development' helps to assess the main difficulties as seen by the most important actors, local communities and experts. Finally, 'sustainability and Europeanisation' were looked at, in an attempt to try to gauge if at all the concept of sustainability was known and supported locally, and in what ways has it considered to be connected to the presence of European values or the European Union itself.

3.1 Heritage and Identity

It is generally assumed that heritage and the relationship to heritage is a significant part of local identities, whereby official definitions of heritage often neglect what is considered important by residents (Harrison, 2010; Oevermann & Szemző, 2023). This premise has been partially reflected by the collected data as well, which clearly showed that heritage means very different things for the various participants, especially what regards the view of experts and residents. Whereas the formers focused more on established sites, locals tended to name less institutionalised sites and intangible heritage as well, like gastronomic traditions.

We were also curious if among interviewed experts a tangible consensus could be detected about what can be regarded as heritage in a given location. So for the sake of analysis we looked at how different heritage types were viewed[2] by them, and based on the extent experts discussed the different heritage types, different scores were given for every type in each territory: thus a heritage type received 4 if all interviewees mentioned it, and 1 if only one of them. The Table 1 below summarises the results of this endeavour.

It shows that even experts differed among themselves about what were the most important heritage sites/attractions of a pilot. In general, it could be observed that much depended on the existence of an already dominant narrative which could "steer" the experts in one direction in their assessment of local heritage values. Thus, for experts in pilots with a dominant landmark, site, or even a tradition it was easier to identify local heritage and find a focus of their heritage related tourism activities. This was very typical for the group of pilots with industrial heritage (like Crespi d'Adda in Italy, Narva, Estonia and Tarnowski Góry in Poland). For experts in most of the other pilots it was either harder to highlight one dominant site, or besides the dominant site the other existing heritage locations/traditions. This divergence also underlines the lack of an overwhelming narrative about a pilot's heritage. But it can also be explained by the fact that interviewees occupy very different positions in the cultural tourism industry, thus have a very different view point about it.

Moreover, it was striking how little was known among experts about the ways the local community uses the heritage sites. Most expert interviews did not mention

---

[2] For details about the heritage types see the differentiation on the TExTOUR website at https://textour-project.eu/heritage-types/.

Table 1 Overview of heritage type assessment by the experts

Pilots/heritage types:	Historical	Archaeological	Natural and geological	Industrial	Gastronomical	Dark	Religious
01. Crespi d'Adda	4	-	4	3	-	-	-
02. Narva	4	-	-	4	-	-	-
03. Umgebindeland	4	-	4	-	-	-	-
04. Via Regia	4	1	3	-	1	-	-
05. Trebinje	4	4	1	-	4	-	1
06. Tarnowskie Góry	3	-	1	3	-	-	1
07. Vale do Côa—Siega Verde	3	4	4	-	2	-	-
08 Anfeh	2	2	4	-	2	-	-
08 Fikardou	2	2	4	-	2	-	2

Source TExTOUR D1.4, "Results from the data collection phase"

this topic at all. The reason behind is hard to assess: it could be connected to the professional attitude of the respondents, but also to the ways the interview questions were asked. However, it also highlights a certain distance of the local population from the interviewed experts themselves. Generally, the role of local community was reflected upon from a contradictory perspective in the interviews. On the one hand several interview partners mentioned such phenomena as the *"spirit of the city is the openness of people"* (Trebinje—representative of a cultural institution) or *"the spirit of welcoming and hospitality"* (Anfeh—local SME representative). These statements always referred to the local community's relation to tourists who are visiting the area. However, many respondents also claimed that the local community was not involved enough cultural tourism locally, and the decision-making around it, although its involvement would be considered desirable.

> Local people don't go to these events and these people (tourists) don't go to the local events. (Narva—cultural institution representative)

In addition, intangible heritage—which is mostly related to the local community's activities—is surprisingly lacking from the interviews. Most people asked focused on tangible heritage and cultural products, while intangible heritage remained hidden. One exception was Vale do Côa in Portugal, where the case of old people sitting outside their houses and telling stories was mentioned:

> (…) can't even realize how much value there can be, if we get that gentleman sitting on the doorstep, in a village, and listen to his stories. Tourists love it. (Vale do Côa—local SME representative)

Finally, it was striking, that the role of natural environment in tourism was a frequently discussed topic, even without specific questions addressing it. Water seems to be particularly cherished by experts, and not surprisingly this happens especially in pilots with rivers and waterfront sites.

Somewhat different is the picture if we look at the results of the focus group discussions. Here the topic of local identity was discussed in more detail than in the expert interviews. Data was gained on the diversity of traditions and the forces that unite these communities. Besides, the involvement of the local population came up as a topic more often during the focus group discussions than in the interviews, and it revealed how the local community uses the certain heritages of the pilot areas. Here, a new pattern emerged, indicating that the local community has a strong connection to the heritages sites around them:

Thus, in Tarnowski Góry in Poland, where the silver mine is designated as the main attraction, locals not only want to show the site to tourists, but they also visit it themselves. The mine is a very attractive place for families with children, who take their children to the mine at least once. In a similar vein, the topic of gastronomy got a stronger focus as in the expert interviews. Participants seem to have deeper knowledge about gastronomic possibilities and they consider it more relevant than experts in tourism development. It was especially revealing in the case of Rivne in Ukraine, Trebinje in Bosnia, Anfeh in Lebanon and Fikardou in Cyprus, where gastronomy turned out to be markedly important. The problem of seasonality is also articulated in a more pronounced way (especially in the cases of Narva and Anfeh) than it emerged from the expert interviews. Finally, participants of the focus groups put less emphasis on natural heritage and the topic of nature around their settlements, while during the expert interviews this was a widely discussed issue.

Surprisingly the topic of UNESCO World Heritage status emerged as an important theme in the case of several pilots, including Crespi, Tarnowski Góry and Vale de Côa. While traces of this was also apparent in the expert interviews; however, the data of the focus group contextualized this matter properly. The UNESCO World Heritage status is clearly part of local identity as it was observed in the case of Crespi d'Adda and Tarnowski Góry, where residents spoke with special pride about it. In Vale de Côa, the UNESCO World Heritage status plays a much less strong role in the local identity, which may be connected to the way the status was gained, through a top-down process.

Finally, it is important to highlight that participants in almost every focus group emphasized the need to involve the local community to a higher degree. They stressed that it would be good to organize similar events in the future. They also agreed that the ideas of the local community cannot be left out when it comes to cultural tourism development. Conversely, the involvement of local community can support the changes. A vivid example of this with the words of one of the participants:

> If you do not burn for a cause yourself, you cannot light a fire in others. (Umgebindeland, focus group participant)

3.2 Barriers to Development

To gauge better how interviewees and focus group participants conceptualise barriers and potentials for sustainable tourism development, the pilots were first classified according to their size (see Table 2). This was done out of the conviction that the size of a settlement profoundly influences both the type of problems (barriers) faced and its potentials for development. Based on this, five pilots were categorised as 'small towns or villages', whereas the remaining four were considered to be situated in 'urban areas'. Despite being one pilot, Anfeh and Fikardou were treated here separately due to their physical distance and the fact that they both conducted individual interviews.

Table 2 Population numbers at the pilot sites

Small town or village	Population	Urban area	Population
Crespi d'Adda	~1000	Narva	~53.000
Cunewalde (Umgebindeland)	~5000	Rivne (Via Regia)	~240.000
Vale do Côa—Siega Verde	~6000	Trebinje	~28.000
Anfeh	~7000	Tarnowskie Gory	~61.000
Fikardou	~15		

Source TExTOUR D1.4, "Results from the data collection phase"

The size of a settlement seems to matter most regarding transportation, which was mentioned as a barrier in pilots which are connected to a village or rural areas. A case in point is Crespi d'Adda, which is a small town in the Lombardy region (Italy). Despite being located between Milan and Bergamo, it is challenging to get there:

> Surely, a first problem is that of connections. Crespi d'adda is a place that is not served by public transport (…) (Local NGO representative)

However, the lack of parking spaces around attraction was mentioned more unequivocally as a barrier, both for small towns and urban areas.

The most frequently mentioned barrier to cultural tourism development seems to be the short stay of visitors. This topic arose regardless of pilot size in every interview in some form. Understandably, it is essential for tourist-oriented services to keep the tourists in their region as long as possible, as this generates revenue for accommodation and service providers like. In parallel, the visitors, who spend more time in a place are also able to engage in less well-known cultural activities and visit lesser-known landmarks. Interviewees referred to this phenomenon as 'long-term tourism', 'overnight tourism' or 'long-stay tourism' which is usually mentioned among the goals to achieve. It is noticeable however, that the wish for 'long-term tourism' is often connected with concepts such as the beauty of rural life, as if that provided a special reason for lengthier stays.

The issue of location was also addressed in some cases, usually not only referring to infrastructural barriers, but also to the lack of promotion and marketing. The pilots, who put most emphasis on it—Crespi d'Adda, Umgebindeland, Rivne, and Tarnowski Góry—are those in remote locations, with a tangible difficulty to be reached.

What regards the lack of sufficient funding and the necessity of a unified communication and marketing strategy, it was underscored by the respondents the most. In all cases, clear expectations have been formulated towards the public decision-makers in the focus group discussions and expert interviews alike. According to the unanimous opinion of most actors, many marketing and promotion issues cannot be solved in a decentralized way or by private actors, but requires a higher-level response, either from the city municipality, or from an even higher, regional or national level. The expert interviewees saw great potential in coordinated marketing and strategic planning, which would bring the desired numbers and types of tourists to their sites.

Lack of accessibility as a barrier is closely related to the presence of isolation without exception. Attracting tourists more successfully can add a lot to the development of these settlements, however there is the parallel risk that they will lose out on the local cultural values that give the character of these places. Often this danger is articulated by the locals although the development of tourism and cultural tourism is a clear goal everywhere. This contradiction is mostly apparent for pilots in Crespi d'Adda, Umgebindeland, Trebinje, Vale de Côa, Anfeh and Fikardou where importance of isolation and the beauty of the simple, rural life was a core part of the local identity, yet it very much contradicts the much desired touristic development.

Natural heritage and the nature around the pilot areas received special attention during the focus group discussions. Although many of the experts included this aspect where it had relevance, a more accurate picture emerges with the involvement of focus group participants. In the case of Crespi d'Adda, Narva, and Vale de Côa the role of the local river emerged as a major factor. Participants articulated that developing the connection to the river would have a positive effect on tourism and the life of the local community as well.

3.3 Sustainability and Europeanisation

What regards the topics of sustainability and Europeanisation, these are discussed here together since many respondents, quite surprisingly, connected them. The original aim of the research was to understand how local residents and stakeholders understood these concepts, so separate questions were devised to detect their attitudes. Nevertheless, there was relatively little response for both topics.

In general experts mostly understood the question of sustainability as an ecological issue rather than an economic or a social one, showing that just as in academic debates, the complex meaning of sustainability proliferates slowly other realms as well. At the same time, as respondents realised that the benefits of cultural tourism, the protection of local lifestyles and the environment was present in the term *sustainable tourism*, they started to resonate better with the question and expressed more detailed opinions about the topic. In some cases, sustainable tourism was contrasted with mass tourism. Whereas the first appeared as a desirable concept all the time, the second was something to avoid. It should be noted however that *over-touristification* is not threatening any of the pilot sites currently, rather there are all interested in increasing their annual number of visitors. As the discussions unfolded, most of the interviewees referred to sustainability as a balance between different aspects:

(...) we must always adhere to environmental standards and take care of both nature and the local population. (Trebinje—tourism bureau representative)

Sustainability is a balance between revenue and responsible impact on the environment. (Via Regia—local NGO representative)

Importantly, the concept of long-term sustainability was also connected to increasing Europeanisation, which was viewed as a key to sustainability. This happened despite the lack of clarity surrounding the term Europeanisation, which was apparent in the interviews and focus groups alike. This vagueness is understandable, as the multitude of meanings associated with the term have been subject to academic debates and papers for a long time. Propelled by research in economics and political science, Europeanisation has been a debated term since the 1970s (Buller & Andrew, 2002; Olsen, 2022; Wach, 2015), but the subsequent accessions waves have only fueled this debate with the focus of the research increasingly narrowing down on the impact of EU membership on member states, the effects of integration and the possible country differences (Exadactylos et al., 2020).

Among the interviewed experts and focus group members many equated Europeanisation with the EU, while others associated the European values in general with it. Overall, two groups of pilots could be distinguished: those within the borders of the EU (Crespi d'Adda, Narva, Umgebindeland, Tarnowskie Góry, Vale do Côa—Siega Verde) and those outside (Via Regia, Trebinje, Anfeh & Fikardou). This distinction framed considerably the responses. The former pilots considered Europeanisation an important factor regarding tourism development and mostly mentioned the possibility of free border crossings and the funding they receive for tourism development. Expert interviews showed that they were very much aware of the possibilities provided by the EU to support tourism development, and some pilots have already applied to funding successfully. This was of course not the case for the group of pilots outside of the EU.

Locals' attitudes towards the EU were somewhat ambiguous, and they tend to see the European Union a remote entity which is not necessarily accessible or easy to relate to. Nonetheless, their attitude towards the EU is mostly positive. Open borders and international cooperation are recognized as having a key role, as the case in Umgebindeland shows:

> The enlargement of the EU has made life on both sides of the border even more common. What is an experience for guests and tourists, i.e. travelling through three countries within a very short time, is normal for the inhabitants and is part of everyday life. (Umgebindeland-tourism bureau representative)
>
> (...) the international character testifies to the diversity of Upper Lusatia, here Europe and internationality is lived every day. (Umgebindeland—focus Group Participant)

4   Conclusions

Sustainability has become the key concept in tourism development. It supports the use of local resources, the development of heritage sites and landscapes in a way that is in line with the wishes and aspirations of the local community. Related to this process in tourism, new approaches have also spread in heritage management that require a deeper understanding of communities and their better, and more meaningful involvement (Oeverman et al., 2023; Patti & Polyák, 2018). All this development presupposes a different dynamic between various stakeholders, where community members are entrusted with heritage protection in a collaborative way, caring for the sites in questions (Veldpaus & Szemző, 2021).

Thus, defining and understanding communities has become a crucial step in tourism development. Whereas the first activity was not in the focus of the current research—for the sake of simplicity it had assumed that local residents, NGOs and SMEs were part of the local community from the start—the second issue was in the centre of its attention. While the results are no way representative, they clearly show that what communities want is often hard to understand and contradictory. This is partially because communities themselves are multi-faceted entities, with diverging interests and understandings about local heritage, its value and its possible social/economic role. But there is also an expert-community divide, creating a schism between these two essential partners, which is undeniably a challenge to be faced.

There are differences between how certain topics, important from the point of view of sustainability are approached by different communities. While the current research could not find general explanatory variables that explain these differences, it seems that the size of a site as well as its geographical position can influence substantially how locals and experts think about tourism development and its potential for the locality. This seems to be underlined by the fact that being close to national borders—like in Narva, Umgebindeland, and Trebinje—seems to explain the positive attitudes towards Europeanisation, and through this gives a different trajectory to tourism development and local identity. Geographical position was also seen important when pilots assessed their potentials and barriers, which were simultaneously connected to the issue of proximity to their given borders or to big cities.

The data collection from the TExTOUR sites also demonstrated, that the existence of an authorized heritage discourse (Smith, 2006) influences strongly the local processes. This creates an advantage for areas with clearly defined heritage sites, providing them with ready answers about local heritage value. And those sites without an acknowledged heritage have more struggles reaching a common understanding about what constitutes their local heritage. Importantly, expert interviews and focus groups both mentioned a diverse list of sites and artefacts, including historical monuments, natural and geographical sites (both protected and not), churches, castles and some local particularities, this lack of consensus between various stakeholders can become a difficulty when developing a tourism strategy.

It seems that despite the obvious requirement about the increasing role of communities for a sustainable development, local experts and local residents approached this topic very differently. While the importance of volunteer work and participation of the community was highly valued in many focus group discussions, even understanding this as something that allows building a "cultural bridge" and connecting countries and people, expert interviews showed significantly less enthusiasm about community involvement. The reason for this was beyond the scope of this research, however one likely explanation is that in reality, the community-driven touristic development is in its initial stages in most of the TExTOUR pilots, thus all actors still need to learn a lot about the nuts and bolts of this difficult cooperation.

Finally, sustainability understood in an environmental sense seems to be a very important topic of development for experts and communities alike. The importance of isolation and the beauty of the simple, rural life are both topics that emerged over and over in the material about local identity. While attracting tourists more successfully can add a lot to the development of these settlements, there is an every growing risk—acknowledged by some locals—that as a result they will lose out on the local cultural values that give character to these places. This contradiction is exemplary, as it showcases the utmost dilemma of sustainable development strategies: finding a balance between its different priorities.

References

Primary sources

Pilot interview transcripts- 4 per each pilot site.
Focus group transcripts—1 per each pilot site.

Secondary sources

Buckley, R. (2012). Sustainable tourism: Research and reality. *Annals of Tourism Research, 39*, 528–546.
Buller, J., & Gamble, A. (2002). Conceptualising europeanisation. *Public Policy and Administration, 17*(2), 4–24. https://doi.org/10.1177/095207670201700202
Butler, Richard W. (1999). Sustainable tourism: A state-of-the-art review. Tourism Geographies, 1: 7–25. Gössling, Stefan, Colin Michael Hall, in Daniel Scott, ur. 2015. The Routledge handbook of tourism and sustainability. London ; New York: Routledge.
European Commission. (2015). Getting cultural heritage to work for Europe: Report of the horizon 2020 expert group on cultural heritage. European Union: Luxembourg.
Exadaktylos, T., Graziano, P., & Vink, M. P. (2020). Europeanization: Concept, theory, and methods. In S. Bulmer & C. Lesquene (Eds.), *The Member States of the European Union* (pp. 47–71). Oxford University Press, Third Edition.
Harrison, R. (2010). *Understanding the politics of heritage.* Manchester University Press.
Harvey, D., & Perry, J. (2015). Heritage and climate change: the future is not the past. In D. Harvey & J. Perry (Eds.), *The future of heritage as climates change: Loss, adaptation and creativity* (pp. 3–21). Routledge.
Hennink, Monique M., & Patricia Leavy. (2015). Focus group discussions. Understanding Qualitative Research. Oxford: Oxford University Press. https://doi.org/10.1093/ACPROF:OSOBL/9780199856169.001.0001.
Jauhari, Vinnie. (2021). Managing sustainability in the hospitality and tourism industry: Paradigms and directions for the future.
Mooney, S., Robinson, R., Solnet, D., & Baum, T. (2022). Rethinking tourism's definition, scope and future of sustainable work and employment. *Journal of Sustainable Tourism., 30*(12), 2707–2725. https://doi.org/10.1080/09669582.2022.2078338
Mowforth, Martin and Ian Munt. (2016). Tourism and sustainability. Fourth edition. Routledge.
Oevermann, Heike, & Hanna Szemző. (2023). What is open heritage? In Open Heritage: Community-Driven Adaptive Reuse in Europe: Best Practice. Eds. Oevermann, Heike, Levente Polyák, Hanna Szemző and Harald A. Mieg. Berlin, Boston: Birkhäuser Verlag, pp. 158–169.
Oevermann, H., Polyák, L., Szemző, H., & Mieg, H. A. (2023). *Open heritage: Community-driven adaptive reuse in Europe: Best practice.* Birkhäuser Verlag. https://doi.org/10.1515/9783035626827
Olsen, J. (2002). The many faces of Europeanization. *Journal of Common Market Studies, 40*(5), 921–952.
Patti, D., & Polyák, L. (2017). *Funding the cooperative city.* Cooperative City Books.
Rastegar, R., Higgins-Desbiolles, F., & Ruhanen, L. (2023). Tourism, global crises and justice: Rethinking, redefining and reorienting tourism futures. *Journal of Sustainable Tourism, 31*(12), 2613–2627. https://doi.org/10.1080/09669582.2023.2219037
Redclift, M. R. (2005). Sustainable development (1987–2005): An oxymoron comes of age. *Sustainable Development, 13*, 212–227.

Sabatini, Francesca. (2019). Culture as fourth pillar of sustainable development: Perspectives for integration, paradigms of action. *European Journal of Sustainable Development, 8*(3), 31–40. https://doi.org/10.14207/ejsd.2019.v8n3p31.

Sadowy, K., & Szemző, H. (2023). Aesthetics, gentrification and new identities: The comparison of adaptive reuse practices in contemporary Budapest and Warsaw. *Journal of Cultural Heritage Management and Sustainable Development.* https://doi.org/10.1108/JCHMSD-09-2022-0172

Smith, L. (2006). *Uses of Heritage.* Routledge.

TExTOUR Deliverable 1.3. (2021). Data collection methodology.

TExTOUR Deliverable 1.4. (2022). Results from the data collection phase.

UNEP and UNWTO. (2005). Making tourism more sustainable: A guide for policy makers, pp. 11–12.

UNWTO. (2021). Yearbook of tourism statistics, data 2015—2019, 2021 Edition. World Tourism Organization (UNWTO). https://doi.org/10.18111/9789284422487.

Veldpaus, Loes, & Hanna Szemző. (2021). Heritage as a matter of care, and conservation as caring for the matter. In Care and the City, Encounters with Urban Studies. Ed. Angelika Gabauer, Sabine Knierbein, Nir Cohen, Henrik Lebuhn, Kim Trogal, Tihomir Viderman and Tigran Haas. Routledge, pp. 194–203. https://doi.org/10.4324/9781003031536.

Vicsek, Lilla. (2006). Fókuszcsoport [Focus Group]. Budapest: Osiris.

Wach, Krysztof. (2015). Conceptualizing Europeanization: Theoretical approaches and research designs. In Europeanization Processes from the Mesoeconomic Perspective: Industries and Policies. Eds. Piotr Stanek and Krysztof Wach. Kraków: Cracow University of Economics, pp. 11–23.

How Cultural Tourism Management Initiatives Come to Light Starting from Local Needs: The Case of the Crespi D'Adda Company Town

Elena Bussolati, Serena Cecere, Roberta De Bonis Patrignani, and Matteo Tabasso

Abstract The article illustrates the interactions and connections between the activities performed within the Horizon2020 project TExTOUR—Social Innovation and Technologies for sustainable growth though participative cultural TOURism—by the Italian partners on the Pilot site of Crespi d'Adda (UNESCO WHS) and the process for the definition of the UNESCO Management Plan for the same site. The timing of the two initiatives allowed to have a continuous exchange of information and, besides the useful integration between the two processes, the main result was that the actions identified within the TExTOUR project, through a bottom-up approach, were included in the Management Plan as a contribution from the European Project. The Management Plan is aimed at defining coordinated activities for the preservation and conservation of the cultural site and the promotion of cultural values. It includes the strategy design and the definition of specific initiatives through the involvement of local stakeholders and residents. Some of the actions that emerged in the TExTOUR project working group, also attended by some of the stakeholders of the Crespi d'Adda site, were included among the actions envisaged by the new UNESCO Management Plan. The paper explains both the participatory processes and the way the actions were identified and customized.

Keywords Cultural tourism · Participatory process · Cultural heritage · Industrial heritage · Sustainable growth · Development strategies

E. Bussolati
Unioncamere Lombardia, Via Ercole Oldofredi, 23, 20124 Milano, Italy

S. Cecere · R. De Bonis Patrignani · M. Tabasso (✉)
Fondazione LINKS, Via Pier Carlo Boggio 61, 10138 Torino, Italy
e-mail: matteo.tabasso@linksfoundation.com

© The Author(s) 2025
B. Neuts et al. (eds.), *Advances in Cultural Tourism Research*, Advances in Digital and Cultural Tourism Management, https://doi.org/10.1007/978-3-031-65537-1_2

1   Introduction

Cultural Tourism (CT) plays a crucial role in today's economy. In 2018 it represented 37% of the total tourism sector, with an annual growth of approximately 15%. With the COVID-19 pandemic, however, the tourism sector has been seriously hit. The OECD estimates that international tourism fell by around 80% in 2020. Many countries are trying to build a more resilient tourism economy, promoting digital transition and rethinking a more sustainable tourism system.

Against this backdrop, cultural tourism can be redesigned by regions and sites that offer a high cultural, social and environmental potential.

To face those challenges, in January 2021, 18 transnational partners, representing the quintuple social innovation helix: knowledge, business, society, government and entrepreneurs kicked off the Horizon 2020 "TExTOUR" Project.

TExTOUR (Social Innovation and TEchnologies for sustainable growth through participative cultural TOURism) aims at designing new strategies for improving the socio-economic development of less known areas, but with a high cultural value. The project co-designs, validates and upscales cultural tourism policies and sustainable strategies. To do this, it works with eight Cultural Tourism Pilot projects located in different EU and non-EU areas and involving various societal players and stakeholders with a relevant role in the Cultural Tourism sector.

2   Theoretical Background

Tourism industry may have diversified effects, both positive and negative, on the people living in touristic areas. (Angelini, 2020). In fact, it is often seen as a generator of the necessary resources to preserve and enhance cultural heritage (Jamhawi & Hajahjah, 2017), thus leading to greater economic development, increase in jobs and services.

According to OECD (2021), culture, and cultural heritage in particular, can play an important role in ensuring inclusive and cohesive societies. Furthermore, culture strengthens local identities and creates a sense of belonging while the promotion of cultural participation and the diversity of the cultural offer can help mitigate factors leading to social and economic marginalization.

On the other hand, negative impacts of tourism can be represented by environmental pollution, overcrowded spaces, loss of cultural identity, speculation on the availability of resources while the positive aspects can be economic benefits and better opportunities for local communities, higher circulation of ideas, more attention on the maintenance of the territory (Solima, 2023).

A possible way to reduce the negative impacts for the local communities is the promotion of cultural tourism based on the valorization of Cultural heritage, a concept associated to the idea of "legacy of physical or intangible elements inherited from past generations, maintained in the present and bestowed for future generations" (UNESCO).

In fact, the concept of cultural tourism is strictly linked to the geographical context, and a territory with a strong cultural identity can be defined as a cultural district that means a geographical area characterized by the ability to create synergies between local stakeholders (both businesses and individuals) (Angelini, 2020).

Furthermore, to reduce negative impacts and meet the needs of local communities it is also very important to develop alternative methods and tools aimed at making the processes of collaboration and involvement more inclusive to ensure the development of a more sustainable tourism.

To this aim, the subjects involved for various reasons, have to be encouraged to participate in the development process of sustainable tourism understood as a sharing space in which the outcomes are not predefined. Thus, co-design related to cultural tourism development can represent an opportunity to bring out new actions and practices from positioning generated within sets of relationships (Liburd, 2020).

The appropriateness of the bottom-up approach to the design of development strategies in depressed areas is reported in numerous published studies. In particular, the bottom-up approach proves to be effective in making up for the lack of knowledge of the territorial reality and the mismatch between the measures envisaged and the actual interests of the local community. In fact, the top-down approach is less effective and barely brings direct benefits to the territories concerned (Ruiz, 2020).

In general, participatory and bottom-up approach can significantly enhance the sustainable management of cultural tourism but this requires that the different stakeholders are systematically involved (Jamhawi & Hajahjah, 2017).

3 The Pilot Site of Crespi D'Adda

Sustainable cultural tourism is the integrated management of cultural heritage and tourism activities in conjunction with the local community creating social, environmental and economic benefits for all stakeholders, to achieve tangible and intangible cultural heritage conservation and sustainable tourism development.[1]

Based on the above definition of sustainable and cultural tourism, and according to the principles of sustainable cultural tourism, in Italy, the pilot site identified is the workers' village of Crespi d'Adda—a hamlet in the municipality of Capriate San Gervasio, near the city of Bergamo—a well-preserved Company town including factories, housing and services. In December 1995, Crespi, together with the factory (still active in that period), was inscribed on UNESCO World Heritage list, as "an outstanding example of the 19th and early twentieth century 'company towns' built in Europe and North America, by enlightened industrialists to meet the workers' needs."

---

[1] www.culturaltourism-network.eu.

The industrial activity of the factory (see Fig. 1), built in 1878, has signifi-cantly declined at the end of twentieth century and closed in 2004. In 2013, a local entrepreneur who decided to use the buildings as headquarters of his companies, purchased the factory, but to date the business has not re-started yet, although a Program Agreement between the owners and the institutions was signed at the end of 2022.

The inhabitants of Crespi d'Adda, who grew up in a symbiotic relationship with the factory, suffer from the fact that the factory is closed and hope that its reopening will become an opportunity to return to their condition before closing, when the life of the Village was focused on work in the factory and so the activities for workers' families. This vision of life, combined with a lack of confidence in the tourist vocation of the Village, means that residents of Crespi mainly grasp the negative aspects and do not evaluate the possible positive effects that tourism could have for them and their quality of life.

The village of Crespi d'Adda is located at the tip of the Isola Bergamasca, a strip of land created by the meeting of the rivers Adda and Brembo and this position deprives the Village of the opportunity to be visited or discovered as a transit place to go elsewhere. You get to Crespi d'Adda if that's where you want to go.

Although there are still no problems of overtourism in Crespi, residents often find the behavior of tourists disrespectful and generally complain about the restriction on buildings resulting from the presence of the UNESCO site. With the aim of fostering the development of sustainable cultural tourism, the municipality therefore decided to use the drafting of the new management plan to initiate participatory design processes and put the local community and the protection of cultural heritage at the center of decision-making processes.

Moreover, although it suffers of isolation due to its geographical location, Crespi d'Adda is located within a territorial system characterized by numerous cultural and natural attractions with which, however, the relationships and synergies are practically non-existent, despite the physical and, in some cases, thematic proximity.

For these reasons, in the framework of TExTOUR project, the pilot area was not limited to the workers' Village but was extended to a wider area that includes 10 municipalities located along the Adda river (see Fig. 2).

4   The Identification of the Actions for the Promotion of Cultural Tourism in Crespi D'Adda and the Surrounding Area

In the framework of the TExTOUR project, in 2022 Unioncamere Lombardia and LINKS Foundation coordinated the participatory process for the development of Cultural tourism in the pilot area.

The process for the identification of actions to be implemented in Crespi d'Adda was based on a co-design approach and involved several local stakeholders based

Fig. 1 The village of Crespi d'Adda with its factory

in Crespi d'Adda and in the surrounding areas along the Adda river. The structure was defined by the University of Bologna during the first year of TExTOUR and it was based on the organization of 4 structured workshops with the involvement of all the local stakeholders according to a bottom-up approach (see Fig. 3). Each session lasted two and a half hours, the first and the third workshop were online,

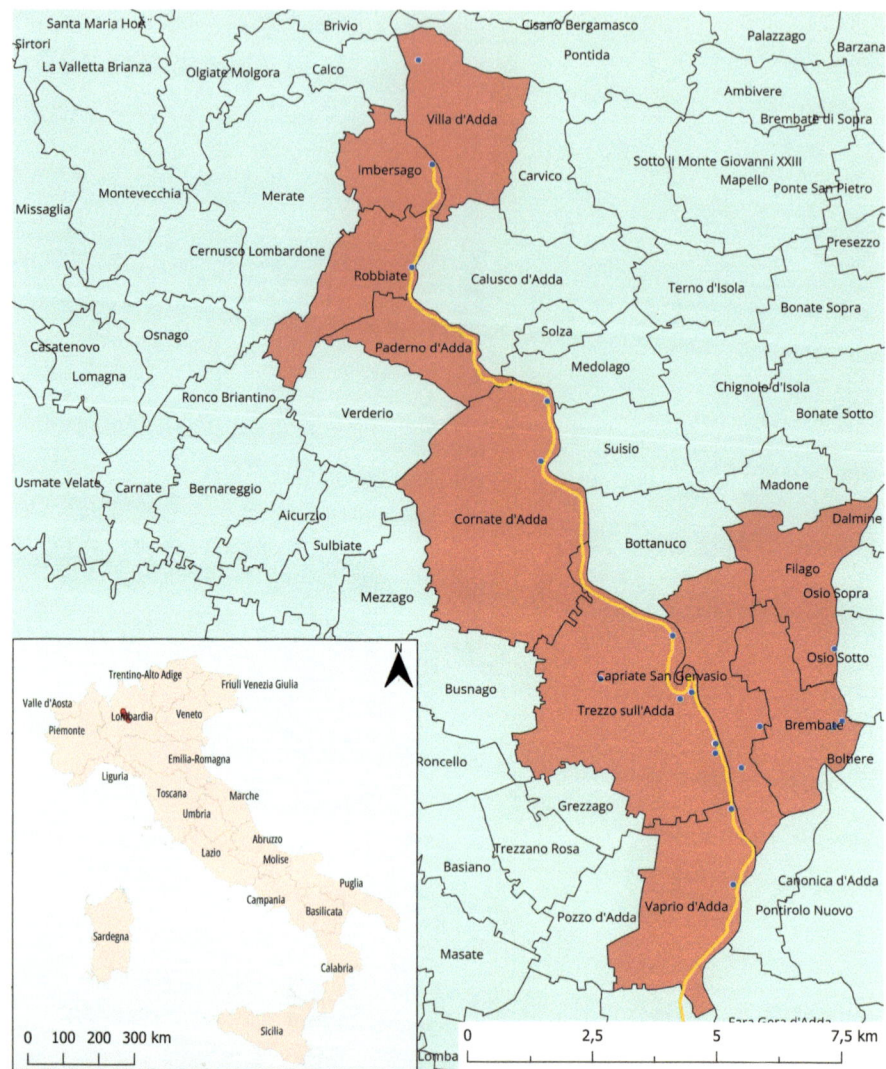

Fig. 2 The pilot area considered within the TExTOUR project

whereas the second was held in presence at the Crespi d'Adda UNESCO visitor center (head office of the Association Crespi d'Adda), the average attendance was of fifteen people in each workshop.

The stakeholders engaged were selected starting with the existing contacts and enlarging the auditors to public and private entities dealing with cultural tourism issues in the surrounding of Crespi d'Adda (i.e., public bodies, non-governmental organizations (NGOs), associations, tourism and Territorial promotion agencies, local stakeholders, etc., …).

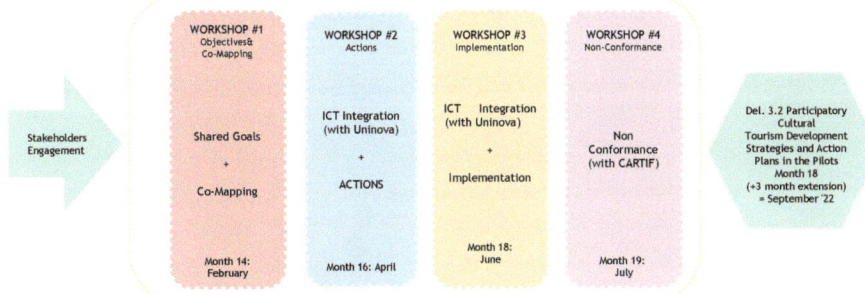

Fig. 3 The 4 steps methodology developed by the University of Bologna

After the stakeholder engagement activities, organized in the previous phase of the project, the **first workshop** (Cultural Heritage Tourism) was dedicated to the definition of the objectives for the area and to the identification and mapping of the cultural sites and attractions located in the proximity of the main pilot site (Crespi d'Adda). The first activity was dedicated to the identification of common goals, values, and objectives and to the identification and mapping of the attractions in the area surrounding Crespi d'Adda, mainly located along the river (see Fig. 4). This process has been made with the help of Miro board Visual collaboration software.

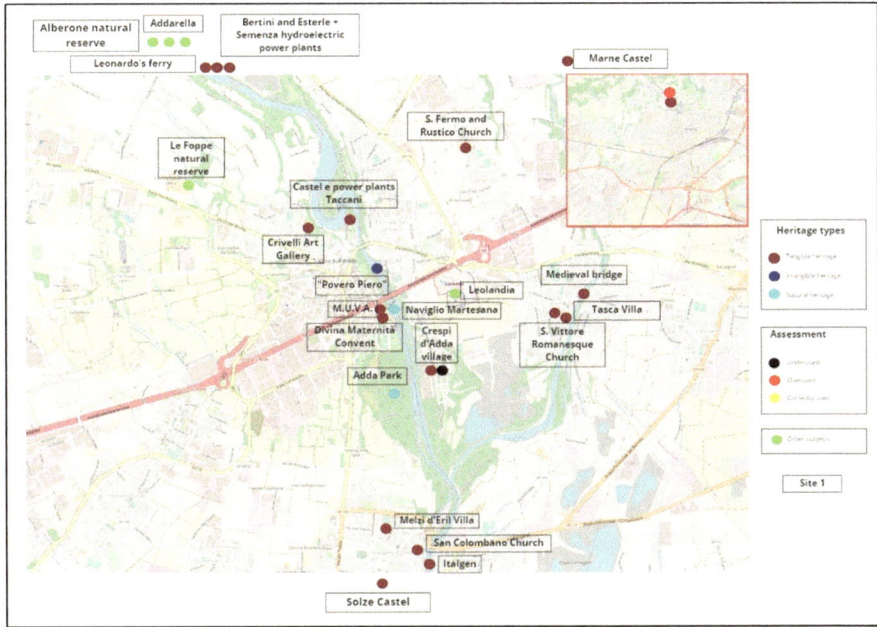

Fig. 4 Map of cultural sites and attractions identified during the first workshop

Fig. 5 The second workshop with local stakeholders held in Crespi d'Adda

The following workshops were dedicated to the definition of several Actions to be jointly implemented.

In particular, the **second workshop** (ICT integration) (see Fig. 5) was aimed at the identification of possible **actions** by the local stakeholders (Crespi d'Adda and surrounding area), taking inspiration from a list of actions proposed by the University of Bologna. Three of the actions proposed were directly inspired by the good practices illustrated in the list:

- #1 Transformation of Rockerill Charleroi factory—use of industrial heritage for touristic purpose
- #2 Village Tourism: 5 villages in East Germany—requalification of traditional villages
- #3 Green Western way: ecotourism in Ireland—routes (mainly hiking) in Ireland

In addition, 12 new actions were proposed collectively within the Workshop 2 and grouped in wider domains:

Institutional actions:

- #4 Consortium among public and private bodies
- #5 Reuse of brownfield areas and spaces
- #7 Development of a municipal App
- #12 Monitoring of tourist flows
- #13 Vademecum for tourists
- #14 Shared timetable of events and site visits

Heritage enhancement projects:

- #6 Lighting of monuments
- #8 Network of cycle and pedestrian paths
- #9 Naturalistic/hydrological/gastronomic heritage network

- #10 Network of cultural sites
- #15 QR-codes in the village of Crespi d'Adda

Events:

- #11 Historical re-enactments

Between the second and the third workshop the actions proposed were revised, shortlisted and aggregated.

At the end of the process the actions identified were 5, but one of them, concerning the Transformation and reconversion of public buildings, was not developed within TExTOUR because it was already included in the UNESCO Management Plan for Crespi d'Adda.

From the process of re-definition, the 4 actions that were confirmed for Crespi d'Adda are the following:

4.1   Action 1: Green and Blue Routes

The action concerns the development of a network of routes (hiking/bicycle/accessible boat) that improve local tourism and increase opportunities for discovering the area. It comes from the integration of the following actions proposed during the second Workshop:

- #3 Green Western way: ecotourism in Ireland.
- #6 Lighting monuments project.
- #7 Development of a municipal App.
- #9 Naturalistic/hydrological/gastronomic heritage network.
- #14 Timetable for guided tours.
- #15 QR-codes in the village of Crespi d'Adda.

The action responds to the need, clarified by many stakeholders, to coordinate the promotion of touristic resources, making them available for tourists in a single website.

4.2   Action 2: Permanent Working Table on Cultural Tourism with Local Stakeholders

This action aims at creating a permanent working table with all the stakeholders that are working on cultural tourism in Crespi d'Adda area in order to exploit opportunities, coordinate communication of attractions and develop new services.

It comes from the integration of the following actions:

- #4 Consortium among public and private bodies.

- #10 Network of cultural sites.

The action responds to the need, common to many stakeholders, to create a table to share, discuss and coordinate all policies and projects on tourism in the area.

4.3   Action 3: Vademecum for Citizens and Tourists

The action aims at defining a *Vademecum* to reduce the externalities of touristic flows on residents. It is focused on various aspects related to the theme of education, declined in different ways and oriented to different targets: tourists, local authorities and citizens.

This includes the following actions:

- #1 Transformation of the old Rockerill Charleroi factories.
- #11 Historical re-enactments.
- #13 *Vademecum* for tourists.
- #15 QR-codes in the village of Crespi d'Adda.

The action responds to the need of residents to see their privacy respected (reducing externalities of touristic flows).

4.4   Action 4: Monitoring System for Touristic Flows Using ICT

The idea of the action is to identify a methodology that helps to monitor the figures and characteristics of tourists in the area.

This is based on the following actions:

- #7 Development of a municipal app.
- #12 Monitoring of tourist flows.

The action responds to the need of the municipality and the Association Crespi d'Adda, to know the characteristics of touristic flows in order to manage them, avoiding overcrowding in certain areas/period of time.

The **third workshop** was then dedicated to the definition of specific Business Model Canvas for 3 of the 4 actions: for the Permanent Working Table on Cultural tourism, it was not considered to develop a model as it mainly represents an organizational and networking activity related to policy.

Since the purpose of the project is more focused on sustainability than on economic, within the TExTOUR project the researchers from the University of Bologna designed a specific model called "Sustainability-Driven Business Model Canvas" (see Fig. 6), specifically tailored for sustainable cultural tourism and

PILOT NAME AND NUMBER				TITLE OF THE ACTION		ACTION #	
Inclusion	**Partners** *Who would you involve to get your action started and completed?*	**Activities** *What are the key steps to move ahead with your action?*	**Propositions/offer** *How will you make your visitors'/beneficiaries life happier?*		**Resources** *What are the resources you need to get this action started and completed?*		**ICT integration and data needed** *What ICT service can be useful for this action? What kind of ICT service can make the action more sustainable?*
	Beneficiaries *Who are your targets audience? What are your beneficiaries? Describe your target audience and/ or your beneficiaries in a couple of words.*	**Cost Structure** *How much are you planning to spend on the action development and marketing (for a certain period)?*	**Channels of communication** *How are you going to reach your visitors/beneficiaries?*		**Revenue Streams** *For what value are the tourists/visitors/users really willing to pay?*		**Social Innovation** *What social innovation is the action producing?*
Sustainability of the Action *How can your action be sustained in the long term? Where to look for funding/opportunities to make it sustainable through the time? What conditions will make this action sustainable in the long run?*							
Economic impact on the territory	Environmental Impact on the territory		Social impact on the territory		Cultural Impact on the territory		

Fig. 6 Sustainability-driven business model canvas developed by the University of Bologna

embracing all four pillars of sustainability (social, economic, environmental and cultural) (Ottaviani, 2023).

A **fourth workshop** was restricted to the TExTOUR partners with the aim of defining the targets that the actions have to meet by the end of the project and match those targets with the Key Performance Indicators (KPIs) defined in the previous phases of the project regarding different domains: economic, social, cultural, environmental (see Fig. 7).

The whole process developed for the area of Crespi d'Adda was interesting for several reasons. In fact, thanks to the bottom-up approach, the actions were not "imposed" by any authority but raised from the local communities' needs. Furthermore, it helped to build trust among the actors of the area and provided a context in which all stakeholders could work together (and, hopefully, will continue, beyond the end of the project).

The methodology tested in Crespi d'Adda and in the other TExTOUR pilot sites can be easily applied to other cultural sites or point of interests. To this purpose, a call to identify new pilot sites for the replication of the method was launched and new sites will be involved to test, promote and extend the methodology to a wider number of Cultural sites.

The project requires huge involvement of stakeholders for the realization of the actions and the process of fundraising is not so easy. Besides, more effort will be needed to involve touristic actors in the development of the actions.

The project's acquired knowledge will be made available on the TExTOUR innovative open access platform for policy makers, practitioners and local communities. This will allow them to assess cultural tourism strategies and services. Other European and non-European cultural sites and ecosystems will have access to the platform so that they can benefit from the project's achievements too.

Fig. 7 The fourth workshop analysis of KPIs and the pilot actions

Index	Categories of tourism industry	Action #1: Green&Blue Routes [Y/N]	Action #2: Permanent Consultation Table on CT [Y/N]	Action #3: Vademecum for Tourist and Residents [Y/N]	Action #4: Digital Services for CT [Y/N]
1	Accommodation facilities	N	Y	N	Y
		N	Y	N	Y
		N	N	N	Y
2	Basic infrastructure	Y	N	N	N
		Y	N	N	Y
		N	N	Y	Y
		N	N	Y	N
		Y	N	N	N
3	Gastronomy	Y	N	Y	N
4	Local products and services				
		N	Y	N	N
5	Local transport	Y	N	Y	Y
6	Organizations	N	Y		
		N	Y	N	N
7	Promotion	Y	Y	N	N
		Y	N	Y	N
8	Revenue	N	Y	N	N
9	Visitors	N	Y	N	Y
10	Attractions	Y	N	N	N
		N	Y	N	N
		N	N	N	Y
		Y	N	N	N
11	Shops/retail	N	Y	N	N
12	Touristic routes	Y	N	N	N
13	Electromobility				
14	Air quality				
15	Water consumption				
16	Waste managements	N	N	Y	N
17	Crime				
18	Employment**	Y	Y	Y	Y
		Y	Y	Y	Y
19	Demography				
20	Climate				
21	Health and safety				
22	ICT technologies				
25	Equality and Inclusiveness				

Fig. 8 Tables for the discussion of the UNESCO management plan

5 The UNESCO Management Plan and the Integration with TExTOUR Project Activities and Results

The process of identification of the actions foreseen by the European project occurred in parallel with the process of definition of the UNESCO Management Plan for the Village of Crespi d'Adda and this allowed a profitable exchange between the two initiatives.

A management plan for a World Heritage site is an integrated planning and action concept that lays down goals and measures for the protection, conservation, use and development of World Heritage sites.[2] With the aim of creating a Management Plan as much as possible oriented towards satisfying the needs and expectations of citizens and stakeholders interested in the future of the Village of Crespi d'Adda, the population was involved in participatory planning activities (see Fig. 8).

The participatory process was aimed to create cohesion between the parties and encourage a renewed social identity according to the new vision of the Village (which emerged from the various meetings). Furthermore, in the long run, the collaboration has the effect of intensifying the engagement of the participants in the activities included in the Plan itself.

The participatory process has given the subjects involved the opportunity to influence the dynamics of urban transformation through their knowledge of the territory. It also represented an opportunity for growth for the participants, who became aware of the plurality of perspectives from which situations must be observed to be able

---

[2] Management Plans for World Heritage Sites – A practical guide (German Commission for UNESCO - Bonn, 2008).

to deal with them effectively, guaranteeing both respect for the cultural heritage and the needs and interests of all, often in conflict with each other.

For the implementation of participatory planning, three meetings were organized, of which: 2 with local actors directly involved in economic and cultural activities and a third to which the entire population of Crespi d'Adda was invited.

After introducing the Management Plan, the importance of participatory planning was highlighted, and some suggestions were given on the aims of the plan and above all on the importance of finding a vision in line with the development path that they hope for the site and for their own town. Finally, it was explained how the individual projects that emerged will contribute to these higher-level objectives. In the first two workshops, groups were formed with different categories of stakeholders, who worked using the Business Model Canvas (see Fig. 9) as a tool aimed at facilitating discussion and collaboration between the participants.

To allow everyone to propose their ideas, the participants of the 3 meetings were then asked to suggest one or more activities or projects in line with the Vision, which could be included in the Management Plan.

In total, more than 70 project files were collected, analysed and aggregated when they referred to similar or complementary actions, and then traced back to 7 macro-themes: Management/Governance; Infrastructure, energy and green; Preservation; Society and economic valorisation; Tourism; Communication.

The 4 actions that emerged from the working tables within the TExTOUR project for sustainable tourism were included within the sphere of actions linked to Tourism, as they combined ideas and purposes in line with the Management Plan and represented some of the activities or objectives included among the 70 proposed by the participants. Namely, the 4 actions are:

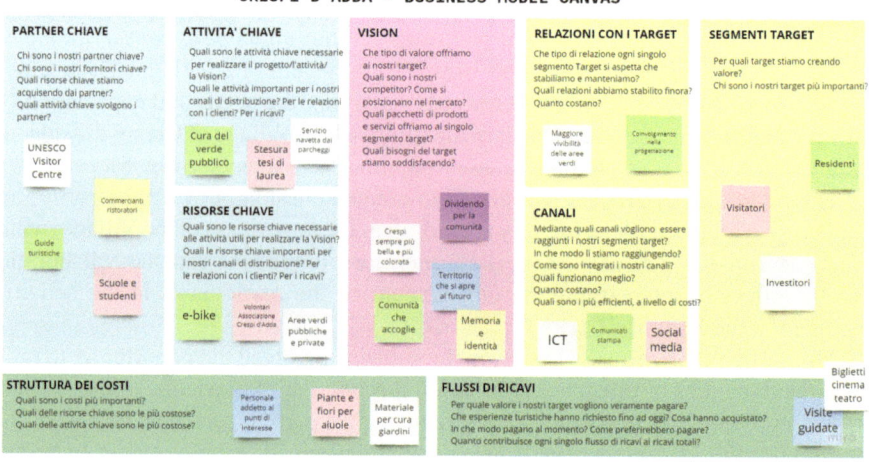

Fig. 9 The business model canvas developed within the preparation of the UNESCO management plan

- Identification of a network of tourist itineraries in the area and between UNESCO sites;
- Establishment of a working table for the organization of the integrated tourist offer;
- Creation of a *Vademecum* for tourists and residents;
- Monitoring of tourist flows.

6 Conclusions

Although Crespi d'Adda suffers from the isolation due to its geographical position, thanks to its cultural heritage and the UNESCO label, at the same time it also attracts a large number of tourists. To make tourism sustainable, therefore, it was necessary to work on the one hand to integrate Crespi and generate synergies with the more structured territorial system (and characterized both by cultural and natural attractions); on the other, to regulate and facilitate coexistence between tourists and residents within the Village on the busiest days.

The participatory process implemented within the TExTOUR project supported the extension of the network of stakeholders involved, from the local level (on which the Management Plan was already working) to a wider territorial area. The integration of the results emerged from the two participatory processes has made it possible to match the local stakeholders' needs and, at the same time, to give visibility and enhance the cultural heritage of Crespi d'Adda within the wider touristic network linked to the TExTOUR project, ensuring greater sustainability over time.

References

ECTN European Cultural Tourism Network website—www.culturaltourism-network.eu, last accessed 2023/06/20.

TExTOUR Project website—www.textour-project.eu, last accessed 2023/06/15.

UNESCO official website. https://ich.unesco.org/en/what-is-intangible-heritage-00003. last accessed 2023/06/15.

German Commission for UNESCO: Management Plans for World Heritage Sites—A practical guide (2008).

Crespi d'Adda Management Plan. https://xoom.virgilio.it/source_filemanager/su/up/supermik/2023_varie/Allegato1_PdG_Crespi_v9_def_protocollo_4631_13_03_2023.PDF.

Angelini, L., Borlizzi, D., Carlucci, A., Ciardella, G., Destefanis, A., Governale, G., & Morfini, I. (2020). Cultural tourism development and the impact on local communities: A case study from the South of Italy.- CERN 2020. https://doi.org/10.23726/cij.2020.1054 (2020).

Solima, L., & Minguzzi, A. (2015). Territorial development through cultural tourism and creative activities. *Mondes Du Tourisme.* https://doi.org/10.4000/tourisme.366

Liburd, J., Duedahl, E., Heape, C. (2020). Co-designing tourism for sustainable development. *Journal of Sustainable Tourism.* https://doi.org/10.1080/09669582.2020.1839473.

Jamhawi, M., & Hajahjah, Z. (2017). A bottom-up approach for cultural tourism management in the old city of As-Salt, Jordan. *Journal of Cultural Heritage Management and Sustainable Development, 7*, 91–106. https://doi.org/10.1108/JCHMSD-07-2015-0027

OECD. (2021). Culture, tourism and local development: new strategies for Italian heritage cities in the post-pandemic scenario. https://www.oecd.org/fr/cfe/leed/italian-heritage-cities.htm.

Ruiz, Á., & Cañizares, M. (2020). Enhancing the territorial heritage of declining rural areas in Spain: Towards integrating Top-Down and Bottom-Up approaches, in Sustainable Rural Development Strategies, Good Practices and Opportunities—Land MDPI ed.

Ottaviani, D., Demiröz, M., Szemzo, H., & De Luca, C. (2023). Adapting methods and tools for participatory heritage-based tourism planning to embrace the four pillars of sustainability. *Sustainability, 15*, 4741. https://doi.org/10.3390/su15064741

Co-Creation Method for Fostering Cultural Tourism Impact

Shabnam Pasandideh⊙, **João Martins**⊙, **Pedro Pereira**⊙,
Alessandra Gandini⊙, **Mikel Zubiaga De La Cal**⊙, **Tarmo Kalvet**⊙,
Tatjana Koor, **Amaia Sopelana**⊙, and **Amaia Lopez de Aguileta**⊙

Abstract This chapter describes the IMPACTOUR co-creation method, which is developed to enhance the impact of cultural tourism in various destinations. The method utilizes effective strategies and actions to monitor and increase the impact of cultural tourism. The primary objective of the IMPACTOUR technique is to support decision-makers in improving the sustainability and competitiveness of cultural tourists in their destinations. The method involves collecting and analyzing data from diverse sources, including tourism stakeholders and specifically local communities to create a comprehensive decision-making system. The resulting recommendations aim to promote the positive impacts of cultural tourism while minimizing negative effects and fostering long-term development. Ultimately, the IMPACTOUR method seeks to assist destinations and attractions in becoming more competitive and attractive to cultural visitors, while ensuring their long-term sustainability.

Keywords Cultural tourism · Decision making · Cultural tourism strategies · Sustainability

S. Pasandideh (✉) · J. Martins · P. Pereira
NOVA School of Science and Technology, UNINOVA-CTS and LASI, Universidade NOVA de Lisboa, 2829-516 Caparica, Portugal
e-mail: Shabnam.pasandide@uninova.pt

A. Gandini · M. Z. De La Cal · A. Sopelana · A. L. de Aguileta
TECNALIA, Basque Research and Technology Alliance (BRTA), Parque Científico y Tecnológico de Bizkaia. Astondo Bidea, Edificio 700. E-48160, Derio, Spain

T. Kalvet
Institute of Baltic Studies, Lai 30, 51005 Tartu, Estonia and Department of Business Administration, Tallinn University of Technology 5, 19086 Tallinn, Estonia

T. Koor
Estonian Tourist Board, Lasnamäe 2, 11412 Tallinn, Estonia

© The Author(s) 2025
B. Neuts et al. (eds.), *Advances in Cultural Tourism Research*, Advances in Digital and Cultural Tourism Management, https://doi.org/10.1007/978-3-031-65537-1_3

1   Introduction

Cultural Tourism (CT) has been identified as a driver of growth, jobs, and economic development in European regions and cities, as well as intercultural understanding and social development. However, there is still a knowledge gap regarding methods to assess multilevel and cross-border strategies, policies, and practices that contribute to sustainable development and Tourism Destination Competitiveness (TDC). Because of the diversity of goals and destinations, it is difficult to grasp concurrent solutions for all types of destinations.

Some places compete to improve their economic development, while others diversify their economies or expand their market share. As a result, sustainability and TDC have been described from several angles. A first point of view holds that a destination should focus on developing value-added items in order to strengthen its market position (d'Hauteserre, 2000). In this regard, organizations are required to improve corporate efficiency, use cutting-edge technologies, seek competitive and sustainable advantages in tourism products and services, compete for a larger market share, and establish proper indicators to monitor their performance.

Moreover, the expansion of tourism has prompted the creation of a number of technologies to aid in management decisions related to tourism. One such technology is decision-making support systems (DMSS), which offer analytical tools to support decision-making in a variety of industries, including tourism.

DMSS has the ability to greatly enhance sustainability and TDC in the tourism industry. The creation and application of DMSS will be more crucial than ever for the cultural tourism sector's long-term sustainability as technology develops.

In this regard, IMPACTOUR methodology is providing the backbone for the DMSS to support decision makers. IMPACTOUR is a H2020 project which brings together CT-related stakeholders and researchers to develop new techniques that take advantage of the vast volumes of information that policymakers confront. By applying DMSS it helps decision-making in cultural tourism destination management by giving a thorough grasp of the location's characterizations and recommends appropriate strategies to improve destination´s sustainability and TDC.

1.1   State of the Art (of Strategic Cultural Tourism Planning)

Strategic tourism planning is a dynamic and future-oriented process or roadmap that sets goals for a destination, tourism organization, or other entity, and produces the direction and specific steps for the future. It is a collaborative management process that can be used to help determine a destination's or organization's present situation, impact factors, vision, goals, objectives, strategies, and actions and give an approach to directing the use of resources and communicating the interests of the stakeholders including community.

Due to the complex context created by the nature of cultural tourism and the challenges of the twin transition, the entities responsible for strategic tourism planning (whether at the local, regional, or national level) need a strong organizational-operational and administrative capacity—qualities that enable an effective management of resources in order to deliver strategic objectives (El-Taliawi & Wal, 2019). Adequate capacity is important throughout the strategy cycle, from strategy development and implementation to monitoring and evaluation.

The characteristics of a successful and competitive destination are (World Tourism Organization (UNWTO), 2019; Morrison, 2018):

- awareness—information and knowledge about the destination
- attractiveness—diverse factors of the destination that attract visitors
- availability—ease of booking options and number of channels
- access—ease and comfort of reaching the destination and moving around there, smart-solutions
- appearance—the impression of the destination when arriving there as well as being there
- activities—opportunities and diversity of activities for visitors
- assurance—guaranteed safety and security
- appreciation—hospitality and welcoming attitude in the destination
- action—long-term tourism planning, marketing activities, crisis management plans
- accountability—destination management and evaluation of Destination Management Organizations (DMO) activities.

Strategic planning may be either a simple straightforward decision-making process or in some cases a complex set of multiple decision directions (Dredge, & Jenkins, 2011). However, in both cases, the strategic planning process should consider economic, environmental, social, and cultural factors, the overall sustainability of the organization or destination (Edgell & Swanson, 2013) and analyze the current situation of destinations, influencing factors, and stakeholders´ awareness, expectations, opinion of importance and needs for development (Mason, 2016; Miočić et al., 2016).

1.2   Purpose and Scope of the Paper

The proposed methodology provides an easy-to-follow guide for decision-making that travel destinations are advised to use when choosing the best development strategy for cultural tourism at their location.

We describe the IMPACTOUR co-creation method, which assists the decision-maker, whether a novice or an expert, in the selection and development of ad hoc selected strategies for boosting cultural tourism impact in their historic context. The framework of the method provides an innovative solution to propose customized plans and actions based on site features, data availability, and monitoring capacity indicators built based on four main domains. These four domains include Cultural, Social, Economic and Environmental domains.

We define the holistic method for sustainable cultural tourism development. The method definition includes setting up the workflow and sequence of steps, the identification of information required, and the information flow needed for the implementation of the method in a real case. The inputs (information type, structure, data management and visualization, semantic organization…) for the calculation of the Key Performance Indicators (KPIs) will be selected, and how strategies are filtered in function of the systematized strategies, according to their replicability, their success factors and the different characteristics and needs of the cultural tourism categories.

The focus of this paper is on the procedure of establishing the recommended strategies and introducing their criteria, main categories and results.

The remainder of this paper is organized as following: Sect. 2, provides different definitions and IMPACTOUR definition on Cultural tourism; Sect. 3, describes the IMPACTOUR methodology; Sect. 4, explains how under the proposed methodology, the impact of the strategies can be measured and finally Sect. 5, concludes the results of the study.

2   Facing Cultural Tourism

Cultural tourism is a type of tourism that focuses on the culture, tradition, and way of life of a specific town or region. It includes things like visiting historical sites, going to cultural events, and learning about local customs (UNWTO). According to Richards and Wilson (Richards & Wilson, 2006), CT is "the subset of tourism concerned with the country or region's culture, specifically the lifestyle, history, art, architecture, religion, and other elements that help shape the identity of the country or region."

In the same way, Sharpley (Sharpley, 2014) characterizes cultural tourism as a type of tourism that involves the pursuit of cultural experiences, specifically those that are unique to a particular destination or community. CT has been also defined as "traveling for the purpose of experiencing the authenticity, history, and character of a place, including its cultural, natural, and built heritage (Rasoolimanesh et al., 2021)".

The motivation and interests of cultural tourists can be described as the activities of tourists who are motivated by cultural interests and activities that include visiting cultural attractions, attending cultural events, participating in cultural activities, and interacting with the local people (Poria et al., 2006).

There are some common themes throughout these definitions notwithstanding their differences. First of all, cultural tourism entails traveling to experience cultural attractions and activities. Second, cultural tourism concentrates on a destination's cultural heritage, which includes its history, architecture, art, and other components that help to define its identity. Thirdly, cultural tourism entails mingling with locals, which is regarded as a crucial aspect of the experience.

2.1 Definition and Driving Indicators

The definition of cultural tourism will be significantly affected by the continually evolving meanings and interpretations of the term "culture," which will be one of the largest problems (Richards, 2018). IMPACTOUR defines cultural tourism as "A type of tourism activity in which the visitor's motivation and aim is to learn, discover, experience, participate and benefit from the tangible and intangible cultural offers in a tourism destination. These offers relate to a set of distinctive material, intellectual, spiritual and emotional features and the relationships with and within a society. It encompasses the places they inhabit, arts and architecture, historical and cultural and natural heritage, landscapes, culinary heritage, literature, music, creative industries and the living cultures with their cultural and social values".

The experience gained during the analysis of existing indicators systems previously performed and the successive interactions with the IMPACTOUR pilots' community drove to the evolution of some baseline indicators, which are required for a dynamic tool able to measure the impact derived by strategies implementation. For succeeding in such an evolution, the results from the Data Gathering process run by the project with the pilots community, as well as the conclusions derived from the benchmarking in relation to the KPIs, were explored and analyzed against two references from UNESCO (the UNESCO Culture 2030 indicators (UNESCO, 2019) and the UNESCO World Heritage Sustainable Tourism Toolkit (UNESCO xxxx) They provide respectively relevant background on the role of culture in the Sustainable Development Goals (SDGs) and best practice approaches to sustainable economic development through tourism.

2.2 Importance of Local Communities

It is crucial to involve the local community in tourism planning and decision-making processes in order to mitigate the negative impacts of cultural tourism on local communities. This can ensure that tourism growth is sustainable and helps the local community as well as outside investors, rather than the other way around. Also, they play a critical role in cultural tourism as they possess unique knowledge and experiences that can be leveraged to create more authentic and immersive tourism experiences.

The study found (Muganda et al., 2013) that local communities desire involvement in tourism policy-making processes to ensure that their needs are met, and their concerns are addressed. They also expressed a desire to participate in tourism development decisions to protect community interests, increase transparency and accountability. The prevailing top-down approach in decision-making for cultural tourism development was widely rejected by the local communities, indicating a need for more participatory approaches. The study suggests a need for policymakers to involve local communities in decision-making processes to ensure the success and sustainability of cultural tourism development initiatives. Using the experiences of local communities to establish cultural tourism initiatives can thus be a useful method to creating more authentic and sustainable tourism experiences.

Participatory planning is one method for utilizing the knowledge of local people to create strategies for enhancing cultural tourism. Engaging local communities in the planning of the tourism industry and incorporating their suggestions and ideas into the final product is known as participatory planning. With this strategy, the development of the tourism product is guaranteed to be respectful of local values, traditions, and customs as well as culturally suitable. Additionally, by fostering community support and buy-in, this strategy may increase the ownership of the tourism product and the likelihood of its long-term success.

3   Methodology: Co-Creation a Method for Fostering Cultural Tourism

The IMPACTOUR method consists of co-creation process of indicators with pilots' community, the process of establishing strategy criteria analysis and propose the strategies based on the pilot´s characterizations which are describe extensively in Sect. 4.

According to the workshops and the successful stories learnt from the pilots /case studies, there are three main attributes to recommend proper strategies: The type of lands, their objectives and cultural activities. Based on the results we suggested the proper strategies to enhance the impact of cultural tourism according to their preferences between domains.

3.1   Building Indicators

The whole process of defining an integrated impact assessment set of strategies for CT has been developed and co-created with the IMPACTOUR Community. An iterative approach between technical and pilot partners was established, based on different participatory activities, which is explained in detail in the following sections.

The exercise provided some insight into the type of indicators and their relationship with some of the identified recommendations. It was the first step to getting pilots familiarized with indicators and start thinking about monitoring the transformative impacts of cultural tourism strategies. Following are the main categorization of the indicators and their connections to recommended strategies:

- Characterization, resilience and social indicators resulted as most relevant for diversification and marketing recommendations and governance recommendations, aiming at better understanding and quantifying the resources of the destination, the existence of recovery plans and funds and the availability of intangible heritage and traditional skills respectively.
- Cultural and environmental groups of indicators were ranked as most relevant for governance recommendations and business recommendations, concerning the promotion of cultural events, cultural tourism contribution to the conservation and restoration of heritage sites, local products availability and participation of local companies in environmental and ecosystems protection.
- Indicators classified in the category "others" apply to all types of recommendations, as their main field of application varies across the above-mentioned domains. Indicators related to accessibility are the most addressed, together with the vulnerability of natural and cultural heritage to over-tourism, branding and economic contribution of cultural industries. With this information, a Baseline Indicator list was developed, aiming to build a cultural tourism assessment framework tailored to different types of destinations and scales and adjusted to real data on destinations.
- Overall, the indicators "Destination Management Organization (DMO)", "Existing contingency and/or recovery plans (vulnerability against Hazards or others)" and "Percentage of local enterprises in the tourism sector actively supporting the conservation of local biodiversity and landscapes" have been rated as highly relevant and included on the top of the benchmarking list.
- Indicators "Tourism pressure to residents", "Alternative Cultural Attractions (considering the surrounding area or territory near to the destination: surrounding resources + diversification options)" and "Employment in cultural tourism activities" even if not selected as highly relevant in the questionnaire were posteriorly included in the benchmarking list, being considered as connected with recommendations.
- Responses with regards to resilience indicators confirmed that the unexpected events putting the CT incomes at risk are highly relevant thus, the decreases should be monitored as well as the affected employment rates. Surprisingly, the measurement of the digital tourism offer receiving an economic return was ranked with very low relevance.
- Those indicators which were not rated as relevant were selected for further discussion in the posterior stages since in some cases the definition initially provided required improvement and adaptation.

The cultural tourism development strategies (Fig. 1) were formulated based on the indicators, previous IMPACTOUR actions results and deliverables, various documents, including reports of other projects and development strategies and suggestions, academic literature review, and discussions with the project partners and pilots.

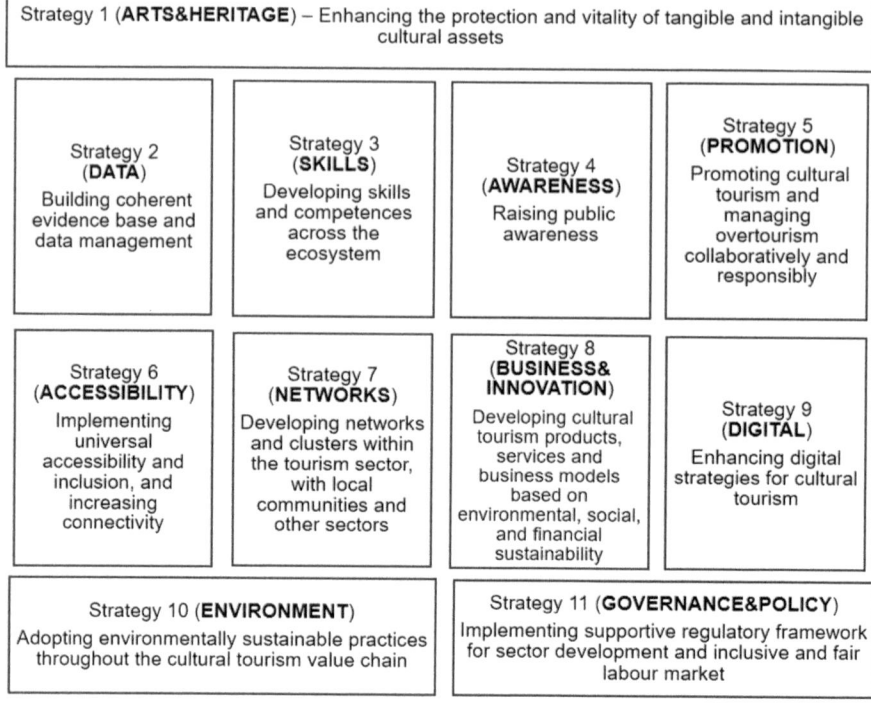

Fig. 1 IMPACTOUR recommended strategies and categories

3.2 Evaluation and Assessment

The IMPACTOUR community evaluated them considering their current practices and expertise and consequently, several indicators were discarded due to the lack of available data or due to the complex process of homogenization in destinations covering different areas with administrative diversity.

Having the data-gathering process finished and following scientific knowledge obtained, a Draft list of impact KPIs was developed, maturing from the Baseline Indicators set. This Draft list of KPIs included all the inputs already mentioned and included some of the indicators initially discarded but which the co-creation process arose as significant ones.

Benefitting from the opportunity of the pilots' attendance at the General Assembly held in the Azores (Atlantic Session), and hosted by one of the pilot sites, a new exercise was proposed to put into practice the interrelated levels mentioned at the beginning in Fig. 2 (strategic, impact and performance indicators levels). Undoubtedly, the impact of IMPACTOUR strategies over the sites should be guaranteed and the measuring framework and its KPIs should be aligned with the strategic objectives they are aiming for.

Fig. 2 Interrelations between the three operative levels

The two main questions were proposed to the attendees during the workshop:

- Are we (as project scientific partners) able to develop all the IMPACTOUR strategies with the information and links we have so far?
- Are we (as project scientific partners) able to measure all the expected from those strategies?

Such an exercise represented a qualitative validation process arranged to allow pilot sites to experience the reflection process of defining their CT plans following the interrelation between KPIs, actions and the IMPACTOUR strategies.

4 Measuring the Impact of Strategies on Cultural Tourism

Building upon the interaction of strategies, actions and KPIs, the site manager is able to monitor the changes in relevant KPIs, according to the action's implementation, considering the extent of the impact of strategies as well.

The information is be provided in two ways:

- The KPIs that directly and indirectly impacted by the implementation of the selected actions.
- In how many KPIs a specific action will impact on, and of these, how many will be directly impacted.

The recommended strategies depend on understanding the generic context of the destination plus its main strategic objectives when facing any transition in CT management.

Therefore, depending on the user's specific characteristics, most proper strategies can be recommended to achieve their objectives as are described in Table 1. Based on the findings of our studies and the practical insights gained from workshops, we figured out these characteristics are the main criteria used to recognize and differentiate the pilot's profile.

By monitoring the KPIs related to the actions and strategies, the stakeholders can modify their strategies and actions accordingly, and ensure that they are effective and aligned with the specific needs of each pilot. Ultimately, this approach can lead to more successful and sustainable tourism development that benefits both the pilots and the broader destination.

Table 1 The main criteria and values for recommending the proper strategies

Criteria	Values	Definitions
Type of site	1. Rural 2. Urban 3. Natural 4. Itinerary	IMPACTOUR partners and the IMPACTOUR Community have been working with four types of sites closely linked to the piloting regions' features: Rural sites, Urban sites, Natural sites and Itineraries
Type of cultural activities (based on)	1. Cultural Heritage 2. Experience 3. Agriculture 4. Natural Heritage	The IMPACTOUR Cultural Tourism definition suggests that an activity can be classified into four types of cultural activities or resources: the Cultural Heritage Based "tangible and intangible cultural offer"; the Experience Based activities such as "learn, discover, experience, participate"; the productive use and/or "culinary heritage" means of a territory (Agriculture Based) is considered a cultural activity itself; and, the Natural Heritage and "landscape", considered a type of cultural activity
Current CT impact on the site	1. No tourism activity 2. Tourism activity but no Cultural Tourism 3. Overtourism 4. Seasonal tourism 5. The touristic activity directly damages cultural heritage 6. Unbalanced impact of tourism 7. Highly dependent of international tourism 1. Lack of knowledge about cultural tourism impact	Aiming to understand how the site manager interprets the current CT impact, the user should select among a list of statements describing the CT situation in their site, so the most appropriate Strategy is provided in each case

5 Conclusion

As aforementioned, the co-creation process held with the IMPACTOUR pilots' community during the project served to build a framework which relies as much as possible on existing data sources. Nevertheless, considering the complexity of gathering sectorial data specific to cultural tourism, the qualitative perspective has also been included.

The IMPACTOUR project has shown that the barriers to be overcome by cultural destinations are different depending on their context, their geography or even their cultural resources. Therefore, their success in achieving the expected impact depends on their regional context. Moreover, the objectives in cultural tourism management depend on the prioritization of those roadblocks to overcome.

Acknowledgements This work was partially supported by the European Commission, grant number 870747 IMPACTOUR, by Portuguese national funds through FCT Fundação para a Ciência e a Tecnologia with reference UIDB/00066/2020 and UIDP/00066/2020, and by the TExTOUR project, which has received funding from the European Union's Horizon 2020 research and innovation programme under grant agreement number 101004687.

References

d'Hauteserre, A.-M. (2000). Lessons in managed destination competitiveness: The case of foxwoods casino resort. *Tourism Management, 21*, 23–32.

El-Taliawi, O. G., & Van Der Wal, Z. (2019). Developing administrative capacity: An agenda for research and practice. *Policy Design and Practice, 2*(3), 243–257. https://doi.org/10.1080/257 41292.2019.1595916

World Tourism Organization (UNWTO). (2019). UNWTO Guidelines for Institutional Strengthening of Destination Management Organizations (DMOs)—Preparing DMOs for new challenges. Madrid. https://doi.org/10.18111/9789284420841.

Morrison, A. M. (2018). *Marketing and managing tourism destinations*. Routledge.

Dredge, D., & Jenkins, J. (Eds.). (2011). Stories and Practice: Tourism Policy and Planning. Ed directions in tourism analysis. Ashgate: Burlington.

Edgell, D. L., & Swanson, J. R. (2013). *Tourism policy and planning: Yesterday, today, and tomorrow* (2nd ed.). London, New York.

Mason, P. (2016). *Tourism impacts, planning and management* (3rd ed.). New York.

Miočić, B. K., Razović, M., & Klarin, T. (2016). Management of sustainable tourism destination through stakeholder cooperation. *Management, 21*(2), 99–120.

Richards, G., & Wilson, J. (2006). Developing creativity in tourist experiences: A solution to the serial reproduction of culture? *Tourism Management, 27*(6), 1209–1223.

Sharpley, R. (2014). Host perceptions of tourism: A review of the research. *Tourism Management, 42*, 37–49. https://doi.org/10.1016/j.tourman.2013.10.007

Rasoolimanesh, S. M., Seyfi, S., Hall, C. M., & Hatamifar, P. (2021). Understanding memorable tourism experiences and behavioural intentions of heritage tourists. *Journal of Destination Marketing & Management, 21*, 100621. https://doi.org/10.1016/j.jdmm.2021.100621

Poria, Y., Reichel, A., & Biran, A. (2006). Heritage site perceptions and motivations to visit. *Journal of Travel Research, 44*(3), 318–326. https://doi.org/10.1177/0047287505279004

Richards, G. (2018). Cultural tourism: A review of recent research and trends. *Journal of Hospitality and Tourism Management, 36*, 12–21. https://doi.org/10.1016/j.jhtm.2018.03.005

UNESCO. (2019). Culture 2030 Indicators: Thematic Indicators for Culture in the 2030 Agenda.

UNESCO. World Heritage Sustainable Tourism Toolkit. Available online: http://whc.unesco.org/sustainabletourismtoolkit/welcome-unesco-world-heritage-sustainable-tourism-toolkit.).

Muganda, M., Sirima, A., & Ezra, P. M. (2013). The role of local communities in tourism development: Grassroots perspectives from Tanzania. *Journal of Human Ecology, 41*(1), 53–66. https://doi.org/10.1080/09709274.2013.11906553

Stakeholders Engagement Processes for Co-Creation of Strategic Action Plans for Circular and Human-Centred Cultural Tourism in European Heritage Sites

Małgorzata Ćwikła[ID]**, Cristina Garzillo, Martina Bosone**[ID]**, and Antonia Gravagnuolo**[ID]

Abstract Sustainable cultural tourism can be a powerful means to enhance communities' wellbeing increasing economic wealth in currently less known and remote areas, as well as residents' awareness on local culture and cultural heritage, environmental preservation and social cohesion. However, tourism activities can threaten cultural and natural resources, especially in fragile natural & cultural areas. Sustainability-led innovation and creativity could contribute to ensure that tourism activity is conducted within a responsible framework, engaging local operators and stakeholders towards reaching shared objectives. The integration of a circular economy oriented approach in cultural tourism strategies can be beneficial to allow sustainable tourism activities which avoid depletion of natural resources, excessive greenhouse gas emissions, over-consumption of cultural resources. Local communities represent the owners and custodians of important natural and cultural resources, thus their active role in cultural tourism strategies development is fundamental to ensure their conservation, regeneration and valorisation over time. Engaging stakeholder groups already at the initial stage of designing changes, can contribute to the development of strategies aiming at implementation of community-based circular and human-centred actions in various areas. The paper describes the co-creation process conducted with various types of stakeholders in six European regions within the Horizon 2020 Be.CULTOUR project. Special attention was given to the process of activating local communities and making them co-create and co-initiative innovative solutions.

Keywords Circular tourism · Cultural tourism · Co-creation · Stakeholders engagement · Innovation · Sustainable cultural tourism · Human-centered approach · Action plans

M. Ćwikła · C. Garzillo
ICLEI Europe, Breisgau, Germany

M. Bosone · A. Gravagnuolo (✉)
CNR National Research Council, Rome, Italy
e-mail: antonia.gravagnuolo@cnr.it

© The Author(s) 2025   47
B. Neuts et al. (eds.), *Advances in Cultural Tourism Research*, Advances in Digital and Cultural Tourism Management, https://doi.org/10.1007/978-3-031-65537-1_4

1 Introduction

Cultural tourism represents a particular tourism sector focused on the appreciation and valorisation of cultural resources, including cultural heritage in both tangible and intangible expressions. As a sub-sector of the whole tourism industry, cultural tourism can generate positive or negative impacts in cities and regions, depending on the way in which it is managed by destination managers and tourism operators, but also on visitors and residents behaviour. Sustainable cultural tourism should avoid the negative impacts of tourism activity, such as overconsumption of environmental and cultural resources, over-crowding, seasonality, commodification of cultural heritage, loss of authenticity and integrity of heritage sites, unfair distribution of economic benefits and other impacts. Particularly, cultural and natural resources should be conserved and maintained, ensuring that these resources are kept available for residents and visitors, as well as for future generations. Diverse research papers, international documents and initiatives underline the importance of sustainability in the tourism industry, which is one of the most relevant sources of jobs especially in European countries, rich in historic and cultural sites (European Union, 2022). However, the Covid-19 pandemic threatened the entire tourism sector due to travel bans and health issues, exposing the fragility of tourism worldwide. Moreover, the environmental crisis highlighted by recent research (Gupta et al., 2019; IPCC Climate Change, 2014; IPCC Global Warming, 2018; IPCC Special Report, 2019; UNEP, 2011; Watts et al., 2018) requires renewed attention towards the depletion of natural resources such as energy, land, water, materials, as well as climate altering emissions, biodiversity preservation and an overall better balance between human activity in all sectors and the need of regenerating natural resources (Fusco Girard & Nocca, 2020). To achieve a long-term sustainability without reducing the level of wealth for all people, many studies, policies and initiatives highlight the urgency to transition from a "linear" production and consumption model based on "take-make-dispose", in all sectors, towards a "circular" development model (Angrisano et al., 2016; Ellen MacArthur, 2013, 2014, 2015a, b; The European Parliament New Circular Economy Action Plan, 2021; European Commission, 2019, 2021a, b) in which no wastes are generated, thanks to processes of reduction of natural resources consumption, recycling of materials and wastes, recovering, reusing, refurbishing. The 'circular economy' raised in the last decade from a niche sector of studies and experimentation to a potential solution to global issues, adopted by governments and private organisations worldwide, and fostered in public policies to accelerate the adoption of a more sustainable production and consumption model at the societal level. The circular economy has been recently explored in the tourism sector to reduce the environmental impact of tourism activity, from sustainable mobility to eco-hotels, 'slow' tourism models, renewable energy generation on site, water recovery systems, etc., evoking a 'circular tourism economy' (Bosone & Nocca, 2022; Nocca et al., 1845; Gravagnuolo & Varotto, 2021; Fusco Girard & Gravagnuolo, 2017; Patti & Messina, 2019; Manniche et al. 2017; Hanza, 2018; Sorin & Einarsson, 2020; Naydenov, 2018; Fusco Girard et al. 2019). Moreover, the circular economy can be relevant for cultural heritage reuse and regeneration (see CLIC project—Circular models Leveraging Investments in Cultural heritage adaptive reuse, 2017) fostering the reuse of abandoned and underused heritage buildings and sites, and introducing circularity principles in construction and conservation interventions. The research studies and practice experiences of circular economy implementation in tourism and cultural heritage sectors led to the development of a new framework for circular cultural tourism which was implemented in the Horizon 2020 project Be.CULTOUR (Horizon, 2020 project, 2020), aiming at exploring and experimenting innovative ways through which the circular economy can contribute to the sustainability of cultural tourism destinations, contributing also to better balance between overcrowded and less known cultural destinations. However, a circular tourism economy, grounded on ecological economics, should also contribute to communities and people wellbeing adopting a human-centred approach where people and nature thrive in higher synergy.

This contribution aims to explore how less known and remote areas can become innovative circular and human-centred cultural tourism destinations, enhancing cultural and natural resources and engaging local communities in the transition towards a more sustainable and circular tourism organisation. Six pilot heritage sites in Europe (Aragon in Spain, Basilicata in Italy, Larnaca in Cyprus, Västra Götaland in Sweden, Vojvodina in Serbia, cross-border region Romania-Moldova) engaged actively to stimulate a collective reflection at local level on the objectives of a circular cultural tourism and the related actions to be implemented in specific heritage sites through a collaborative effort with local tourism operators, public bodies, cultural and creative industries, agricultural activities, research and innovation actors, as well as active citizens to co-design and co-implement a new sustainable and circular model of tourism in European cultural destinations.

2   Methodology: Stakeholders' Engagement to Co-Design Innovative Circular and Human-Centred Cultural Tourism Destinations

Human-centred design in the innovation processes continually gains attention of the researchers and practitioners (Bosone et al., 2019; Fusco Girard, 2019; Giacomin, 2014a; Krippendorff, 2004; Munhoz et al., 2020). In relation to sustainability, a human-centred approach is crucial to ensure social relevance of the transformative ambitions and build an affirmative foundation for change that is not only implemented but first of all co-created by people themselves (European Commission, 2020a, b). The six pilot heritage sites of Be.CULTOUR project started a co-design journey to stimulate a collective reflection on the meanings and objectives of a circular and human-centred cultural tourism and how this model could support the sustainable development of less known and remote cultural heritage destinations. Strategic co-design experimentation was implemented in the pilot areas to set the what, why, and how of circular and human-centred cultural tourism in the remote areas participating in the project.

The aim of the strategic co-design experimentation was to show the process of awakening creativity and empowering the ecosystems of local stakeholders, called to reflect on the relevance of cultural tourism as an opportunity for sustainable development of remote areas and to actively shape the path of their strategic development as circular cultural tourism destinations. The overall methodology adopted was grounded on solid research and experimentation previously conducted within other European heritage sites, and particularly within previous Horizon 2020 projects in which action plans or similar strategic documents for cultural heritage conservation in relation to environmental challenges were developed. This included other Horizon 2020 projects such as CLIC (CLIC Project, 2021), Open Heritage project (Open Heritage Project Organizing, 2019), ILUCIDARE project (ILUCIDARE, 2020), ROCK project ().

The co-creation process was organized in three main steps, including: problem exploration, problem definition, problem solving (see Fig. 1). In all phases, a human-centred approach was adopted, focusing on stakeholders' and communities' needs and people wellbeing and health as a priority, strictly linked to ecosystems regeneration, as a key objective of every strategic design and policy in line with the circular economy approach.

The first phase of problem exploration was dedicated to the identification of specific challenges for circular cultural tourism in the target areas, identifying strengths and weaknesses in terms of cultural heritage valorisation, infrastructure development, accessibility, services and facilities, policies, investments and incentives beyond the tourism sector and including cultural and creative industry, agricultural activities in rural landscapes, circular economy sector, technological and social

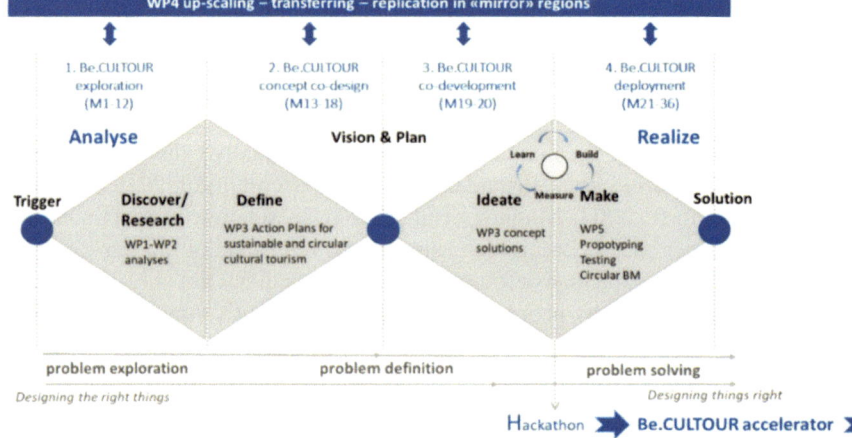

Fig. 1 Co-creation methodological framework in Be.CULTOUR. *Source* Gravagnuolo et al. (2021a, b)

innovation. After conducting an initial mapping of stakeholders, from the first phase onwards the project made efforts to balance different interests among the identified stakeholders. The second phase of problem definition focused on the co-design of possible solutions to overcome barriers and achieve specific objectives related to local challenges. In this phase, strategic Action Plans were co-created with local stakeholders in each pilot area, defining the targets to be reached and the monitoring framework. This strategic thinking and co-design exercise was particularly relevant as stakeholders were supported to strengthen their collaboration capacity through a series of facilitated co-design workshops during which diverse aspects of circular and human-centred cultural tourism were debated, analysed and synthesized into clear objectives and actions to be undertaken in the pilot sites. This was achieved through facilitated dialogue, consensus building, collaborative decision-making, adaptive management and transparent communication. The workshop organisers were provided toolboxes supporting facilitation. All exercises in the toolboxes were designed to overcome power imbalance as well as overcoming the challenge of limited resources in remote and smaller regions. Finally, the third phase of problem solving included diverse activities towards the implementation of the actions defined in the action plans, ranging from co-development of innovative solutions through hackathon and business acceleration process, as well as the implementation of collaborative actions by local organisations leading the action plan co-design process. This phase was important to start-up the action plans and test the feasibility of the proposed solutions, through a continuous monitoring, co-evaluation and feedback loop in the territories, which is fundamental to progress for turning 'usual' behavioural patterns into different actions that are able to contribute to intentionally reach the targets and objectives.

2.1 The Human-Centred Approach in the Be.CULTOUR Strategic Co-Design Experimentation

The human-centred approach provided a basis for new solutions towards circular cultural tourism in the Be.CULTOUR project (Bosone et al., 2019; Fusco Girard, 2019; Giacomin, 2014a; Krippendorff, 2004; Munhoz et al., 2020). It highlighted several aspects resulting from the empowerment of the people involved in the co-creation process (European Commission, 2020a, b). Local communities were considered to be experts in understanding of their place and potential and thus genuine cultural tourism attractiveness (in relation to opportunities as well as risks). People, organisations, individuals and communities, were involved in the design process in all pilot sites as holders of knowledge and awareness of the uniqueness of the area (Bosone et al., 2019; Gravagnuolo et al., 2021). At the same time, however, communities living in a given space need to see their surroundings with new eyes to restore local 'pride' and re-discover hidden 'treasures'. In working with various groups facing similar challenges, numerous approaches based on cooperation and analysis of problems from the perspective of people experiencing them were applied. Examples include Action Research, Participatory Action Research, community-based participatory research. References were made to these methods during particular exercises (e.g. serious game, stakeholder mapping, iteration in various workshop co-design modules), however the general approach in the co-creation was more creativity and innovation oriented. This enabled the communities to think about cultural heritage as a means of re-establishing local identity, to consider themselves at the same time as service providers, beneficiaries and visitors in the region who are taking advantage of what it has to offer and are also shaping this offer by understanding how to meet the needs of people coming from other areas. The famous sentence *Belief in your creative capacity lies at the heart of innovation* by David Kelley (IDEO) served as inspiration for developing this concept of work on the ground, facilitated by the local coordinators with the support of mentors and experts. In this way, as highlighted in the literature on human-centred approach, reference was made to the users and simultaneously to the principles of design for all (Clarkson & Coleman, 2010), human-centred city (European Commission, 2020a, b). Objectives of using this methodology and also adapting elements of other approaches in particular exercises delivered during workshops (e.g. customer journey mapping, scenario development, role-playing) were fostering innovation, deepening awareness of the challenges resulting from the environmental crisis and developing unique answers that can be applied locally and also replicated in other less-known cultural tourism destinations.

With the strong focus on human-centred approach in six Pilot Heritage Sites, while developing the framework for the process involving real communities with their values, needs, working conditions and organisational culture, it was necessary to know the advantages and disadvantages of the methods and tools themselves (Brandsen et al., 2018; Watts et al., 2018). The questions connected to the empathy and ethics included the issues of how to centre attention on humans while solving environmental problems caused by humans, how to ideate rapidly giving the diverse participants with various skills and abilities the opportunity to contribute, how to deal with the authorship of ideas in open innovation, how to use the unique creativity of the participants of the process and taking a responsibility once the tasks foreseen in the project are completed. The solution to these problems was to develop a Community of Practice stimulating mutual trust and collaboration. This applied to both the relationships within the international community of practice generated by the Be.CULTOUR network and within the local stakeholder ecosystems. This whole process of *supporting the development* of the Action Plans can be intended as a meta-reflection of the process of the *development* of the Action Plans—iterative, enabling feedback loops, inclusive and affirmative. On the basis of interviews, documentation, discussion, bilateral talks and community meetings, problems were identified and specific solutions were sought.

3   Towards a Replicable Model for Co-Design of Circular and Human-Centred Cultural Tourism Destinations

The aim of the strategic co-design exercise was to develop first concept ideas of innovative solutions for circular cultural tourism in the target areas. According to the human-centred approach, this phase was collaborative, inclusive, and iterative to ensure equal participation of diverse stakeholders. Local communities were working together to ideate concepts responding to the identified needs and reflecting to identify sustainable, circular solutions. The co-design process was developed in several sub-tasks:

1. Building 'Heritage Innovation Networks' in Pilot Heritage Sites and mapping stakeholders
2. Organise Local Workshops (three in each Pilot Heritage Site)
3. Define the initial collaboration Pact ("Local Pact")
4. Identify specific Innovation Areas of circular cultural tourism, as well as transversal innovation approaches and emerging trends, which are relevant for the pilot heritage site
5. Identify actions linked to potential innovative solutions in line with the Innovation Areas defined
6. Adopt the Action Plan and monitor progress

At the local level, the following Be.CULTOUR Innovation areas were taken into consideration while defining actions, sub-actions and innovative solutions: Rural co-living, Sensorial Heritage Experience, Contemporary Meanings of Heritage, Spiritual Travel Experience, Nature as Heritage, Industrial Heritage Experience, along with the following transversal innovation approaches: Circular tourism, Cultural Europeanisation, Human-centred, fair and responsible tourism, smart destination management.

3.1   Strategic Action Plans Co-Creation Methods

Collaborative innovation has been defined as the pursuit of innovations through the sharing of ideas, knowledge, expertise and opportunities (Ketchen et al., 2007). It can encompass a broad spectrum of external parties (e.g. customers, suppliers, competitors, universities and research institutes) and cover a range of collaboration forms and approaches (Chesbrough, 2003), including alliances, partnerships, networks and cooperative agreements (Feranita et al., 2017). Research and practice stress the relationship between collaboration in tourism innovation and the implementation of sustainable tourism. In this context, collaborative innovation through co-creation and co-design of sustainable products, services and experiences is key for capturing needs of residents and visitors (Font & Lynes, 2018) and ensure ongoing engagement and interest. A review of research highlights the importance of collaborative

Fig. 2 Workshops
methodological scheme

Local Workshop 1 - **Problem exploration**

↓

Local Workshop 2 - **Problem definition**

↓

Local Workshop 3 - **Problem solving**

innovation as a driver of (Marasco et al., 2018): superior performance (e.g. profitability) and innovativeness of tourism firms; new service market outcomes, new service development speed, quality of new services; democratized citizenship and creative practices for the innovation of urban tourism concepts/services; destination competitiveness through new or improved services and smart innovations; knowledge sharing of tacit and explicit knowledge among different stakeholders in networks; spin-offs and spill-overs.

In addition to the multi-stakeholder approach, the place-based dimension of collaborative innovation is crucial. Innovation takes place in a precise location, which suggests that the physical proximity of innovation players matters (Cohan, 2018; Misuraca et al., 2017). The strategic Action Plans were developed by the six communities primarily during the local workshops. The workshops provided a framework for the whole communities to meet and work together, while other activities (like community meetings and bilateral calls) included research partners and local coordinators. The entire process was conducted for one year including the preparatory phases, and the 18 workshops in total were delivered from November 2021 to June 2022. As shown in Fig. 2, the logic of the process followed three steps: problem exploration (workshop 1), problem definition (workshop 2), problem solving (workshop 3).

The Action Plans are therefore based on three pillars—diagnosis (of the local potentials, needs and challenges), mission (agreeing as an ecosystem of stakeholders—Heritage Innovation Network—on the path towards circular cultural tourism), and vision (concrete steps that will be implemented within indicated time frame). Additionally, the Action Plans:

- Contribute to the development strategies of pilot heritage sites and local governments
- Map the circular economy concept in the unique context of the local heritage and in connection to circular cultural tourism and beyond
- Refer to cultural Europeanisation, highlighting the European value of heritage in the pilot areas
- Valorise or re-valorise concrete intangible and tangible cultural heritage assets
- Use principles of human-centred approach (applied to both communities and visitors, all understood as beneficiaries of the revitalisation of the territory)
- Focus on Be.CULTOUR innovation areas
- Cover short-term and long-term perspectives going beyond the implementation of the project

- Be feasible in a given region and possible to be implemented by the local authorities or external stakeholders.

The process of Action Plans development was rooted in the preliminary work conducted to identify challenges and potentials of the heritage sites and overall cultural destinations, based on interviews to stakeholders, surveys to visitors and residents, statistical and territorial data collection and interpretation. This continuity was crucial in guaranteeing the relevance and importance of the Be.CULTOUR Action Plans in synergy with existing strategies and resources at territorial level, starting from building the knowledge framework and local context conditions. In this way it was also possible to identify stakeholders with various level of interest and influence on the project and approach them all, despite the power relations. Based on the identified gaps and potential, Action Plans contribute in innovative ways to existing plans and strategies and put the local communities at the centre of positive change.

In reference to the human-centred approach methodology, the workshop preparation process was based on the use of visual elements in co-creation exercises and processes (McKim, 1980; Norman, 2002). On the one hand, this meant using images in the materials. On the other hand, the goal was to encourage participants to form ideas in drawings, schemes, posters. In selected exercises local maps, newspapers, postcards and photos were used enabling visual storytelling fostering the co-creation process. Visual materials also served to widely disseminate the project approach and results (see Fig. 3). Within the Action Plans preparation process, the six pilot heritage sites were invited to interact on a collaborative digital board and reflect on the visual metaphor that best shows their experience in aligning bottom-up community plans with municipal, regional and national strategies. The exercise was inspired by the book *Images of Organization* by Alexander and Morgan (Alexander & Morgan, 1988) and concerned four selected metaphors (brain, machine, organism, instrument of domination) that illustrate complex relationships in a simple way. The aim was to provoke self-reflection of the participants and possible search for better ways of cooperation and communication between the various levels in the further work on Action Plans.

3.2   Results of the Six Strategic Action Plans in the European Pilot Heritage Sites

The core of the co-creation processes in human-centred approach during the Be.CULTOUR workshops was the empowerment of the communities involved in creating actions, based on the capacities and needs of representatives of various groups. Participants of workshops at the community level had the opportunity to address the development of circular and sustainable cultural tourism in the field of heritage via innovative activities, currently in the process of being implemented (2022–2023). In these community driven, bottom-up strategic visions, sustainability and circularity were "mediated" in two ways. First through culture as a means of

Fig. 3 Visual co-creation in Pilot Heritage Sites. Copyrights: Be.CULTOUR project, pictures by local coordinators taken during the local workshops from left to right: Romania-Moldova, Vojvodina, Aragon)

regional development, embedded in the local history potential that can be economically and socially beneficial for the community and offering visitors a unique experience. Second, through capitalization of cultural tourism as a potentially sustainable business activity. In all six Pilot Heritage Sites, 148 actions in total were designed and proposed by the stakeholders (Aragon—6, Basilicata—19, Larnaca—13, Romania/ Moldova—8, Västra Götaland—48, Vojvodina—54). As mentioned in the Action Plan from Basilicata pilot site, the human-centred approach was *"focusing on the relationship between people and with places, aiming at re-discovering and enhancing the "Genius loci" of the sites, from forests and astonishing lakes to cities and towns inhabited since ancient times"* (Ćwikła et al., 2022) (p. 283). This ambition, which additionally refers to the life-centred approach as well as to the departure from the conventional thought of the Anthropocene (Bonneuil & Fressoz, 2017), is also reflected in other Action Plans (e.g., Aragon and Västra Götaland). In all six Pilot Heritage Sites, it was thus crucial to recognize the entanglement between cultural and natural heritage, temporary visitors and permanent residents (vulnerable social groups representatives) around identified assets and within the system of stakeholders (Fig. 4).

Fig. 4 Stakeholders' categories involved in the co-creation process of the Action Plans

The issue of inclusion was not understood purely as "participation." The aim was to tailor the actions to specific needs of different people. As a result of defining the path towards circular tourism, the benefits are to be felt both by the local communities and the visitors (e.g. in Romania/Moldova the "Stephen the Great VR route" action). In addition, the communities designing actions highlighted the importance of specific groups, including: education (in Romania/Moldova and in Basilicata), youth and ageing population (in Aragon and in Västra Götaland), women (travelling alone or gaining new opportunities to run their own business, taking over leadership roles which is considered not sufficient in Vojvodina and in Aragon), and diverse communities (in Vojvodina specific actions have been proposed to reflect on the inclusion and social cohesion).

Accessibility has been reflected in various ways in the actions in terms of marking the interesting spots in a simple yet communicative way, offering translation in several languages, including people with disabilities, creating friendly offers for families, minorities, diverse genders. Inclusion is rooted in European identity and history, from great ethnical variety (Vojvodina), through traces from the history (Jewish and Mudejar heritage in Aragon) to relative social homogeneity in a country with high percentage of foreign-born population (Västra Götaland). Each Pilot Heritage Site has a unique connection with European culture and contributes to its diverse identity (e.g. the legacy of Emperor Federico II in Basilicata and Stephen the Great in Romania/Moldova). In addition, the shift from linear to circular tourism was considered a financial opportunity to save resources and develop new businesses models enhancing economic opportunities for individuals and communities. The actions proposed in the six Pilot Heritage Sites reflected the Be.CULTOUR Innovation Areas and interpret the emerging trends identified in the project concept are based on unexceptional, engaging storytelling, authentic yet unusual understanding of heritage, and seek for place-based and people-based solutions. Those context-specific reflections on circular tourism aim at turning visitors into temporary residents and residents into temporary visitors. The stories told to explain ambitions towards circular tourism and beyond should bring benefits to communities, tourists, industries and businesses, and the environment.

One clear conclusion from the process across the pilots is that the co-design is key to unlocking innovation for circular tourism. Its success and influence, particularly regarding novelty for the tourism sector, lies therein with its governance structure allowing co-decisions and co-implementation. For further consideration in replication and upscaling efforts following trends highlighted by the Be.CULTOUR community of practice it could be inspirational to reflect upon the following aspects:

- *Highlighting nature in areas with unique cultural heritage*—Pilot Heritage Areas recognized as
- assets not only the intangible and tangible cultural heritage, but also the surrounding nature (e.g., the "Innovative Ecosystem Centre" in Aragon; the "Monticchio lakes paths and natural heritage valorisation in Rionero and surroundings"in Basilicata; "The Bison's Land Heritage" in Romania/Moldova; in Vojvodina the "Monastery product development").

- *Sensorial and experiential stays*—(e.g., in Basilicata "Astrotourism projects linked with ancient heritage sites and remains; in Västra Götaland "new winter experiences, skiing, skating, ice fishing"; Vojvodina's. "Development of human-centred, total wellness tourism"; in Larnaca, spiritual journeys).
- *Digital environment*—The presence of digital tools, accelerated by the COVID-19 pandemic, can be seen as opportunities and in the case of the Be.CULTOUR Pilot Heritage Sites this assumption contributes to fairly novel approaches. For example, the historic, religious assets in Vojvodina will be linked with sustainable tourism via digital presence. This idea combines two worlds: the virtual one as space for promotion of tourist destinations and the physical one as terrain for local entrepreneurs taking financial advantage of novel approaches to cultural heritage. In Larnaca the on-line tools have practical function facilitating the organisational processes while in Vojvodina herbs are to be used not only in culinary products but also be part of digital archive documenting the heritage of the region.
- *Hubs and labs for innovation, business, and entrepreneurship*—As stated in the document from Basilicata *"The strategic Action Plan of Vulture—Alto Bradano for circular cultural tourism aims at re-interpreting in innovative ways the rich tangible, intangible and natural heritage of this unique area of Basilicata to make it a driver of new attractiveness and wellbeing for residents and visitors"* (Ćwikła et al., 2022) (p. 284). In Västra Götaland the actions on "Attracting new inhabitants by interpretation campaign" and in Vojvodina "Business Hub Establishment in Sremski Karlovci" should create new opportunities for entrepreneurs and businesswomen (and businessmen). In Larnaca a living lab will be created as an open, innovative ecosystem enabling further innovations in the areas and their implementation based on public–private-people partnership.

The key commonalities that have emerged from the Action Plans can be summarised.

by the following observations: reducing environmental impact, taking care for both residents and the visitors, striving for balance in exploitation of the assets and their protection, establishing new opportunities for just transition and resilient entrepreneurial models based on cultural and natural heritage in circular and human-centred cultural tourism. All Action Plans put people at the centre of actions, keeping in mind the crucial relation with nature, balance in developing innovative solutions and the boundaries needed to be respected. At the same time, all actions are embedded in the local circumstances which influence their uniqueness in cultural, economic and social aspects. Thus, some actions are more natural heritage oriented (Aragon), some are rooted in the historical stories (Basilicata), other in focusing on the needs of the residents (Västra Götaland), several are based on comprehensive strategies of development (Vojvodina), other aim at defining new goals and opportunities for the communities resulting from shift towards circular tourism (Larnaca) and some are using archetypal figures from the past in shaping the newest European history attractive for visitors (Romania/Moldova). Furthermore, all Action Plans are contributing to the existing ambitions aiming at sustainable development in the given regions (Table 1).

Table 1 Overview of chosen strategic documents Action Plans are contributing to. *Source* Ćwikła et al. (2022, p. 56)

Pilot heritage site region	Strategic document	Level
Aragon	Sustainable Tourism Strategy 2030	Regional
Basilicata	Touristic Promotion Plan (2021–2024)	Regional
Larnaca	Cyprus Action Plan for the transition to a circular economy 2021–2027,	National
Romania/ Moldova	National Sustainable Development Strategy SDD2030 (Romania), various regulations of the Ministry of Culture and the Ministry of Environment (Moldova)	National
Västra Götaland	Regional Development Strategy 2021–2030, Västra Götalands Smart Specialization Strategy (3S), Regional Cultural Strategy 2020–2023	Regional
Vojvodina	National and Provincial Policies and Legislation, EU Framework for Sustainable and Cultural Tourism	Various

3.3 Key Achievements and Future Outlook in Six Pilot Heritage Sites

The project focused on stakeholder engagement and the integration of circular economy principles to create a more inclusive, resilient, environmentally friendly as well as innovative and inspiring cultural tourism models. Key achievements can be summarized in the following way. The project successfully engaged various stakeholders, including local communities, tourism businesses, government agencies, cultural and research organizations. Regular consultations, workshops, and webinar were organized both at the project level and at the local coordinator level to ensure active participation and collaboration during co-creation and co-implementation phases. Stakeholders were involved in decision-making processes, allowing them to contribute their local knowledge, cultural heritage, and concerns. This participatory approach fostered a sense of ownership of the co-created Action Plans and cooperation among stakeholders.

The resulting Action Plans promoted the adoption of circular economy principles within the cultural tourism strategies of remote European destinations. This involved reducing waste, optimizing natural resources use, enhancing skills and capacities between tourism operators and stakeholders, adopting green and slow mobility systems in the areas, and encouraging sustainable practices. Local businesses were stimulated to co-implement specific measures such as waste recycling, energy-efficient infrastructure, and sustainable sourcing of goods and services. This happened while rethinking the potential of the cultural and natural heritage assets.

Last, but not least, Action Plans particularly focused on preserving and enhancing the less-known cultural and natural heritage of these remote European destinations. Cultural heritage recovery, regeneration and valorisation involved mapping cultural and natural assets, identifying intangible cultural practices, and developing sustainable tourism and place-branding strategies that aim to respect local traditions and values, avoiding commodification processes of local cultural heritage, often at the risk of disappearing due to abandonment and neglect. Plans for allowing cultural visitors to discover local heritage were developed, including use of digital infrastructure to actively engage with local communities, learn about their traditions, and contribute to their preservation.

Compared to initial context situations, it could be observed as an increase in knowledge and awareness of stakeholders on circular economy, networking and collaboration benefits, innovation and strategic planning. New EU funded projects and local initiatives were starting, such as the Single Market Programme "TRACE" (SMEs transition towards a European circular tourism ecosystem) running in 4 out of 6 pilot heritage sites, engaging tourism operators and stakeholders in transitioning to circular economy updating and enhancing their skills and business model and accessing environmental certifications. Moreover, a series of cultural initiatives and festivals were launched under the Action Plans implementation, and new financial resources were attracted to territories for developing bike-sharing projects and bike routes, digital supporting tools for enhanced visit to cultural and natural sites, as well as intangible heritage recognition and valorisation.

Clearly, the launch of several initiatives does not ensure that all objectives and results will be reached, however it can be foreseen that the enhanced capacity and knowledge of stakeholders in the target areas will be key for monitoring, adjusting and implementing sustainability and circularity actions in the longer term, beyond the EU funded project timespan.

The next session discusses the strengths and barriers encountered during the co-creation process in the pilot heritage sites of Be.CULTOUR project, proposing conclusive reflections on next research needs towards a more circular and sustainable cultural tourism.

4   Discussion and Conclusions

The outcomes of Action Plans can be used as a blueprint for similar initiatives in other remote European destinations. During the Be.CULTOUR project, replication and peer-learning was discussed with 16 additional cultural tourism ecosystems and 3 experienced advisor organisations (CreaTour network, Historic Environment Scotland, Future for Religious Heritage) to co-learn and exchange ideas and reflections. Further collaboration with tourism authorities and organizations at the regional, national, and international levels was fostered to facilitate the scaling up and replication of the project's achievements and thus ensure longer term sustainability. Understanding the needs of the stakeholders and embracing emerging technologies and innovative solutions will be crucial for developing circular cultural tourism in remote European destinations.

Continuous education and awareness campaigns targeting both tourists and locals will play a vital role in promoting sustainable tourism practices. In Be.CULTOUR, this is part of the place-branding strategies tailored at the local level and developed with the stakeholders. First ideas of tangible-intangible products and services rooted in natural-cultural heritage are not only results of human-centred approach as business strategy (Giacomin, 2014b) but can also go beyond human-centred approach as creative strategies highlighting phenomena in the living systems (Jones, 2022) that are to be considered part of the circular cultural tourism. The holistic approach to these major challenges requires not only what can be provided within a framework of a project, based on proven methodologies, but needs to trigger actions fuelled by the cultural values, artefacts and assumptions the heritage is manifestation of. The already mentioned local knowledge needs further place-based and people-based sources of information. Thus, in relation to the research literature, the experience of the six Be.CULTOUR pilot heritage sites could be seen as an example of generating situated knowledge. Highlighting the better understanding of the local heritage with intuition and generational expertise in dealing with uncertainty from this point of view could be an added value of the project, arguing the limits of dualistic approach in perceiving and tackling climate change with innovative circular solutions in cultural tourism and beyond.

Throughout the period of work on Action Plans co-creation (Autumn 2021 to Summer 2022), research actors, local leaders and stakeholders were involved in the process, defining and implementing the methodology and tools to support the collaborative work. During the process, the project encountered various barriers and obstacles (natural in collaborative efforts) that were collectively addressed, taking into account the external and internal environments of the organizations and groups involved in the co-creation process. The external environment refers to the broader perspective encompassing organizations, individuals, and factors that influence stakeholder networks' functioning both during the project and beyond. On the other hand, the internal environment pertains to the relationships among stakeholders directly engaged in the Action Plans, including interactions during individual meetings and all three workshops (Fig. 5).

Fig. 5 Stakeholders' categories involved in the co-creation process of the Action Plans

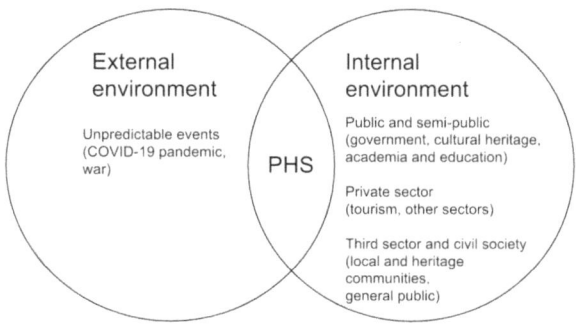

External environment had an influence on the process, from the covid-19 pandemic to the war in Ukraine, at the border of Romania-Moldova pilot heritage site. The uncertainty is often discussed at the local levels with the authorities and for example tour operators or other professionals from the tourism industry.

Despite the Action Plans implementation is currently not concluded, some considerations on the methodology and results can be made.

First, it should be noted that stakeholder engagement requires time, resources, and expertise. However, stakeholders, particularly local communities and small businesses, may have limited resources and capacities to actively participate in the co-creation process. This issue entails the local innovation ecosystem, which should be progressively enhanced at the European level shifting the focus from big innovative cities to small urban areas and remote, rural contexts. Between the pilot areas, diverse levels of engagement and advancements could be observed in Be.CULTOUR project. The relationship between the local innovation ecosystem, the capacity of collaboration and level of trust, and the results obtained will be objects of further exploration to identify the main drivers and barriers of co-creation processes for circular cultural tourism in remote and rural areas. So far, peer-learning and exchange of best practices was observed to be very beneficial to enhance the level of knowledge of stakeholders and small businesses who could have difficulties in becoming more innovative and entrepreneurial.

Another issue could be related to the lack of continuity in the long term. Sustaining the participants' initial level of engagement proved challenging due to the extended co-working period spanning several months. However, the workshops were designed to be inclusive, allowing for new participants to join and contribute. Additionally, in some areas multiple projects can be ongoing involving local stakeholders. Thus, participants often have to allocate resources to other activities. Private enterprises and start-ups faced greater difficulties in this regard compared to public organizations. To accommodate the needs of this group, the workshop dates, times, and formats were adjusted accordingly, with some exercises conducted online and others in person. The local coordinators and facilitators made continuous efforts to maintain participants' involvement, overcome biases, and foster an inclusive environment. For instance, additional webinars and consultations were organized to demonstrate the project's ability to adapt and respond to changing circumstances and requirements.

An important issue during the co-creation process concerned reaching not only the 'usual suspects' but also other stakeholders. For this purpose, a stakeholder ecosystem mapping was carried out, repeated and deepened during the workshops, opening the invitation to smaller businesses, minority cultures and diverse social groups, both individuals or representatives of diverse organisations. The resulting Action Plans show a mix of small-scale actions conducted by informal groups and more infrastructural investments fostered by the authorities. The needed synergies to carry out the actions at all levels are continuously monitored and object of discussion with the local coordinators, adjusting and integrating the efforts during all phases of implementation taking into account the needs of diverse community groups. At the end of the co-creation process, participants could commit to a 'Local Pact' as an expression of interest in further collaboration.

The utilization of co-creation processes in developing strategic Action Plans can serve as valuable tools to initiate a reflection based on values in cultural tourism destinations. These processes aim to identify the objectives (what) and the underlying motivations (why) for achieving them. The initial reflection phase was considered essential and emerged as the most crucial step prior to devising actions and solutions. It played a significant role in fostering shared values among stakeholders and establishing a consensus on the desired future development of the cultural tourism destination. Community engagement and participatory decision-making can enhance opportunities for collaboration, however it should be also taken into account that the diverse stakeholders involved may have diverse interests, priorities, and perspectives. Balancing these interests and finding common ground can be challenging. For example, local communities may prioritize cultural preservation, while tourism businesses may focus on economic growth. However, apparently conflicting interests could be put in synergy through creative solutions. Instead of adopting "business as usual", creativity and innovation was fostered in all pilot heritage sites to combine heritage conservation, communities' needs and economic opportunities. Moreover, exercises such as 'future newspaper' and other visualisation techniques proved to be a valid support to enhance stakeholders' capacity to identify common objectives and pursue them over time, sharing similar visions. Clearly, stakeholders' engagement could be not enough to ensure that co-created action plans are implemented in the long term. Institutional commitment at the local and regional level could greatly contribute to stimulate mutual trust and cooperation, stimulating further investments in terms of human resources, capacity building, and financial support.

Also, lack of knowledge and understanding of circular economy, sustainable cultural tourism, cultural heritage regeneration, collaboration and innovation, could hinder not only the implementation, but also the effectiveness of the co-creation processes. Thus, initial knowledge sharing activities involving researchers, public officers, innovators and diverse community groups would be largely beneficial to enhance local capacity (human capital) and increase the likelihood of effective and feasible action plans preparation, enhancing their implementation over the longer term.

Finally, availability of reliable data and data management and interpretation capacity at the local level can be key to support action plans choices, monitoring and review processes, adjusting targets, resources and timing based on evidence of the impacts and effectiveness of diverse actions, projects and initiatives. In remote areas, data management can be particularly challenging, as less data are available compared to large cities or well-known tourism destinations. However, a focused effort in retrieving and analysing data should be foreseen to allow better management and understanding of ongoing processes.

The experience of Be.CULTOUR pilot heritage sites in co-creating strategic action plans for circular and human-centred cultural tourism can be a relevant background for other less known and remote destinations to co-develop collaborative strategies for cultural tourism innovation, enhancing cultural heritage regeneration, people wellbeing, and generating long-lasting local economic wealth grounded on a circular ecological economy model to benefit people and nature at the same time.

Acknowledgements A.G. developed the overall research concept and co-creation methodology, introduction and research questions, identification of pilot case studies, coordination of the research, discussion and conclusions, as well as funding acquisition. M.C. developed the specific tools for co-creation, coordinated the developing and monitoring of Action Plans in all pilot heritage sites, results of co-creation process and co-developed conclusive reflections. C.G. co-developed the research and co-creation methodology, introduction and conclusive reflections. M.B. developed literature research background, and contributed to monitoring of Action Plans and conclusive reflections.

Funding This research was funded under the framework of Horizon 2020 research project Be.CULTOUR "Beyond cultural tourism". This project has received funding from the European Union's Horizon 2020 research and innovation programme under grant agreement No 101004627.

References

Alexander, J. W., & Morgan, G. (1988). Images of organization. *Am. J. Nurs.*, *88*, https://doi.org/10.2307/3425778.

Angrisano, M., Biancamano, P. F., Bosone, M., Carone, P., Daldanise, G., De Rosa, F., Franciosa, A., Gravagnuolo, A., Iodice, S., Nocca, F. et al. (2016). Towards operationalizing UNESCO Recommendations on"Historic Urban Landscape": A position paper. *Aestimum, 69*. https://doi.org/10.13128/Aestimum-20454.

Bonneuil, C., & Fressoz, J.-B. (2017). *The shock of the anthropocene*. Verso.

Bosone, M., & Nocca, F. (2022). Human circular tourism as the tourism of tomorrow: The role of travellers in achieving a more sustainable and circular tourism. *Sustainability, 14*, 12218. https://doi.org/10.3390/su141912218

Bosone, M., Micheletti, S., Gravagnuolo, A., Garzillo, C., & Wildman, A. (2019). Towards a circular governance for the adaptive reuse of cultural heritage. *BDC. Boll. Del Cent. Calza Bini, 19*, 279–305. https://doi.org/10.6092/2284-4732/7270

Brandsen, T., Steen, T., & Verschuere, B. (2018). *Co-production and co-creation: Engaging citizens in public services.*

CenTour project CEnTOUR—Circular Economy in Tourism.

Chesbrough, H. W. (2003). *Open innovation the new imperative for creating and profiting from technology Xerox PARC the achievements and limits of closed innovation*. Press.

Chesbrough, H. W., & Appleyard, M. M. (2007). Open innovation and strategy. *Calif. Manage. Rev., 50*.

Cirtoinno project—Destination: A circular tourism economy Cirtoinno project—Destination: A circular tourism economy.

Clarkson, J., & Coleman, R. (2010). Inclusive design. *Journal of Engineering Design, 21*, 127–129. https://doi.org/10.1080/09544821003693689

CLIC project *CLIC Pilot Local Action Plans: One Approach, Diverse Outcomes*. (2021).

CLIC project—Circular models Leveraging Investments in Cultural heritage adaptive reuse Horizon 2020 project "CLIC project—Circular models Leveraging Investments in Cultural heritage adaptive reuse."

Cohan, P.S. *Startup Cities*; 2018;

Ćwikła, M., Garzillo, C., & Silverton, S. (2022). *Action Plans and concept solutions for sustainable cultural tourism in pilot heritage sites*

Ellen MacArthur Foundation Towards the Circular Economy: Economyc and business rationale for accelerated transition. (2013). *J. Ind. Ecol.*

Ellen MacArthur Foundation; McKinsey & Company Towards the Circular Economy : Accelerating the scale-up across global supply chains. (2014). *World Econ. Forum.*

Ellen MacArthur Foundation *Growth within: a circular economy vision for a competitive Europe.* (2015a).

Ellen MacArthur Foundation *Towards a Circular Economy: Business Rationale for an Accelerated Transition.* (2015b).

Ellen MacArthur Foundation What is a circular economy?

European Union *Transition Pathway for Tourism.* (2022).

European Commission *The Human-Centred City: Recommendations for research and innovation actions*; Luxembourg (2020a).

European Commission *The human-centred city. Opportunities for citizens through research and innovation.* (2020b).

European Commission *The European Green Deal.* (2019).

European Comission New European Bauhaus. *Europa.Eu.* (2021a).

European Commission EU taxonomy for sustainable activities. *Eur. Comm.* (2021b).

Feranita, F., Kotlar, J., & De Massis, A. (2017). Collaborative innovation in family firms: Past research, current debates and agenda for future research. *J. Fam. Bus. Strateg. 8.* https://doi.org/10.1016/j.jfbs.2017.07.001.

Font, X., & Lynes, J. (2018). Corporate social responsibility in tourism and hospitality. *J. Sustain. Tour. 26.*

Fusco Girard, L. (2019). The human-centred city development and the circular regeneration. In *Matera, città del sistema ecologico uomo/società/natura il ruolo della cultura per la rigenerazione del sistema urbano/territoriale*; Fusco Girard, L., Trillo, C., Bosone, M., Eds.; Giannini Publisher: Naples. ISBN 978-88-6906-120-2.

Fusco Girard, L., & Gravagnuolo, A. (2017). Circular economy and cultural heritage/landscape regeneration. Circular business, financing and governance models for a competitive Europe. *BDC. Boll. Del Cent. Calza Bini 1/2017*, 35–52.

Fusco Girard, L., Nocca, F., & Gravagnuolo, A. (2019). Matera: City of nature, city of culture, city of regeneration. Towards a landscape-based and culture-based urban circular economy. *Aestimum 74*, 5–42, https://doi.org/10.13128/aestim-7007.

Fusco Girard, L., & Nocca, F. (2020). Climate change and health impacts in urban areas: Towards hybrid evaluation tools for new governance. *Atmosphere (basel).* https://doi.org/10.3390/atmos11121344

Giacomin, J. (2014). What is human centred design? *Des. J. 17.* https://doi.org/10.2752/175630614X14056185480186.

Giacomin, J. (2014b). What is human centred design? *The Design Journal, 17*, 606–623.

Gravagnuolo, A., & Varotto, M. (2021). Terraced landscapes regeneration in the perspective of the circular economy. *Sustain, 13*, https://doi.org/10.3390/SU13084347.

Gravagnuolo, A., Micheletti, S., & Bosone, M. (2021a). A participatory approach for "Circular" adaptive reuse of cultural heritage. Building a heritage community in Salerno, Italy. *Sustain. 13, 4812.* https://doi.org/10.3390/SU13094812.

Gravagnuolo, A., Marasco, A., Fasciglione, M., Xydia, S., Matei, A., Garzillo, C., & D'Auria, I. (2021b). *Protocol / methodology for human-centred innovation in sustainable and circular cultural tourism (v1).*

Gupta, J., Hurley, F., Grobicki, A., Keating, T., Stoett, P., Baker, E., Guhl, A., Davies, J., & Ekins, P. (2019). Communicating the health of the planet and its links to human health. *Lancet Planet Heal, 3*, e204–e206.

Hanza, R. (2018). Contributions regarding the research of the sustainable development in agrotourism from a circular economy perspective, Universitatea „Lucian Blaga" din Sibiu.

Horizon 2020 project "Be.CULTOUR—Beyond CULtural TOURism: heritage innovation networks as drivers of Europeanisation towards a human-centred and circular tourism economy."

ILUCIDARE project *Evaluation Report on Focus Groups and Co-Creation Ateliers.* (2020).

IPCC *Climate Change 2014: Synthesis Report. Contribution of Working Groups I, II and III to the Fifth Assessment Report of the Intergovernmental Panel on Climate Change.* (2014). ISBN 9789291691432.

IPCC *Global warming of 1.5°C*. (2018). ISBN 9789291691531.

IPCC *Special Report: Global Warming of 1.5 C*. (2019).

Jones, H. (2022). Beyond human-centred design. Mapping Empathy in Living Systems. In *Metadesigning Designing in the Anthropocene*; Wood, J., Ed.; Routledge: New York, pp. 1–14.

Ketchen, D. J., Ireland, R. D., & Snow, C. C. (2007). Strategic entrepreneurship, collaborative innovation, and wealth creation. *Strateg. Entrep. J. 1.* https://doi.org/10.1002/sej.20.

Krippendorff, K. (2004). Intrinsic motivation and human-centred design. *Theor. Issues Ergon. Sci. 5.* https://doi.org/10.1080/1463922031000086717.

Manniche, J., Larsen, K. T., Broegaard, R. B., & Holland, E. (2017). *Destination: A circular tourism economy*

Marasco, A., De Martino, M., Magnotti, F., & Morvillo, A. (2018). Collaborative innovation in tourism and hospitality: A systematic review of the literature. *International Journal of Contemporary Hospitality Management, 30,* 2364–2395. https://doi.org/10.1108/IJCHM-01-2018-0043

McKim, R. H. (1980). *Thinking visually: A strategy manual for problem solving.* Dale Seymour Publications.

Misuraca, G.; Pasi, G.; Abadie, F. Innovating EU Social Protection Systems through ICTs. *JRC Insights—Soc. Policy Innov. Ser.* **2017.**

Munhoz, D. R. M., Fadel, L. M., Spinillo, C. G., Oliveira, A. E. F. de, Assis, K. M. M. de., Júnior, D. J. L. R. (2020). A human centred-design approach to a serious game in health training for the open university of the unified health system (UNA-SUS/UFMA) in Brazil. *Eur. J. Teach. Educ. 2,* 24–34. https://doi.org/10.33422/ejte.v2i3.493.

Naydenov, K. (2018). Circular tourism as a key for eco-innovations in circular economy based on sustainable development. *Int. Multidiscip. Sci. GeoConference Surv. Geol. Min. Ecol. Manag. SGEM 18,* 135–142. https://doi.org/10.5593/sgem2018/5.3/S28.017.

Nocca, F., Bosone, M., De Toro, P., & Fusco Girard, L. (1845). Towards the human circular tourism: Recommendations, actions, and multidimensional indicators for the tourist category. *Sustainability, 2023,* 15. https://doi.org/10.3390/su15031845

Norman, D. (2002). Emotion & design: attractive things work better. *Interactions, 9.*

Open Heritage project *Organizing, Promoting and Enabling Heritage Reuse through Inclusion, Technology, Ac-cess, Governance and Empowerment.* (2019).

Patti, S., & Messina, A. (2019). From linear to circular tourism: Environmental challenge for tourism. *Adv. Integr. Approaches to Environ. Econ. Policy Emerg. Res. Oppor.* 120–139. https://doi.org/10.4018/978-1-5225-9562-5.ch007.

The European Parliament New Circular Economy Action Plan. *Integr. Secur. Wester Eur.* (2021).

ROCK project *Integrated Management Plans (IMPs).* (2021).

Sorin, F., & Einarsson, S. (2020). *Circular Economy in Travel and Tourism: A conceptual framework for a sustainable, resilient and future proof industry transition.*

UNEP *Decoupling Natural Resource Use and Environmental Impacts from Economic Growth.* (2011). ISBN 9789280731675.

Watts, N., Amann, M., Arnell, N., Ayeb-Karlsson, S., Belesova, K., Berry, H., Bouley, T., Boykoff, M., Byass, P., Cai, W., et al. (2018). The 2018 report of the Lancet Countdown on health and climate change: Shaping the health of nations for centuries to come. *Lancet, 392,* 2479–2514.

Cultural Tourism in the Cyclades Before and After the Pandemic: A Stakeholders' Perspective

Theano S. Terkenli◉ and Vasilki Georgoula◉

Abstract The paper engages in a critical assessment of the changes in cultural tourism largely due to the COVID-19 pandemic, from the period before to the period after the pandemic, as regards both the supply and the demand sides of tourism, through the eyes of local/regional/national stakeholders, in the case of the Cyclades, Greece. Methodologically, the study relies on a series of stakeholders' interviews, a round-table discussion and a short questionnaire, undertaken in the context of the H2020 EU project SPOT, during the years 2020–2022. This material is then combined, using a SWOT analysis, in the context of a discussion and assessment of the problems, pitfalls and potential ensuing from the pandemic in Cyclades cultural tourism, towards a resilient, sustainable, or transformative future for the islands' tourism and cultural sectors. The paper begins with an overview of relevant scientific literature, it continues with the presentation of the study's research questions and data collection, and then proceeds to the analysis and discussion of the stakeholders' opinions, perspectives, visions and recommendations on the changing relationship culture-tourism and the SWOT analysis. A general conclusion is that current and emerging trends and patterns seem to reinforce the reciprocal relationship culture-tourism, but also to reconfigure it, in line with new and evolving trends and patterns of cultural tourism.

Keywords Cultural tourism · Tourism sustainability · Local sustainability · Post pandemic · Cyclades · Greece

T. S. Terkenli (✉)
Department of Geography, University of the Aegean, University Hill, Mytilene, Greece
e-mail: terkenli@aegean.gr

V. Georgoula
Department of Tourism Economic and Management, University of the Aegean, Michalon 8, Chios, Greece
e-mail: v.georgoula@aegean.gr

1 Introduction

The COVID-19 pandemic (2020–2022), currently at its end, instigated a long series of serious impacts on tourism and related sectors and activities. Some of its repercussions seem destined to alter or at least modify 21st mobility patterns and travel cultures, while others seem to have dissipated into a return to 'business as usual'. Greek tourism strongly reflects these trends, with the Cyclades, reaching record highs, at the tail-end of the pandemic.[1] In 2022, the country welcomed over 31 million airport arrivals, whereas the overall number of inbound visitors in Greece had peaked at roughly 34 million in 2019 (INSETE, 2020; The National Herald, 2023). Specifically, Greek islands, and particularly the Cyclades marked a 39.8 percent increase in tourist arrivals to 1.1 million in the January-August 2022 period or up by an additional 313,000, compared to the same period in record year 2019[2]. This article tackles the lessons, insights, and prospects that the pandemic imparted on Cyclades cultural tourism, which must, nevertheless be placed in their broader context of a series of hatching and incumbent crises of global scope, in all sectors of life, including tourism, towards a resilient or transformative and sustainable future for the islands' tourism and cultural sectors.

The role, position, and potential of 'culture' in/ for tourism during this volatile and transformative period was and continues to be less straightforward than that of 'nature', where a turn towards 'greener' and more sustainable tourism, at more remote and 'safe'/ protected, less crowded destinations, has gained ground. Not only does 'culture' defy prescriptive and reductionist approaches to its study and understanding, but it is also always under flux and regeneration. Furthermore, culture represents an often-unstated motive for travel and tourism, that spans an endless gamut of attractions, which elude statistical recording and proper scientific analysis, rendering continuous research into culture-motivated tourism ('cultural tourism') an important scientific objective on a permanent basis (Jacobsen et al., 2021; UNWTO, 2020).

This paper explores cultural tourism trends, insights, and prospects as they have emerged from the period of the pandemic, in a comparative study of pre- and post-pandemic stakeholders' opinions, perspectives, visions and recommendations on the changing relationship culture-tourism, in the Cyclades, Greece. It engages in a critical assessment and SWOT analysis of the changes in cultural tourism largely due to the COVID-19 pandemic, from the period before to the period after the pandemic, as regards both the supply and the demand sides of tourism. It achieves this goal through the eyes of local/regional/national stakeholders, with the aid of qualitative data collection undertaken in the context of the H2020 EU project SPOT[3] during the years 2020–2022. The approach is a case-study analysis, purporting to contribute to theory and empirical knowledge on current change in the tourism sector, and

---

[1] https://www.schengenvisainfo.com/news/greece-aegean-islands-register-record-tourist-arrivals.

[2] https://news.gtp.gr/2022/10/03/greek-islands-win-share-8-month-tourism-arrivals.

[3] http://www.spotprojecth2020.eu/.

specifically in heavily tourism-dependent economies/ societies, such as the Greek islands.

2 Theoretical Background

Tourism studies and practices have increasingly tended to engage with or consider culture, as a pivotal factor contributing to or affected by processes of production of tourism spaces/ places/ landscapes, movement, sustainability, development, identity, etc. Even though culture is a complex concept and constantly in flux and redefinition (Richards, 2018), it lies at the crux of the tourism phenomenon. Broadly defined as the highest-level, most deeply-ingrained, comprehensive and stable system of reference in human life (Throsby, 2008; Williams, 1958), culture represents all tangible and intangible manifestations of human life and creativity, which, in turn, may generate recreational/ tourism mobilities, termed 'cultural tourism' (Mandic & Kennell, 2021; Pandora, 2009; Richards, 2018).

For the purposes of our study, we adopt the definition of cultural tourism as the compound set of activities of tourism planning, effectuating, and experiencing a destination, with the—broadly defined—motive of culture (Mandic & Kennell, 2021). Furthermore, for our study purposes, we establish that we embrace culture in its broader sense, as encompassing all relevant tourist motives and typologies (Kaufman & Scantlebury, 2007; McKercher & Cros, 2003; Sayeh, 2022; Weaver et al., 2001), with special attention not to delimit it to 'high culture' or 'heritage' applications to tourism, as is often cultural tourism in Greece misleadingly confounded with.

The last few decades have witnessed significant research advances in cultural tourism (Chen & Huang, 2017; McKercher, 2002) through various perspectives, with a special emphasis on its complex and variegated motivational aspects of cultural tourism (Kay, 2009; McKercher & Cros, 2003; Weaver et al., 2001). According to Richards (2021) (Richards, 2021), the clear challenge posed in defining cultural tourism seems to be the conceptualization both of cultural products offered for tourist consumption and of the cultural processes which generate the motivation to participate in cultural tourism. Cultural tourists, thus, are not homogeneous; they may respond to a series of different aspects of attractions/ products that may relate to any number of distinctive material, intellectual, spiritual, and emotional features offered by a destination (UNWTO, 2017). Relevant research inroads, however, seem to have been seriously compounded by the COVID-19 pandemic (Jacobsen et al., 2021; Knezevic et al., 2021), which, nonetheless, presented new grounds for furthering the study of cultural tourism, by developing pertinent knowledge in times of great fluidity and future uncertainty. Our study is placed in the latter context and perspective.

Despite the major upheaval that the COVID-19 pandemic wrought into the tourism sector, up until 2020, tourism arrivals and expenditure had continued to grow (UNWTO, 2020), a trend that also reflects tourism trends at the top Greek destinations (INSETE, 2020, 2021). The Cycladic Islands, among the most world-renowned tourism destinations in Greece, belong to the Southern Aegean archipelago, and represent a highly competitive top global destination (Berg & Edelheim, 2012; INSETE, 2020). All in all, the Southern Aegean islands (Cyclades and Dodecanese) tend to attract 1 out of 4 tourists visiting Greece (Bank of Greece, 2023; INSETE, 2020; Statista, 2021). Cultural tourists do not all travel with the same motivations or engage similarly in cultural activities at their destination; rather some of them may be characterized as casual, incidental, or serendipitous cultural tourists (McKercher, 2002), with reference to their declared or underlying motives. Accordingly, although an unstated fact, the Cyclades' cultural heritage and assets tend to be their most significant comparative advantages distinguishing and upholding them as tourism destinations, vis-à-vis their competitors. The broad spectrum of these cultural assets elicits variable cultural tourism, a form of tourism that has been significantly affected by the pandemic and its global and local repercussions (Iaquinto, 2022; Jacobsen et al., 2021; Knezevic et al., 2021).

Moreover, the Cycladic islands have always been extremely dependent on tourism for their economic survival (INSETE, 2020). What makes this island archipelago especially dependent on tourism, is the fact that the growth and development of all other sectors of local/ regional economy in the Cyclades (such as primary-sector activities, services, culture, gastronomy etc.) tend to follow those of tourism, which constitutes the main—and rather fragile and vulnerable–source of income for the whole region. Despite the fact that a lot of recent research has been focusing on the impacts of the pandemic on tourism, such research is obviously not definitive on the matter. More research is called for to assess such impacts on such destinations (i.e., small tourism-dependent Mediterranean islands), considering the issues brought up by the pandemic, in their broader past and future perspective (Ferretti, 2021).

3   The Research Design

The Cyclades were selected as our study area, as a significant global tourism destination, but also based on their especially rich present and past cultural heritage. The Cycladic islands generally feature small- and medium-scale tourism, as opposed to 'industrial tourism', since they are not as heavily reliant on mass/ package tourism (with the exception, perhaps, of Mykonos and Santorini), a trend also reflected in the locally supplied types of accommodation (Sarantakou & Terkenli, 2019; Sarantakou & Tsartas, 2015).

The study's research questions were as follows:

1. What were the distinctive characteristics of cultural tourism in the Cyclades, before the pandemic?
2. How were these affected by the pandemic?
3. What is the outlook for cultural tourism in the Cyclades, after the pandemic?

To achieve the study's objective, the following methodological steps were undertaken in the context of the H2020 EU project SPOT during the years 2020–2022:

Table 1 The methodology of data collection and stakeholder types, in three stages (2020–2022)

Interviews in late summer 2020	Roundtable discussion July 2021	Short questionnaire in fall 2022
• Deputy Mayor of Syros for tourism • Deputy Mayor of Syros for culture • Deputy Mayor of Santorini for culture • Head of culture/ heritage NGO, Syros Institute	• National Tourism Organization of Greece (EOT) representative in Andros • Cyclades Chamber of Tourism representative • Cyclades Ephor of Antiquities (Ministry of Culture)	• Scientific Director of the Greek Tourism Confederation (SETE) • National Tourism Organization of Greece (EOT) representative in Andros • Deputy Mayor of Syros for tourism

(a)   a series of stakeholders' interviews, September 2020
(b)   a round-table discussion, July 2021
(c)   a small, targeted questionnaire, November 2022

The motivation for choosing three different methods in the three subsequent years of our study duration lay in capturing the progress of the pandemic impact on cultural tourism in the Cyclades. The research was conducted by the authors themselves and included the following types of stakeholders in culture, tourism, and cultural tourism, both locally, as well as at the regional and national levels (Table 1). They were drawn from the total pool of our case study's stakeholders; those that ended up participating in the different stages of our research were those that responded positively to our invitation. Nonetheless, the resulting sample ended up being quite representative of both sectors (culture, tourism) and the three levels of governance. Each research step built on and supplemented the previous one: the stakeholders' interviews were of more general content and scope, rather exploratory in character, aiming to cover all aspects of the study's subject matter, at the beginning of the pandemic; the round-table discussion was our core research tool, encompassing a series of targeted, in-depth questions[4] on same aspects of culture, tourism and cultural tourism at the three governmental levels, at the mid-point of the pandemic; and the end questionnaire included only three open-ended questions that purported to assess the stakeholders' perceptions of the changes brought about by the pandemic on issues and aspects of cultural tourism in the Cyclades and Greece, at its tail end.

The material collected through this research was then combined using a SWOT analysis, in order to discuss and assess the problems, pitfalls and potential of the changes ensuing from the pandemic in Cyclades cultural tourism, towards a resilient or transformative and sustainable future for the islands' tourism and cultural sectors.

4   Research Findings: Analysis and Discussion

Research Question 1. findings on the distinctive characteristics of pre-pandemic Cyclades cultural tourism

---

[4] The roundtable discussion focused on questions regarding the definition of cultural tourism; policy formulation promoting the development of cultural tourism, its implementation, monitoring, and evaluation; relevant infrastructures; local engagement/ benefits from cultural tourism; sustainable local development and the 'Green Agenda'; innovation and shared future visions; and finally, the impact of COVID-19 pandemic on cultural tourism, at all levels.

As world-wise tourism scientific and grey literature attests to, the Cyclades, and espe-cially the islands of Mykonos and Santorini, are among the most world-renowned and highly competitive global-tourism destinations in Greece (INSETE, 2020; WTTC, 2020), with significant implications for these islands' economic survival and devel-opment (Coccossis, 2001; DiaNeosis, 2015). Indicatively, international tourist air arrivals in the Cycladic islands in 2019 reached 994,000 according to official statis-tical data (INSETE, 2020). Besides their strong 3Ss (sea-sand-sun) allure, the Cyclades also boast striking natural/ environmental assets, great landscape diver-sity, and rich cultural traditions and heritage, dating back to the antiquities (Berg & Edelheim, 2012; Prokopiou et al., 2018). As already mentioned, cultural tourism differs from island to island, and it does not represent a conscious tourism motive for most Cyclades visitors; however, broadly defined, culture remains the factor that underlies tourists' decision to visit these islands.

Cycladic culture encompasses both tangible and intangible, folk, historical/ arche-ological and contemporary sites, monuments, practices, and landscapes, i.e., distinc-tive traditional Aegean architecture and townscapes, gastronomy and music, art and crafts, feasts, and festivals, etc. On the negative side, incoming tourists may not only enjoy the assets, but also suffer the limitations, of their fragile insular char-acter (smaller-scale destinations, insularity-induced resource limitations etc.), often resulting in traffic congestion, infrastructure overload, and problems in environmental quality and service satisfaction (Tsartas et al., 2020). On the positive side, however, local Cycladic communities seem to be more close-knit and tightly linked with their cultural traditions than other parts of Greece or other island groups (Dianeosis, 2015; Stewart, 2016). Consequently, it is their cultural attractions, taken all together, that render them a most significant pole of both local and international tourism attraction.

Our study stakeholders implied and underlined these facts, but focused more on the situation at the time, as regards tourism, culture, and the ways they come together in cultural tourism. According to all our study participants, although tourism had generally been thriving in most Cycladic destinations before the pandemic, cultural tourism suffered from an overconcentration in specific sites/ attractions, a lack of organizational coordination, inadequate infrastructures, and circumstantial clien-tele. Although there seemed to be tourist satisfaction with locally provided cultural tourism aspects/ attractions and apparent interest in all types and forms of cultural tourism, admittedly several aspects of existing current Cycladic cultural tourism leave much to be desired (number, diversity, pricing, and quality of offered cultural activities). As the Vice Mayor of Syros asserted in his interview, cultural tourism for "our" islands has, so far, been tourism "complementary to the main sea-sand-sun type of tourism" they attract. Indicatively, out of the 3 million tourists in Santorini in 2019, only 450,000 visited its most significant cultural attraction, the archeological site of Akrotiri. The understandings of all sides involved in our research matched the state and challenges of cultural tourism in the Cyclades, eliciting the desire for more and more diverse and geographically dispersed attractions/site/events in this area.

The role and significance of culture in Cyclades tourism was highly advocated and extolled by all our stakeholders and other surveyed sides (residents, tourists, entrepreneurs) at all stages, throughout our study, even though culture was viewed as the realm most susceptible to adverse tourism impacts. A propos, the representative of the Cyclades Chamber of Commerce highlighted the importance of preserving local/ regional culture, heritage, and traditions as a living part of island life and the present way of living, and not stage them only for external consumption, that is for sale to tourists: "you either make it your reality or you lose it". He further discussed this issue with the aid of the example of fishing boats: "there can be no cultural tourism if we wipe out traditional ship-making and local shipyards—which the State has steadily elicited for many years now, either purposefully or inadvertently. This is very serious for the islands, where boats and other traditional sea-vessels are of utmost importance for island life—indeed, a crucial part of island traditional life".

One of the structural problems in Greece vis-à-vis culture is that it tends to be confounded with 'high culture', a tendency that was obvious throughout, as well as in the more quantitative survey findings of our case study work in the context of the SPOT project.[5] Cultural tourism, as conventionally promoted by the Greek State and other top-down institutions, refers mostly to archeological sites, museums, galleries, and theaters, and certainly reinforces those heritage aspects of the islands' place identity, tourism growth and local sustainable development. However, as it is based on relics of the past and high culture, such cultural tourism does not elicit further growth, creativity, and diversification in matters of culture and/ or tourism development/ enrichment. This understanding of 'culture' was succinctly echoed by the Cyclades Ephor of Antiquities input to the roundtable discussion and highly representative of the predominant national (Ministry of Culture) position and attitude towards culture, more generally (top-down perspective). This shortcoming has over-arching repercussions on the development, management/ protection, and promotion of all (other) cultural artifacts, sites, events, and other assets for the Cyclades and for Greece. As pointed out by most local actors/ tourism-related parties (bottom-up perspective), the remediation of this problem will have the additional beneficial effect of attracting and/ or creating a far broader market spectrum for Cyclades domestic and international cultural tourism.

As pointed out by all our stakeholders, tourism in the Cyclades had been continuously growing in the pre-pandemic decades. Furthermore, cultural tourism had helped enhance and promote tourism flows in the region; it had directly and indirectly contributed to economic growth, to population retention, to an increase in employment opportunities, to variable (infrastructural and other) investments, and to overall local and regional development, including cultural development, thus sustaining a beneficent cycle of further cultural tourism development. However, it did so, despite the absence of the State. The general opinion of our stakeholders here was that "there is no central planning for cultural tourism in the Cyclades. Many factors come into play as regards the development of cultural tourism here, but no pertinent tourism policy exists" (Ephor of Antiquities), coupled with a lack of cooperation among all interested and involved parties, regarding cultural tourism. The regional representative of the National Tourism Organization of Greece (EOT) recounted that:

---

[5] http://www.spotprojecth2020.eu/reportsandoutcomes.

As regards the role of local communities in the development of cultural tourism here, after the 1970s, many stakeholders from many sides started to mobilize and get involved in the cultural tourism sector; this trend flourished in the 1980s; and, in many cases, it went on: these parties continued to do what they had been doing, now in an official local government framework. This tradition has gone on for a long time already, has come full-circle and cannot deliver anything new in this regard. We have seen new schemata emerge since then, of people (individual citizens, groups of various sorts, cultural clubs, official organizations, NGOs etc.) who are interested in and determined to offer new, innovative, digital etc. approaches and initiatives to matters of culture and cultural tourism, with successful results in some cases— and not in other cases, due to the aforementioned hostile general environment, in which they are called to operate.

According to the same stakeholder, "this is an area of tourism growth necessitating more integrated and participatory planning, both from the side of the public sector and local authorities and from the side of the civil society. The latter must commit to joint actions in planning and synthesizing these actions in common goals…towards (a) tourism promotion/ marketing and (b) tourism product organization/ enhancement/ maturation". A propos, the Chamber of Commerce representative pointed out that they:

Have not yet managed to activate local interest and participation in such events/ undertakings: a cultural deficit, indicating a vacuum for the islands …Because there are no organized cultural institutions in Greece, which could assume this task; it is all unchartered territory, to be handled… by those genuinely interested in doing so. Normally and habitually, these efforts are 'officially' undertaken under the protective and regulatory guidance mainly of the Municipalities…but there is so much that a Municipality can do… without any central planning, which means that each island has its own cultural production/ consumption characteristics and identity/ profile …As regards progress in these matters, in the past few years, and the espousing of new technologies, innovation, green development etc., there has been rather balanced growth and development in all Cycladic islands, although each island has its own character and place in such progress.

Research Question 2. findings on how culture and cultural tourism were affected by the pandemic.

The onset of the pandemic certainly ushered a change in mindsets as regards tourism and many other sectors of social life, both in Greece and beyond. The pandemic brought new ways of looking at existing issues, situations, issues, problems etc. and a turn away from mass tourism towards more sustainable forms of tourism mobilities (INSETE, 2021; Jacobsen et al., 2021; Knezevic et al., 2021). During the summer of 2020, the pandemic altered local priorities in Cyclades (cultural) tourism, shifting them towards more realistic goals of survival, at least from the supply side. From the demand side of Cyclades cultural tourism, market priorities shifted more towards individualized and 'protected' modes of travel, to domestic but often remote and non-urban destinations; domestic tourism took over and predominated in 2020. Furthermore, the pandemic revealed and exposed a series of structural and functional inefficiencies and longstanding problems in the Greek tourism industry, while it brought to the fore relevant exigencies and urgencies. All the progress that had been achieved in the years prior to the crises, in terms of more sustainable/ 'green', innovative/ creative, and technologically upgraded cultural (tourism) development, was put on hold by the grave socio-economic crisis (2008–2015) and the pandemic, with unpredictable future repercussions.

Data collected in the context of the SPOT project during the early pandemic times (summer 2020) indicated high tourist interest in the Cyclades for gastronomic events or sites, folklore-related activities, and other local cultural events and festivals. However, these activities were served a serious blow, despite the fact that Greece was considered to be a relatively safe national and international tourism destination at the time, due to successful measures taken by the Greek government at the time (Constantoglou & Klothaki, 2021; National Geographic, 2020). Tourism mobilities were significantly curtailed, in terms of type of tourism, ratio of domestic vs. foreign tourism, frequency of traveling, length of stay at destination, type of transport used, preferred type of destination, behavioral patterns during traveling, cultural activities at destination, etc. However, the very high percentage of repeat-travelers to the Cyclades, even in times of the pandemic, indicated a degree of customer loyalty to the destination (http://www.spotprojecth2020.eu).

At the outset of the pandemic (summer 2020), the supply side of Cyclades tourism, culture, and cultural tourism expressed great concern with regard to addressing and overcoming the challenges of the COVID-19 pandemic in these sectors (SPOT findings[6]). Local tourism entrepreneurs expressed a fatigue in having to assume the brunt of efforts to sustain the islands' tourism sector on their own, without the State's help, called to operate in a 'hostile environment' (Terkenli & Georgoula, 2021). Our round-table discussants referred to the State's misguided actions in combatting the pandemic and its repercussions, leading to an even more pronounced and grave loss of cultural traditions/ heritage, jobs, and opportunities for a sustainable future in local culture and island life. New parameters were reportedly brought to cultural tourism by the pandemic, such as the opportunity for post-pandemic regeneration, "but with several collateral losses, e.g., many people employed in the sector of culture have already changed profession" and several businesses closed permanently.

Culture has habitually been considered as the realm most susceptible to adverse tourism impacts and repercussions. A great number of cultural activities ingrained in local ways of life were banned or did not take place at all during 2020, especially those conducive to large concentrations of participants/ spectators, such as religious feasts and all sorts of cultural festivals. The Chamber of Commerce representative asserted that the gravest impact of the pandemic was on culture, while the EOT representative explained:

> All parts of the cultural sector have been gravely affected, as regards all aspects of these sectors, so much so that people in the sector did not believe that it would be possible for them to return to their professions and creative activities/ occupations, after all these crises are over. But also we, as spectators, are held back by both the pandemic and the concomitant State measures (both psychologically and institutionally) in enjoying culture as we did before. If you cannot dance at a local feast, it is no longer such a feast. The sense of letting loose, of co-existing/ communicating with other people in the realm of culture has been all but lost,

---

[6] http://www.spotprojecth2020.eu/reportsandoutcomes.

even though it has been facilitated by new technologies and the digitalization of culture and cultural activities—but that cannot substitute the actual experiences in their actual contexts.

On the other hand, the tourists who visited the Cyclades in the summer of 2020 imbibed in more expenses and/ or spent more money at the destination (Kathimerini Newspaper, 2021); as pointed out by one of our interviewees, "they sought to invest in the crisis". Furthermore, the Vice Mayor of Santorini for Culture pointed out that the respite from rampant tourism growth and activity on Santorini that the pandemic brought about allowed for a period of recollection and re-evaluation of shortcomings in the sectors of culture and cultural tourism, towards more sustainable future solutions, as well as to the turn towards these sectors' digitalization. For instance, the so called 'overtourism' problems (i.e., traffic congestion in Santorini and Syros) reportedly abated during the summer of 2020. Although tourist satisfaction during the pandemic was generally lower than that before the pandemic, there was a significant number of tourists who reported a similar or better experience now (in pandemic times) as compared to the past. Such findings of our case study work in the context of SPOT highlight the durable and sustained popularity of (cultural) tourism in the Cyclades and indicate the capacity of Cycladic tourism to cater to the needs and demands of a loyal and growing clientele, responding to tourism changes brought about by the COVID-19 pandemic.

Research Question 3. Findings regarding the post pandemic outlook for cultural tourism in the Cyclades

Our stakeholders overwhelmingly considered the COVID-19 pandemic as an opportunity to address old impediments to future tourism growth and development. They stated that emphasis on 'green', sustainable, and milder forms of tourism had been evolving in the Cyclades even before the pandemic and were cut short by it; they postulated that these developments would become more and more important in the future. The SETE Director additionally emphasized the significant outlook for the digitalization of (cultural) tourism in the post pandemic era, with the aid of new ICTs (i.e., augmented, and virtual reality), but also the opportunity to take a better look into and remedy the ills and deficiencies of (cultural) tourism that the pandemic exposed. He pointed out the dynamic potential of cultural tourism development in the Cyclades, to restitute the two major problems of the islands' tourism sector: seasonality and predominance of 'mass'/ organized tourism. Both he and the Deputy Mayor of Syros for Tourism advocated the great internal cultural variability/ diversity in the Cycladic Archipelago as a valuable basis and promising competitive edge for the future development and diversification of Cyclades cultural tourism. Future visions and goals, as described by the Ephor of Antiquities for the Cyclades, point to "a different type of tourism that does not destroy the landscape (either built or not) and the tourism product itself (e.g. turn islands into 'tourism paradises'), but rather protects and promotes the intangible heritage of the islands, ways of life and activities in rural areas and in the sea: these are clearly deteriorating and in the process of being irrevocably lost".

A general realization was that there was not a lack of visions vis-à-vis culture and (cultural) tourism in the Cyclades, but rather a lack of planning, of synergies, of infrastructures and of mechanisms to materialize these visions and produce tangible results towards their future sustainable development. In accordance with other stakeholders' opinions, the EOT representative stated that she believed that,

> After the end of the pandemic, people will crave for more culture and return enthusiastically to it, as will the organizers of such activities/events ...but also new forms of culture and cultural expression will emerge/develop. These developments may lead to forms of cultural tourism that are more remote (spatially) and engage smaller numbers of people/ participants, more abstract types of experiences, more authentic experiences, more controlled and hybrid big-event activities, simultaneously digitalized: these developments will also favor those parts of the society with moving disabilities and other particularities, who were formerly unable to attend to/participate in these activities/events.

A result of successive and unfolding recent crises, our stakeholders deemed that the future of the Cyclades ought to be grounded on the principles of sustainability, as regards both cultural tourism and life, in general. All our stakeholders expressed the need to coordinate and regulate tourist inflows better, to realize such alternative types of tourism, acknowledging the importance of culture for tourism, and cultural tourism itself as "the future of the islands". The Cyclades Chamber of Commerce representative especially rallied for the preservation or re-instatement and further development of the islands' culture, as a tangible fact of everyday life. The EOT representative brought up the post-pandemic fact that the Cyclades risk becoming an unaffordable destination for domestic tourism, due to the rising cost of the whole tourism product, caused by the various ongoing crises in Greek society. For these and all other previously mentioned inefficiencies and shortcomings in the cultural tourism sector, our stakeholders proposed a series of amendments and measures addressed to all levels of government in culture, tourism, and cultural tourism.

There was a call for integrated planning and management of, on the one hand, cultural traditions, and production and, on the other hand, of tourism activity, in collaboration with the local societies, in terms of environmental, social, and economic sustainability. The establishment and development of synergies and partnerships in all sectors of economy and society were deemed essential for any sustainable future growth and development of (cultural) tourism, towards local/ regional (tourism) development and societal well-being. These need to involve all relevant parties (tourism-related businesses, the authorities, and the cultural sector) and to be initiated both from the top-down and from bottom-up, with the role of the State being crucial and key to all such development.

The qualitative thematic analysis of the random sample of 150 reviews identified relevant codes from frequent words and sentences, related to visitor experience to the historic city centre of Ghent. The analysis revealed several relevant categories—each with a unique set of keywords. Most analysed reviews included multiple categories across themes, for example.

Table 2 SWOT analysis of Cyclades cultural tourism

Strengths

Natural beauty: Stunning beaches, clear blue waters, unique land formations and landscapes.

Cultural heritage: Rich cultural heritage with many ancient & historical sites, lively festivals, gastronomy, picturesque villages.

Accessibility: Easily accessible by ferry or plane; tourists may visit multiple islands in a few days.

Tourism infrastructure: good, with wide range of hotels, short term rentals, restaurants, sports & leisure services.

Weaknesses

Seasonal demand: Tourism is highly seasonal, with the majority of visitors arriving during the summer months.

Lack of know-how: Many tourism-related businesses are family-owned/ operated; lack of experience in managing a business.

Workforce shortages: Serious post-pandemic problems in recruiting enough workers to cope with the demand.

Absence of State: In tourism planning and management.

General infrastructure: Inadequate and poor condition; limited resources for waste management, energy and water supply.

Opportunities

Diversification possibilities: In tourism offerings, by catering to niche markets that can attract visitors during the off-season.

Digital marketing: Such strategies may help reach new markets and promote the region's unique offerings to a wider audience.

Partnerships: Possibility for synergies/ partnerships with other nearby destinations to share their cultural resources and infrastructure. Promotion of multi-destination trips and multiple cultrural assets can attract a broader range of clientele and extend the season.

Threats

Competition: heavy competition in Greece and abroad.

Climate change: threats to the region's natural beauty, cultural heritage and infrastructure.

Economic instability: risk of a decrease in tourism demand and negative impact on the economy.

'Overtourism': risk for resource overuse if carrying capacity is exceeded in certain sites

Dependence on tourism: Heavy economic dependence on tourism leads to vulnerability to global risks and unforeseen events such as natural disasters or pandemics.

5 Swot Analysis and Conclusions

Conclusively, a valuable asset for the Cyclades sustainable future (tourism) development, cultural tourism, was significantly affected by the COVID-19 pandemic and its global and local repercussions. The significance of culture for tourism and concern about the cultural impacts of tourism were explicitly expressed by various sides. The culture–tourism relationship was generally viewed as holding great potential for all sides involved and for local cultural and overall sustainability, despite the broad acknowledgement that the great potential for cultural tourism in the study area is, to date, far from met. Nonetheless, current, and emerging trends and patterns seem to reinforce the reciprocal relationship culture-tourism, but also to reconfigure it, in line with new and evolving trends and patterns of cultural tourism.[7] Strengths, weaknesses, opportunities, and threats pertaining to cultural tourism in the Cyclades, in its fluid and changeable current context, are presented in Table 2.

In the current turbulent and transitional times for tourism, issues of sustainability and changing market demands, become especially poignant, pressing, and pivotal for tourism and destinations in general, calling for change and adaptation to emerging trends, attitudes, needs, challenges and prospects, despite an attempted return back to business-as-usual and a post-pandemic recovery led by private business interests. Nonetheless, in the aftermath of the pandemic and in light of the heightened awareness and re-prioritization of sustainable development and economic self-sufficiency, the value and significance of protecting the islands' physical environment, local character, cultural heritage and cultural production were highly advocated, through a series of proposed measures addressing longstanding deficiencies and/or future risks

---

[7] Examples of post-pandemic actions prioritizing sustainable tourism practices in the Cyclades: (a) strategic actions at the national level https://insete.gr/wp-content/uploads/pdf/proorismoi/exe cutive-summary-kuklades.pdf; (b) the 'Hotel Footprinting Action' by the Center for Sustainable and Circular Bioeconomy and (c) HERMeS NGO.

(i.e. imposing more restrictions on hotel constructions and other tourism infrastructure, as well as on mass/ package tourism). In this regard, the importance of further advertising and communicating the natural and cultural beauties of the Cyclades was raised, in conjunction also with the urgency of regulating tourism flows ('overtourism' in Santorini) in the islands. Further, 'greener', sustainable and 'alternative' (special interest/ purpose) tourism development, supported by new ICTs, seemed to be highly favored by our stakeholders throughout the study. Funding and infrastructure provision were deemed essential, as well as tourism vocational training; information provision to tourists; the digitalization of the tourism sector; and safeguarding local culture from tourism commodification. Finally, there was general agreement that all sectors and levels of government ought to be involved in the islands' cultural tourism development and governance, in collaboration with all relevant local/ regional parties (tourism-related businesses, the cultural sector, NGOs and civil societies).

Acknowledgements This research is part of the EU SPOT project, funded by the European Union's Horizon 2020 program for research and innovation under grant agreement no. 870644.

References

Bank of Greece. (2023). Statistics, external sector, balance of payments, travel services. Retrieved 26 March, 2023, from https://www.bankofgreece.gr/en/statistics/external-sector/balance-of-payments/travel-services.

Berg, I., & Edelheim, J. (2012). The attraction of islands: Travellers and tourists in the Cyclades (Greece) in the twentieth and twenty-first centuries. *Journal of Tourism and Cultural Change, 10*(1), 84–98. https://doi.org/10.1080/14766825.2012.660946

Chen, G., & Huang, S. S. (2017). Understanding Chinese cultural tourists: Typology and profile. *Journal of Travel & Tourism Marketing, 35*(2), 162–177.

Coccossis, H. (2001). Sustainable development and tourism in small islands: Some lessons from Greece. *Anatolia Int. J. Tour. Hosp. Res., 2001*(12), 53–58.

Constantoglou, M., & Klothaki, T. (2021). *Journal of Tourism and Hospitality Management, 9*(5), 288–313. https://doi.org/10.17265/2328-2169/2021.05.004.

DiaNeosis. (2015). Numbers: Greece in wef's tourism competitiveness report. Retrieved 6 April, 2019, from https://www.Dianeosis.Org/2015/07/poso-antagonistiki-einai-iellada-ston-pagkosmio-tourismo.

Ferretti, G. M. M. (2021). The travel shock. Hutchins Center on Fiscal and Monetary Policy Working Paper #74, August 2021. The Brookings Institution.

Iaquinto, B. L. (2022). Locating pro-environmental vernacular practices of tourism. Geography Compass, pp. 1–12.

INSETE. (2020). Key figures of incoming tourism in Greece (in Greek). Retrieved 4 November, 2021, from https://insete.gr/statistika-eiserxomenou-tourismou.

INSETE. (2021). Megatrends. Greek Tourism: Action Plans 2030 (Greek Tourism. Action Plan 2030) (In Greek). Athens: SETE Institute.

Jacobsen, J. K. S., Farstad, E., Higham, J., Hopkins, D. & Landa-Mata, I. (2021). Travel discontinuities, enforced holidaying-at-home and alternative leisure travel futures after COVID-19, Tourism Geographies.

Kathimerini Newspaper. (2021). Tourists come with a bigger wallet this year. Economy section, Sunday 28/11/2021: 5.

Kaufman, T. J., & Scantlebury, M. (2007). Cultural tourism and the vacation ownership industry. *Journal of Retail & Leisure Property 6* (Aug), 213–220.

Kay, P. L. (2009). Cultural experience tourist motives dimensionality: A cross-cultural study. *Journal of Hospitality Marketing & Management, 18*(4), 329–371.

Knezevic, C. L., Antonucci, B., Cutrufo, N., Marongiu, L., Rodrigues, M., & Teoh, T. (2021). *Research for TRAN committee – Relaunching transport and tourism in the EU after COVID-19.* Tourism sector, European Parliament, Policy Department for Structural and Cohesion Policies.

Mandic, A., & Kennell, J. (2021). Smart governance for heritage tourism destinations: Contextual factors and destination management organization perspectives. *Tourism Management Perspectives, 39*, 1–14.

McKercher, B. (2002). Towards a classification of cultural tourists. *International Journal of Tourism Research, 4*(1), 29–38.

McKercher, B., & Du Cros, H. (2003). Testing a cultural tourism typology. *International Journal of Tourism Research, 5*(1), 45–58.

National Geographic. (2020). How Greece is rethinking its once bustling tourism industry. Retrieved from https://www.nationalgeographic.com/travel/article/how-greece-is-coping-without-tourism-due-to-covid.

Pandora, L. K. (2009). Cultural experience tourist motives dimensionality: A cross-cultural study. *Journal of Hospitality Marketing & Management, 18*(4), 329–371.

Prokopiou, D. G., Mavridoglou, G., Manologlou, S., & Tselentis, B. S. (2018). *Tourism development of the Cyclades islands: Economic, social and carrying capacity assessment and consequences, WIT transactions on ecology and the environment, 217: 09–521.* WIT Press.

Richards, G. (2018). Cultural tourism: a review of recent research and trends. *Journal of Hospitality and Tourism Management 36*(Sep), 12–21.

Richards, G. (2021). *Rethinking cultural tourism.* Edward Elgar Publishing.

Sarantakou, E., & Terkenli, T. S. (2019). Non-institutionalized forms of tourism accommodation and overtourism impacts on the landscape: The case of Santorini. *Tourism Planning & Development, 16*(4), 411–433.

Sarantakou, E., & Tsartas, P. (2015). A critical approach to the new framework for creating tourism investment during the current period of economic crisis 2010–2014. *Greek Econ. Outlook, 26*, 46–55.

Sayeh, S. (2022). Tourists' segmentation based on culture as their primary motivation. *Athens Journal of Tourism, 9*(3), 183–193.

Sheller, M., & Urry, J. (2006). The new mobilities paradigm. *Environment and Planning A, 38*(2), 207–226.

Statista. (2021). Number of international air arrivals on the Greek island of Santorini from 2010 to 2020. Retrieved 30 December, 2021, from https://www.statista.com/statistics/880883/santorini-international-air-arrivals.

Stewart, C. (2016). *Demons and the devil: Moral imagination in the modern Greek culture.* Princeton University Press.

Terkenli, T. S., & Georgoula, V.: Tourism and cultural sustainability: Views and prospects from cyclades, Greece. *Sustainability, 14*(1), 307. MDPI AG., https://doi.org/10.3390/su14010307.

The National Herald. (2023). In 2022, Greece Saw Record 31 million Tourists Arrive at Airports. Retrieved 27 March, 2023, from https://www.thenationalherald.com/in-2022-greece-saw-record-31-million-tourists-arrive-at-airports.

Throsby, D. (2008). Linking ecological and cultural sustainability. *Int. J. Divers. Organ. Communities Nations, 8*, 15–20.

Tsartas, P., Zagotsi, S., & Kyriakaki, A. (2020). Τουρίστες, Ταξίδια, Τόποι. Κοινωνιολογικές Προσεγγίσεις στον Τουρισμό (Tourists, Travels, Places, Sociological Perspectives to Tourism) (in Greek) Athens: Kritiki Publications.

UNWTO. (2017). Tourism and culture, definition of cultural tourism. Retrieved 14 May, 2022, from https://www.unwto.org/fr/tourism-andculture.

UNWTO. (2020). United Nations World Tourism Organization statistics. International Tourism Highlights, 2020 Edition.

Weaver, P., Kaufman, T. J., & Yoon, Y. A. (2001). Market segmentation study based on benefits sought by visitors at heritage sites. *Tourism Analysis, 6*(3–4), 213–222.

Williams, R. (1958). *Culture and society 1780–1950*. Chatto & Windus.

WTTC. (2020). Travel and tourism-global economic impact & trends 2020. London: WTTC.

Responsible, Circular, and Human-Centred Regional Development Potential

A Framework for Responsible Tourism in Scotland's Historic Environment: Experiences from Transforming Tourism at a Film-Induced Heritage Visitor Attraction

Vanessa Glindmeier and Gary Treacy

Abstract Global recognition of the importance of responsible tourism and its benefits, which can be enjoyed by all, both now and in the future, without detriment to communities and the environment, is growing. While tourism is a major component of the Scottish economy, it also contributes to climate change through associated greenhouse gas emissions. Heritage and cultural tourism contributes to making better places for people to live in, and better places for people to visit, whilst contributing significantly to Scotland's green recovery from the pandemic and its transition to net zero and a climate-resilient society, when responsible tourism principles are at the heart of decision making. Historic Environment Scotland (HES), Scotland's lead public body for the historic environment and largest operator of paid-for visitor attractions published its HES Responsible Tourism Framework in March 2023, determining how the organisation will adopt responsible tourism principles to transform its approach to tourism operations, equally respecting the needs of local communities, visitors, the environment, and of the cultural heritage itself. In 2019, HES obtained funding to deliver a pilot project at Doune Castle, alongside which the Framework has been developed. The castle was chosen as a case study as it, and the village it is located in, has experienced pressure through increased footfall following its appearance on the hit TV series 'Outlander'. This paper presents how the HES Responsible Tourism Framework has been applied at Doune Castle, supporting the transformation of heritage and cultural tourism to the site to a more responsible model.

Keywords Responsible heritage tourism · Climate change · Local communities

V. Glindmeier (✉) · G. Treacy
Historic Environment Scotland, Edinburgh, Scotland
e-mail: vanessa.glindmeier@hes.scot

G. Treacy
e-mail: gary.treacy@hes.scot

© The Author(s) 2025   87
B. Neuts et al. (eds.), *Advances in Cultural Tourism Research*, Advances in Digital and
Cultural Tourism Management, https://doi.org/10.1007/978-3-031-65537-1_6

1 Introduction

Historic Environment Scotland (HES) is the lead public body established to investigate, care for, and promote Scotland's historic environment. Responsible for 336 properties of national importance, such as buildings and monuments including Edinburgh Castle, Skara Brae, and Fort George, HES is the largest operator of paid-for visitor attractions in Scotland, drawing more than 5 million visitors to staffed sites in 2018.

Both a rise in visitor numbers and the changing climate have put pressure on Scotland's built and natural heritage assets. In addition, the sector has been immensely affected by the global coronavirus pandemic, which has brought international travel and tourism to a standstill for intermittent periods from early 2020 to as far as early 2023 in some parts of the world. An opportunity to move away from previous, less sustainable approaches to tourism has been identified, to ensure that built and natural heritage can be enjoyed by future generations. The threats to our cultural assets from climate change are increasingly understood, for example through exemplary work identifying Coastal Resilience and Adaptation Options for the Bay of Skaill (Rennie et al., 2021) and the Guide to Climate Change Impacts on Scotland's Historic Environment (2019), but perhaps less well articulated is the significant contribution that the historic environment sector, including its connection to tourism, can make to transition to a low carbon economy. Responsible heritage and cultural tourism can contribute to making better places for people to live in and better places for people to visit, by supporting a green recovery from the pandemic and Scotland's transition to net zero and a climate resilient society (Historic Environment Scotland, 2022).

Heritage and cultural tourism can support low-carbon activities by using sustainable supply chains, reducing energy use and waste generation on sites, and developing lower-carbon and regional itineraries. It can work for the local area when good quality, local jobs are created and sustained, and local businesses and communities are included in decision-making.

HES has been identified as a 'Major Player' under the Climate Change (Scotland) Act 2009, which puts a duty on the organisation to act as an exemplar and contribute to climate change mitigation and adaptation, and to act sustainably (Climate Change (Scotland) Act, 2009; The Scottish Government, 2011).

This paper presents the newly developed HES Responsible Tourism Framework, which aims to transform tourism in Scotland's historic environment to ensure it can be enjoyed by all, now, and in the future. The paper provides an example of the Framework's application at a film-induced heritage visitor attraction in HES's care, Doune Castle.

2   Tourism in Scotland

Tourism is a major component of the Scottish economy, with £3.20 bn spent by domestic visitors, and £2.54 bn spent by international visitors, in 2019 (VisitScotland Insights Department, 2019). According to the 'Scotland Visitor Survey 2015 & 2016', 51% of European survey respondees, and 52% of international survey respondees indicated that their trip to Scotland was motivated by history and culture, and 60% of overall visitors to Scotland have engaged with the historic environment at least once during their trip by visiting historic houses or stately homes. 12% of survey respondees from Europe or a long-haul market such as Australia, were prompted to visit by one or more TV shows featuring Scotland, most notably *Outlander*. The 1995 movie *Braveheart* was quoted most where a film featuring Scotland has prompted a visit, mainly with 16% by French, German, and Spanish respondees (VisitScotland, 2017).

3   Heritage and Cultural Tourism and Climate Change

While tourism can deliver benefits for communities and foster understanding and respect, contributing to community wealth building, it also impacts the natural environment. Increased footfall to an area can lead to soil erosion, the loss of natural habitats of both flora and fauna, and increased pollution, including littering. Tourism contributes to global climate change through associated greenhouse gas (GHG) emissions, such as those generated through the production and consumption of products and services which account for 80% of Scotland's carbon footprint (Zero Waste Scotland, 2021), as well as transport, including international and domestic aviation, accounting for 25.9% of net GHG emissions in Scotland (Transport Scotland, 2023). The industry has been identified by the Scottish Government as a key sector in the green economic recovery and just transition to net zero by 2045 (The Scottish Government, 2018).

Scotland's national tourism strategy 'Scotland Outlook 2030—Responsible Tourism for a Sustainable Future', developed by the Scottish Tourism Alliance with HES represented on the Strategy Steering Group, sets out the vision for Scotland to become a leader in twenty-first century tourism. It addresses climate change and supporting the inclusive economic recovery of the Scottish tourism sector at its core (The Scottish Tourism Alliance et al., 2020). Subsequently, Scotland's National Tourist Organisation (NTO) VisitScotland became part of the Drafting Committee of the Glasgow Declaration (One Planet Network, 2021), and the first NTO to declare a Climate Emergency, and has developed a Responsible Tourism Promise (VisitScotland, 2021).

4   The HES Responsible Tourism Framework

In response to the growing recognition of responsible tourism and its benefits, which can be enjoyed by all without detriment to communities and the environment, HES has developed a new Responsible Tourism Framework (Historic Environment Scotland, 2023). The Framework outlines the way in which the organisation adopts responsible tourism principles to transform its tourism operations. The approach reflects HES's role in caring for Scotland's historic environment, managing historic sites to tell Scotland's story in an inclusive and respectful way, with regard to the needs of the environment, local communities, visitors, and of the cultural heritage sites themselves.

The Framework highlights the opportunities of adopting a responsible tourism model for HES, including increased resilience and independence from carbon and resource-intensive operational models. Further, it responds to changing visitor behaviour and numbers, as well as growing visitor expectations for ethical, low-carbon tourism experiences. It is a driver for innovation in new ways to welcome visitors. In order to empower everyone to participate in decision-making, HES plans to work in partnerships across the tourism sector, community groups, and beyond, with the aim of maximising local economic and wellbeing benefits and increasing cultural awareness, identity and inclusion, by unlocking local knowledge.

4.1   The Principles

The HES Responsible Tourism approach is guided by five interlinking principles, which have been adapted from those laid out in the Cape Town Declaration on Responsible Tourism of 2002 (Responsible Tourism Partnership, 2008). The five principles adopted by HES link back to pertinent Scottish policies (see Fig. 1).

4.2   Priority Areas and Outcomes

The Framework proposes actions across three priority areas, with each priority area containing outcomes around which HES will develop the potential of its operational activities.

Our Responsibility for the Historic Environment. The priority area concerned with the historic environment includes efforts to decarbonise HES's tourism operations and maximise the positive impact on the environment through the integration of circular business models and sustainable procurement, as well as enabling and educating visitors to be responsible consumers through providing low-carbon visitor experiences.

Fig. 1 HES responsible tourism principles and guiding national policies. © Historic Environment Scotland

Our Responsibility for People. Our Responsibility for people covers activities related to HES's visitors and members of local communities within which their historic sites are situated. Outcomes in this priority area are co-creating experiences that enhance the well-being of both communities and visitors while fostering respect between visitors and residents, and improving access to heritage tourism experiences for all, all year round and across Scotland.

Our Responsibility for Capacity Building. Our responsibilities for capacity building priority area proposes activities which support local economic benefit generation from tourism, strengthen skills development opportunities in responsible heritage tourism, as well as quality career pathways in the sector, through collaboration with learning institutions and supporting others in adopting responsible tourism principles into their business models.

4.3 Exemplar for Responsible Tourism in the Historic Environment

To ensure user-friendliness, application quality, and its practicability, the HES Responsible Tourism Framework has been developed alongside pilot projects and initiatives. One such pilot project is the Doune Sustainable Tourism project.

The Doune Sustainable Tourism project aims to raise awareness and community involvement with Doune Castle, focusing on the reduction of the carbon footprint of tourism operations, encouraging social and cultural diversity and maximising the benefits of tourism for communities, such as increasing dwell time and spend in the village and locale, all of which contribute to sustainable development of the site and its surrounding areas.

The project focuses on new approaches through familiar tourism functions, which are: *Sustainable Travel, Commercial Operations, Visitor Experience, Access, Landscape & Biodiversity, Infrastructure,* and *Community Engagement.* In addition, the project goes beyond the boundaries of Doune Castle, taking a regional destination approach by working with local organisations, the local authority, and national agencies such as VisitScotland. This supports our holistic approach to the project and its stakeholders.

A visualisation of how project activity maps across to the HES Responsible Tourism Framework is included in the Appendix.

Doune Castle. Doune Castle (see Fig. 2) is located on the banks of the River Teith in the rural village of Doune, to the north-east of Stirling in central Scotland. Most of the curtain-walled castle can be dated back to the fourteenth century, with some of the fabric dating back to the thirteenth century. In 1361, Robert Stewart, the 1st Duke of Albany and Governor of Scotland, also known as 'Scotland's uncrowned king', acquired the castle and his rich tastes can be seen clearly in the architecture of the medieval courtyard castle (Historic Environment Scotland, 2017).

Doune Castle was used by the Jacobites as a prison for government troops during the 1745/6 Jacobite Rising. Following the Rising, the castle fell into disuse, resulting in a semi-ruinous state. George Philip Stuart, 14th Earl of Moray, restored parts of Doune Castle to its current state during the 1880s, including re-roofing parts,

Fig. 2 Aerial photograph of Doune Castle. © Historic Environment Scotland

partly furnishing the castle and restoring interiors. Based on its cultural significance, including national importance, the castle, including its defences and earth-
works, has been designated a Scheduled Monument and put into State care (Historic
Environment Scotland, 2011).

Today, Doune Castle is popular with visitors from all over the world and forms a
fundamental part of the identity of the village. While tourism to the village presents
economic opportunities, it also puts pressure on its infrastructure. Doune Castle also
has a long-standing collaboration with the local primary school, where its pupils guide
visitors around the castle as part of the Junior Guides scheme (Historic Environment
Scotland, 2017).

As Fig. 3 illustrates, HES's care covers the castle itself, Doune Roman Fort, and
the surrounding area covering around 16.2 hectares, including the promontory and
point where the River Teith and Ardoch Burn meet. Within the Property in Care (PIC)
boundary lie several buildings part of the Moray Estate, including a former steading
and cottage that today functions as a workshop for HES's Monument Conservation
Unit, the ruin of a mill, and an icehouse (Historic Environment Scotland, 2017).

A car park with a capacity for about 25 cars is located close to the castle. An
adjacent cottage serves as an office for HES staff, as well as housing visitor welfare
facilities. Visitors can enjoy an audio guide narrated by Monty Python's Terry Jones
and Sam Heughan of *Outlander*, and graphic interpretation covering the history of
the castle, and its role in popular culture as a filming location. The current visitor
offer also includes a small shop, boasting a selection of TV and movie memorabilia
alongside historic souvenirs (Historic Environment Scotland, 2017).

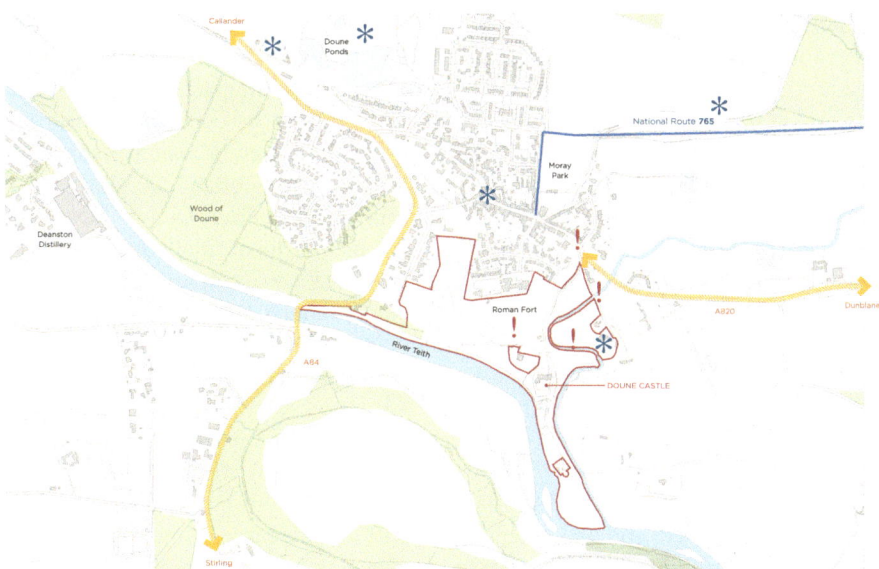

Fig. 3 Map of Property in Care (PIC) boundaries at Doune © Historic Environment Scotland

Fig. 4 Winterfell sign at Doune Castle. © Julie Howden

Doune Castle is a popular filming location and has been featured in *Monty Python and the Holy Grail*, *Game of Thrones* and *Outlander* (see Figs. 4 and 5), attracting around 147k visitors to the site in 2019/2020. A proportion of today's visitors are heavily motivated to visit the castle by its position in popular culture, and the interface of reality and fiction forms an important part of their visitor experience. It is this connection, however, which also poses a risk of negative impacts on key historical features of the castle and the visitor experience of those not associating the castle with TV and film, highlighting the importance of best practices in visitor management and responsible tourism by HES. (Historic Environment Scotland, 2017).

Challenges and Opportunities at Doune Castle. The Doune Sustainable Tourism Project has been developed in response to local challenges identified, predominantly around increased visitation to the site due to its inclusion in the notable TV series *Outlander*. What is now coined the 'Outlander Effect' has driven visitor numbers from around 49.5k in 2024/15, the year that *Outlander* first aired, to around 147k in 2019/2020, when tourism at Doune was at its height.

This increase in visitor numbers has contributed to several challenges at and around Doune Castle. It has had a detrimental effect on the natural and built historic environment, with archaeology in the grounds surrounding the castle starting to be exposed through the increased footfall. The state of pre-project infrastructure was susceptible to congestion and unable to support the increased number of visitors to the village, especially when they arrived as part of a coach trip, which reduced the overall economic benefit to the village.

Fig. 5 Behind the scenes of *Outlander*. © 2014 Sony Pictures Television Inc. All Rights Reserved

A major barrier to addressing these challenges and realising opportunities is a lack of key infrastructure. Prior to the project, there had been no obvious routes between Doune Castle and Doune Village and therefore, the majority of visitors to Doune Castle were not exposed to the other attractions in Doune and the surrounding area including the River Teith, Ardoch Burn, Doune Ponds Nature Reserve, and a village centre with quality retail and food & drink offering (see Fig. 6).

As Fig. 6 shows, there are numerous established visitor attractions in the vicinity of Doune complementing the heritage-based visitor offer at Doune Castle to provide a more complete visitor experience. This includes support to the local economy at the Deanston Distillery, promoting and engaging with local biodiversity through the community-managed Doune Ponds Nature Reserve and Argaty Red Kites along with sharing resources with other nationally recognised visitor attractions, such as the Blair Drummond Safari Park.

In addition to established visitor attractions, there are opportunities to align with other initiatives within the region, such as the extension of the national cycle route, National Route 765, from Doune to Callander, which should provide opportunities for low-carbon and active travel to the village and castle, whilst tapping into a whole new connection of visitors from the Loch Lomond and The Trossachs National Park.

Activity. Supported by the VisitScotland Rural Tourism Infrastructure Fund (RTIF), which supports projects delivered in collaboration to improve visitor experiences in rural parts of Scotland that have seen increased pressures on infrastructure and communities caused by rising visitor numbers, HES was able to deliver a series of individual projects to initiate the 'Doune Sustainable Tourism Project'. These

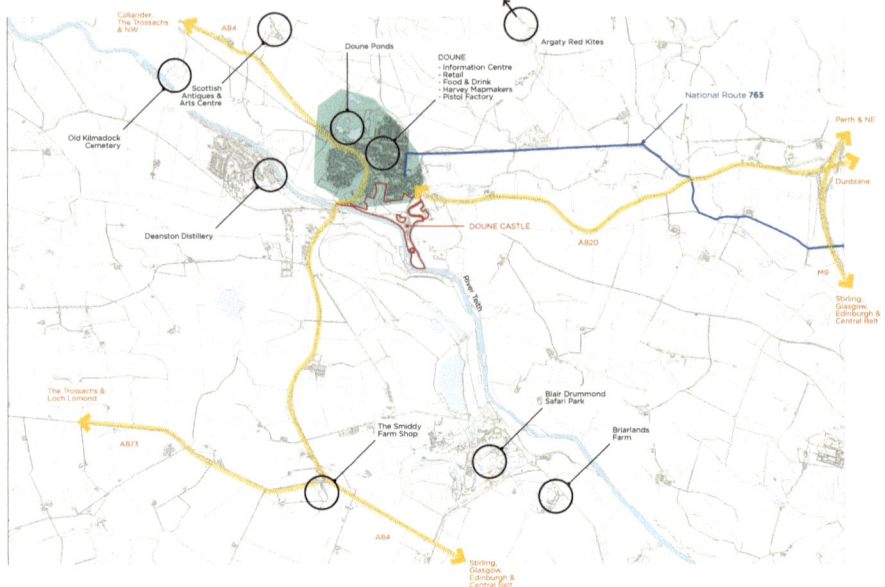

Fig. 6 Map of wider Doune visitor offer opportunities. © Historic Environment Scotland

projects have been developed and carried out in collaboration with Stirling Council and representatives of the local community including the Kilmadock Community Development Trust and Kilmadock Community Council. They focus on sustainable infrastructure to subsequently maximise benefits to local businesses from tourism and minimise the negative environmental and social impacts of tourism in the Doune area.

Since receiving funding in June 2019, HES has been fortunate to be able to deliver the projects as intended, despite the challenges brought by the COVID-19 pandemic. The first RTIF project was completed in early 2021. This created a new physical link from the Castle towards Doune Village, using a new stepped ramp and path (see Fig. 7), which goes past the site of the Roman Fort leading to and from the Castle.

This was followed by the most significant RTIF project: a new pedestrian bridge (see Fig. 8) crossing the Ardoch Burn by the Mill of Doune. Setting an example for future projects, the bridge was built applying sustainable practices, for example using homegrown Scottish Larch sourced from the woods of the Moray Estate, the large estate where Doune Castle is located, felling and cutting the timber within the local area. Locally sourced stone was used to clad the foundations of the bridge with HES's apprentice team learning and applying traditional skills to cut and lay it. By using locally sourced materials and working with local businesses, HES was able to cut supply chain-associated carbon emissions significantly, demonstrating the application of sustainable resource use.

Completed in January 2022, this new route leading from Doune Castle to Castle Farm reconnects the surrounding landscape to the castle and the local community,

Fig. 7 New stepped ramp leading from Doune Castle past the Roman Fort. © Historic Environment Scotland

Fig. 8 A new pedestrian bridge linking Doune's heritage assets with its natural environment and the local village. © Rob McDougall

increasing access along the Ardoch Burn. Following the principle of environmental stewardship, this enhances the visitor experience and well-being, enabling visitors, staff, and the local community to enjoy and engage with the impressive natural environment and other cultural assets that form the setting for Doune Castle. Visitor Enjoyment scores have risen significantly from 2020 to 2022—from 7.61 to 9.22 out of 10.

In March 2021, in collaboration with Artlink Central, a local community organisation, HES carried out a mapping exercise that identified current local priorities for learning, engagement, and visitor experience, and potential partners. Delivering on the principle of community involvement, various community workshops and interviews were held online, and links to local community groups were strengthened.

Subsequently, work began on the installation of a new Signage & Interpretation route, including information signage at Doune Castle on attractions and services in the village, maps and wayfinding signage to promote a circular walking route through the village, and interpretation panels of key places of historical interest (see Fig. 9). By highlighting local businesses in this way, HES hopes to encourage longer dwell time and spend in the local and wider area, to maximise local economic benefits from tourism. The HES team on site engage with visitors to direct them on the walking route and to local businesses.

An in-person engagement event 'Doune Together' was held with partners in April 2022 to review achievements and consider future plans, which include trialling a

Fig. 9 Doune historic village panel © Historic Environment Scotland

discount flier for local businesses handed out to castle visitors and supporting the community with the revitalisation of a business network.

As the new pedestrian bridge is now connecting the village, Doune Castle, and auxiliary buildings such as the Mill of Doune and Castle Farm, this work has become a springboard for future activity. Already, delivery of the HES Climate Action Plan objectives has started through several projects. The Castle Farm Cottage is currently undergoing traditional building retrofitting targeting Passivhaus standards. A material pilot study into Scottish mass timber is taking place at The Mill of Doune, and following circular economy principles, the Castle Keeper's Cottage visitor facilities are being upgraded. Finally, options are under consideration to decarbonise the operation of Doune Castle and generate energy for the site from renewable sources.

This activity is also aligned to and supporting initiatives in the wider community including the completion of a new visitor Park & Stride transport hub within the village, including EV charging and active travel infrastructure, a pilot scheme to develop the public transport connections to Doune attractions and Dunblane train station, and the development of the wider Local Place Plan by the Kilmadock Development Trust.

5   Conclusion

Following the success of the 'Doune Sustainable Tourism Project' pilot and the launch
of the HES Responsible Tourism Framework in March 2023, HES is expanding the
application of responsible tourism principles into projects and initiatives across its
estate. For example, the Framework, and other relevant HES policies, have informed
the development of a 'Strategic Tourism Infrastructure Development Plan' for Blackness, a village which is also experiencing challenges due to a steep increase in visitor
numbers to Blackness Castle, cared for by HES, following its appearance in the TV
show *Outlander*. Funded by VisitScotland's RTIF and working with Falkirk Council,
HES aims to transform tourism at Blackness Castle by applying responsible tourism
principles to address challenges, similar to those in Doune, including congestion
during the peak season.

The HES Responsible Tourism Framework proposes an alternative approach to
pre-pandemic tourism models and forms a new lens through which the organisation
will consider future investment planning and prioritisation. It supports resolving the
challenges heritage and cultural tourism face by encouraging responsible visitation
while transforming business models to be more circular. This could be an inspiration
for others, who may see challenges only resolved by reducing numbers and actively
using disincentives to dissuade visitors. Instead, responsible tourism principles lie at
the heart of decision-making to ensure the short- and long-term benefits of tourism
are spread to communities, local businesses, local amenities, and both the historic
and natural environment, as well as enjoyed by the tourists themselves.

The project highlights how the holistic approach provided by the Responsible
Tourism Framework can be applied. The individual initiatives within the project
tie back to all three priority areas, from integrating circular economy principles
into tourism operations, the use of locally sourced material for construction, and
enabling visitors to engage responsibly with the biodiversity and landscape in and
around Doune Castle, to working in close partnership with others, especially local
community groups and businesses to better share economic benefits from tourism.
It demonstrates the importance of ensuring that solutions meet the needs of the
community and local businesses, and the environment, as well as tourists.

The Framework's implementation is not without its challenges. The development
of the Framework has been informed by a wide-reaching internal cross-organisational
consultation, and a formal public consultation carried out through an online survey.
The survey was shared through the required statutory structure of public consultations in Scotland, which can prove to be rigid and a challenge to engage with all.
Therefore, care has been taken to maximise the reach of consultation through available traditional and social media platforms. Further work needs to be carried out to
optimise inclusive and meaningful community engagement around the development
of responsible tourism at HES sites, including training staff and exploring innovative
engagement methods.

Furthermore, the tourism sector is currently facing competing demands in its
recovery from the COVID-19 pandemic. The Framework provides the basis on

which activities on site can be transformed, to reflect that responsible tourism can contribute to the green recovery and a move to a well-being economy, without adverse effects on the environment and communities. More physical exemplars will showcase responsible tourism's benefits and support the wider adoption of this approach.

Lastly, HES is conscious that the application of responsible tourism principles will look different from site to site, location to location, based on local circumstances, knowledge, and capacities. The Framework allows for such flexibilities, but future applications, such as at Blackness Castle, will be valuable in gaining further understanding of its resilience.

Appendix

See Table 1 (Historic Environment Scotland, 2023).

Table 1 Depicts how activity within the Doune Sustainable Tourism Project maps across the outcomes of the HES Responsible Tourism Framework

HES responsible tourism framework outcomes	Doune sustainable tourism project
Our responsibility for the historic environment	
01 We will integrate circular economy practices into our operational model.	✓ Embeds resource efficiency and prioritises reused or remanufactured goods over new ✓ Builds strong and fair partnerships with suppliers ✓ Targets high-performance retrofit standards, such as PassivHaus EnerPHit, to explore the limitations within a sensitive cultural context
02 We will protect and enhance the natural capital and biodiversity of our historic environment.	✓ Promotes and implements best practices, avoiding or minimising the negative impacts of tourism activities on the environment through enhanced active travel infrastructure and signage

(continued)

Table 1 (continued)

HES responsible tourism framework outcomes	Doune sustainable tourism project
03 We will enable and promote low carbon visitor experiences.	✓ Embeds sustainable and active travel as a core consideration in the development of strategies ✓ Adopts a shared destination approach with partners to develop low-carbon travel routes between attractions
Our responsibility for people	
01 We will co-create experiences enhancing the wellbeing of communities and visitors.	✓ Leads proactive dialogue with communities to explore opportunities within social carrying capacity thresholds ✓ Supports the development of a baseline to understand and recognise differing levels of community engagement ✓ Supports the development of long-term relationships supporting groups who would otherwise struggle to engage actively with heritage and the historic environment
02 We will improve physical, intellectual, cognitive and cultural accessibility to heritage tourism experiences for all.	✓ Enhances accessibility and connection of the site with the surrounding environment and community, through improved infrastructure and wayfinding
03 We will increase the seasonal and geographic spread of our outstanding experiences for more communities to benefit from tourism.	✓ Enhances the visitor offer, influencing visitors to spend more time in the area

(continued)

Table 1 (continued)

HES responsible tourism framework outcomes	Doune sustainable tourism project
Our responsibility for capacity building	
We will improve and support the generation of local economic benefits from tourism.	✓ Increases HES awareness of regional tourism strategies to identify areas for effective support and collaboration
We will strengthen the provision of skills development and quality career pathways in the heritage tourism sector.	✓ Contributes to the development of a knowledge base and best practice catalogue, to ensure consistency across the organisation
We will support heritage and tourism organisations and businesses in their efforts to move to business models reflecting responsible tourism principles.	✓ Contributes to positively influencing behaviour and inspiring others within the heritage tourism sector towards taking responsibility for net zero activities

References

Climate Change (Scotland) Act 2009. Retrieved 15 June, 2023, from https://www.legislation.gov.uk/asp/2009/12/contents

Historic Environment Scotland. (2011). *Designations—Doune castle*. Retrieved 14 June, 2023, from http://portal.historicenvironment.scot/designation/SM12765

Historic Environment Scotland. (2017). *Statement of significance Doune castle*. Retrieved from https://www.historicenvironment.scot/archives-and-research/publications/publication/?publicationId=7546c7d2-2a7f-477f-a26c-a57000c9b439

Historic Environment Scotland. (2019). *A guide to climate change impacts on Scotland's historic environment*. Retrieved from https://www.historicenvironment.scot/archives-and-research/publications/publication/?publicationId=843d0c97-d3f4-4510-acd3-aadf0118bf82

Historic Environment Scotland. (2022). *Green recovery statement For Scotland's historic environment*. Retrieved from https://www.historicenvironment.scot/archives-and-research/publications/publication/?publicationId=8a0b75d5-0776-4587-8dd5-ae8201362dd4

Historic Environment Scotland. (2023). *Responsible tourism framework—transforming heritage tourism.* Retrieved from https://www.historicenvironment.scot/archives-and-research/publicati ons/publication/?publicationid=30eaf2e3-9e8a-47c3-b9c9-afcb00eca788

One Planet Network. (2021). *Tourism climate action—Glasgow declaration.* Retrieved 14 June, 2023, from https://www.oneplanetnetwork.org/programmes/sustainable-tourism/glasgow-dec laration

Rennie, A. F., Hansom, J. D., Hurst, M. D., Muir, F. M. E., Naylor, L. A., Dunkley, R. A., & MacDonell, C. J. (2021). *Dynamic coast: Adaptation and resilience options at the Bay of Skaill.* Scotland's Centre of Expertise for Waters (CREW). Retrieved from https://www.dynamiccoast. com/files/dc2/_DC2_WS4_BayOfSkaill_FINAL.pdf

Responsible Tourism Partnership. (2008). *Cape Town declaration on responsible tourism.* Retrieved 14 June, 2023, from https://responsibletourismpartnership.org/cape-town-declaration-on-res ponsible-tourism/

Transport Scotland. (2023). Chapter 13—environment. In *Scottish transport statistics 2022.* Retrieved 14 June, 2023, from https://www.transport.gov.scot/publication/scottish-transport-sta tistics-2022/chapter-13-environment/

The Scottish Government. (2011). *Public bodies climate change duties: Putting them into practice.* Retrieved from https://www.gov.scot/binaries/content/documents/govscot/publications/adv ice-and-guidance/2011/02/public-bodies-climate-change-duties-putting-practice-guidance-req uired-part/documents/0113071-pdf/0113071-pdf/govscot%3Adocument/0113071.pdf

The Scottish Government. (2018). *Update to the climate change plan 2018—2032: Securing a green recovery on a path to net zero.* Retrieved from https://www.gov.scot/binaries/content/docume nts/govscot/publications/strategy-plan/2020/12/securing-green-recovery-path-net-zero-upd ate-climate-change-plan-20182032/documents/update-climate-change-plan-2018-2032-sec uring-green-recovery-path-net-zero/update-climate-change-plan-2018-2032-securing-green- recovery-path-net-zero/govscot%3Adocument/update-climate-change-plan-2018-2032-sec uring-green-recovery-path-net-zero.pdf

The Scottish Tourism Alliance et al. (2020). *Scotland outlook 2030—responsible tourism for a sustainable future.* Retrieved from https://scottishtourismalliance.co.uk/wp-content/uploads/ 2020/03/Scotland-Outlook-2030.pdf

VisitScotland. (2017). *Scotland visitor survey 2015 and 2016—full version.* Retrieved from https:// www.visitscotland.org/binaries/content/assets/dot-org/pdf/research-insights/scotland-visitor- survey-2015-2016.pdf

VisitScotland. (2021). *Scotland's responsible tourism promise.* Retrieved 14 June, 2023, from https://www.visitscotland.com/travel-planning/responsible-tourism/responsible-promise#:~: text=I%20promise%20to%20care%20for%20Scotland's%20communities.&text=Respect% 20the%20locals%20and%20their,that%20are%20found%20throughout%20Scotland

VisitScotland Insights Department. (2019). *Key facts on tourism in Scotland.* Retrieved 14 June, 2023, from https://www.visitscotland.org/research-insights/about-our-industry/statistics

Zero Waste Scotland. (2021). *Carbon cost.* Retrieved 8 June, 2023, from https://www.zerowastesco tland.org.uk/resources/carbon-cost

Heritage and Territory: Tangible and Intangible Cultural Resources as Drivers of Regional Development in Croatia

Zvonimir Kuliš⬤ and Blanka Šimundić

Abstract This paper investigates the relationship between cultural heritage, tourism demand, and regional development in Croatia using a spatial econometrics approach. A composite Cultural Heritage Index was created based on UNESCO and national material and immaterial cultural assets within the framework of the Horizon 2020 SmartCulTour project. The spatial autoregressive (SAR) model was employed to analyze the impact of cultural heritage and tourism demand on regional development across Croatian NUTS 3 regions while accounting for control variables such as gross value added and trade openness. The findings reveal that cultural heritage has a positive and statistically significant effect on regional development, both directly and indirectly. Tourism demand also plays a vital role in regional development, with the potential for enhancing positive spillover effects. These results contribute to the literature by quantitatively demonstrating the link between cultural heritage, tourism, and regional development in the Croatian context, providing valuable insights for policymakers to foster sustainable cultural tourism activities.

Keywords Cultural heritage · Tourism demand · Regional development · Spatial regression · Croatian NUTS 3 regions

1 Introduction

Within the context of a span covering six decades, the tourism industry has evidenced extraordinary escalation on an international scope, a trend that is also mirrored within the confines of the European Union (Šimundić, 2017). Nonetheless, the unprecedented advent of the COVID-19 pandemic has instigated a severe dislocation in

Z. Kuliš (✉) · B. Šimundić
Faculty of Economics, Business and Tourism, University of Split, Cvite Fiskovića 5, 21 000 Split, Split, Croatia
e-mail: zkulis@efst.hr

B. Šimundić
e-mail: blans@efst.hr

© The Author(s) 2025

B. Neuts et al. (eds.), *Advances in Cultural Tourism Research*, Advances in Digital and Cultural Tourism Management, https://doi.org/10.1007/978-3-031-65537-1_7

the global tourism landscape. This disturbance owes its severity to a myriad of factors, including the enforcement of social distancing regulations, the curtailment of international transport services, as well as the implementation of governmental decrees such as quarantines and travel prohibitions (Gunter et al., 2022). As such, academics and industry professionals alike have increasingly recognized the COVID-19 crisis as an opportunity for an introspective reevaluation of the prevailing tourism paradigm. There is growing advocacy for a transformative redirection towards a more sustainable future in tourism (Yang et al., 2021).

The special form of tourism that can enable and drive regional development, as well as contribute to the sustainability and resilience of destinations within the EU, is cultural tourism (Directorate-General for Education, 2019; Directorate-General for Internal Market, 2022; Lykogianni et al., 2019; Neuts, 2022; Neuts et al., 2021; Petrić et al., 2020, 2021; Russo & Borg, 2006; Stoica et al., 2022). Cultural heritage holds immense significance in Europe, which serves as a prominent cultural tourism destination due to its unparalleled and abundant cultural assets, thereby positioning it as the foremost global tourist macroregion with a dominant share of tourism demand (Cultural Heritage). In an analysis by ESPON (Lykogianni et al., 2019), cultural heritage has been acknowledged not merely as a reservoir of knowledge, facilitator of social welfare, a conduit for a sense of community identity, and a promoter of societal cohesion, but also as a critical element of Europe's socio-economic asset base. Despite being an inheritance from previous generations, cultural heritage maintains a contemporary relevance as a "living" cultural asset, spurring an array of economic pursuits and permeating the wider economic landscape. Further, the positive societal impact of cultural heritage is evident in its contributions to employment rates and gross domestic product growth. This report also underscores that in the past decade, there has been a rising cognizance among policymakers regarding the strategic importance of cultural heritage for fostering sustainable territorial development and bolstering economic expansion, a fact evidenced in numerous policy manuscripts within the European context. Additionally, it highlights the advocacy for a more comprehensive and interdisciplinary methodology in relation to cultural heritage, a notion that is manifested across multiple European policy domains, such as the cohesion policy, research and innovation, environmental stewardship, as well as neighborhood and foreign policy.

Naramski et al. (2022), drawing on an OECD report, estimated that approximately 40% of tourist trips in the twenty-first century involve cultural components, with this proportion rising to 50% in European and American tourism. Jelinčić and Senkić (2017) noted that, prior to the COVID-19 pandemic, the global market for cultural tourism was estimated to be valued between 800 billion and 1.1 trillion USD. Croatia, experiencing the second-highest annual growth in tourism overnights in the EU during the second decade of the twenty-first century (Kovačević, 2020; Šimundić et al., 2022), has emerged as a significant international tourist destination highly regarded for its rich cultural heritage among foreign tourists (Kordej-De Villa et al., 2021). In fact, according to a study on the attitudes of respondents from outbound markets, 54% of surveyed tourists from these markets selected cultural heritage as a key motivator for their visit to Croatia (2019; Ministry of Tourism & Sport,

2022). Demonja (2013) highlights that the abundance of both tangible and intangible Croatian cultural heritage serves as a foundation for the development of various forms of cultural tourism, including heritage tourism, UNESCO sites, museums, archaeological sites, and rural and eco-ethno tourism. Indeed, Croatia possesses an abundance of cultural assets, garnering recognition on international and national levels. Šimundić et al. (2022) note that Croatia is included among the 16 European Union member states that boast ten or more sites listed by UNESCO. At present, a total of 31 cultural heritage assets from Croatia, 10 tangible and 21 intangible, are acknowledged in the UNESCO Lists (Ministry of Culture & Media). Additionally, as documented in the Register of Cultural Property of the Republic of Croatia, managed by the Ministry of Culture and Media (Ministry of Culture & Media), over 6,400 properties, inclusive of more than 200 intangible assets, are cataloged in The List of Cultural Goods.

Thus, it is not surprising that, as highlighted by Tomljenović (2021), since the adoption of Croatia's first national cultural tourism strategy in 2004, cultural heritage tourism has become vital for dispersing tourists and fostering regional development. As the same author explains, the tourism industry acknowledges the potential of cultural heritage and activities to attract tourists via supply-driven strategies, particularly in Croatia's continental regions, while also mitigating seasonality and appealing to higher-spending tourists. The cultural and heritage sectors recognize their role in promoting tourism and economic development. The 2011–2015 Strategy of Conservation, Protection, and Sustainable Economic Use of Croatian Cultural Heritage aimed to bolster the economic utilization of culture and heritage, promote cultural entrepreneurship, and support regional and economic development through cultural tourism. However, a recent study by Šimundić et al. (2022) contends that the integration of cultural heritage into the tourism supply remains inadequate, despite the considerable potential and accessibility of such heritage resources. This conclusion is also echoed in the recently adopted Sustainable Tourism Development Strategy until 2030 (Ministry of Tourism & Sport, 2022), which acknowledges that, although certain destinations within Croatia have effectively promoted and emphasized their cultural-historical heritage, a considerable portion of this heritage remains unutilized for tourism purposes (e.g., castles, fortresses, small historic towns, etc.), in spite of its unmistakable potential. The document underscores the significance of cultural heritage in shaping the country's new tourism vision and identifies cultural tourism as one of the most important tourist products, as well as a key driver for future tourism development.

Hence, Croatia, characterized by its extensive and diverse cultural resources, which have not yet been fully exploited, and building upon the recent methodological frameworks established in the Horizon2020 SmartCulTour project (Neuts, 2022; Neuts et al., 2021; Petrić et al., 2020, 2021), provides an exceptional context for examining the potential of cultural resources as a form of territorial capital that can be utilized for regional development. This paper seeks to investigate the role of tangible and intangible cultural heritage in catalyzing regional development in Croatia through cultural tourism. By shedding light on the interplay between cultural heritage, tourism, and regional development, the paper aims to contribute to the ongoing discourse on cultural tourism and its role in fostering economic growth, sustainability, and resilience. In the subsequent sections, this paper will provide a comprehensive review of the pertinent literature regarding the role of cultural heritage and tourism in regional development, present the data and the spatial regression model, and delve into a discussion on research methodology and results. Additionally, the paper will address the findings and opportunities in capitalizing on cultural resources for regional development. Ultimately, the paper will put forth policy recommendations and suggestions for future research.

2   Theoretical Background

Panzera (2022) posits that cultural heritage can indeed serve as a catalyst for development in a unique and distinctive manner due to its diverse and multifaceted values. She explains, when viewed as an economic resource, cultural heritage can have a considerable influence on local economies due to its economic value (e.g. tourist consumption, associated investments, and sales). Neuts et al. (2021) outline some of the primary benefits of cultural heritage, including: (i) enhancing the appeal of regions, cities, towns, and rural areas; (ii) offering investment opportunities in cultural tourism; (iii) acting as a catalyst for innovation and creativity; (iv) promoting sustainable heritage-driven revitalization; and (v) enhancing the overall quality of life.

The most salient and observable connection between cultural heritage and economic development can be found in tourism. Beginning in the 1970s and expanding more extensively in the 1980s, heritage tourism emerged as a growing phenomenon. Local cultural resources, including cultural heritage, have begun to be viewed as factors contributing to territorial attractiveness, distinction, and competitiveness, and the link between cultural heritage and tourism was increasingly seen as inseparable (Panzera, 2022). Richards (2018) emphasizes that while the relationship between culture and tourism has always been inherently connected, it is only in recent decades that their association has been explicitly identified as a unique form of consumption, termed cultural tourism. Škrabić Perić et al. (2021) expound that culture holds potential in cultivating destination distinctiveness within the tourism sector, while tourism simultaneously offers prospects for bolstering cultural production and enhancing the economic performance of the cultural sector. The symbiotic relationship between culture and tourism is also acknowledged by UNWTO (2018). In a survey conducted among UNWTO Member States, participants were prompted to identify the various elements of culture and heritage incorporated into their classification of "cultural tourism." The majority of participants indicated their inclusion of both tangible and intangible elements of cultural heritage. Tangible aspects consisted of both global and national monuments, historical edifices, locations, and cultural pathways. Intangible elements, on the other hand, incorporated traditions, gastronomy, craftsmanship, festivals, and similar elements. Timothy (2021) delineates that the phrases "cultural tourism" and "heritage tourism" are habitually referenced in professional sectors and academic literature as separate, albeit related or overlapping, phenomena. He further encapsulates that cultural heritage tourism is inclusive of built heritage, enduring cultural practices, ancient artifacts, as well as contemporary art and culture. Furthermore, he underscores that although some scholars prefer to discern cultural tourism from heritage tourism, contingent on individual motivations or the nature of the resources involved, any extant distinctions are typically slight, thereby allowing the two terms to be used interchangeably. More recently, Matteucci and Von Zumbusch (2020) propose a re-conceptualization of cultural tourism. According to their definition, cultural tourism is a distinct variety of tourism in which tourists interact with heritage, local cultural and creative endeavors, and the daily cultural routines of host communities. This engagement aims to facilitate the exchange of experiences characterized by their educational, aesthetic, creative, emotional, or recreational qualities.

Cultural heritage stands as one of the most prominent resources utilized by tourism (Csapo, 2012) and serves as a crucial factor in crafting a destination's distinctiveness while providing a foundation for authentic and differentiated tourism experiences (Romão, 2018). Timothy (2021) posits that a majority of contemporary tourist attractions and destinations are based on cultural heritage elements. This notion is corroborated by Gómez-Vega et al. (2021), who conducted a DEA-MCDM approach using the Travel and Tourism Competitiveness (T&TC) report as the primary data source for a sample of 136 tourist destinations. Their analysis revealed that, among the 14 pillars of T&TC, cultural resources were of the utmost importance. Panzera (2022) elucidates that despite considerable efforts in scientific literature, a definitive consensus regarding a quantifiable link between cultural heritage endowment and tourism attractiveness remains elusive. Generally, when examining the role of cultural heritage in stimulating tourism demand, UNESCO World Heritage Sites are the most commonly employed proxy for tangible forms of cultural heritage. Nevertheless, the findings in the existing body of literature are inconclusive (Cellini & Cuccia, 2016). For instance, in a study analyzing the impact of cultural indicators on tourism performance at the national level within EU countries, Škrabić Perić et al. (2021) discovered that the number of UNESCO Heritage Sites had no significant influence on the number of tourism overnights but positively affected international tourism receipts and tourism employment. In the regional context of European NUTS 2 regions, several papers have identified a positive correlation between regional endowment in cultural resources and the volume of tourism demand (Panzera et al., 2021; Romão, 2015; Romão & Neuts, 2017; Romão et al., 2017).

Panzera (2022) presents empirical findings that reinforce the significance attributed to tourism within the realm of economic literature. This is primarily due to the role of tourism attractiveness as a key conduit for the influence of tangible cultural heritage on the economic growth of European regions. Using a structural equation model that includes two specific indicators—UNESCO World Heritage Sites and regional monument counts, Panzera validates the mediating function of tourism in this context. Nonetheless, Camagni et al. (2020) emphasize that, despite its undeniable importance, cultural tourism is not the exclusive mechanism through which tangible cultural heritage can impact local performance, as more abstract and complex processes may be involved. They introduce the idea that cultural heritage forms one component of "territorial capital"—an ensemble of territorial resources that foster endogenous development. Their empirical findings suggest that the impact of cultural heritage on local development is a product of its interaction with other elements of territorial capital, specifically the intangible territorial components such as creativity, identity, and governance quality. Moreover, Panzera (2022) presents a novel pathway related to the influence of cultural heritage in shaping or strengthening territorial identities and their consequent economic ramifications. Furthermore, Cerisola (2019) advances the debate by conceptually and empirically broadening the idea that creativity, manifested in various forms, can function as a mediating factor, clarifying the local ability to capitalize on cultural heritage for economic objectives. Investigating the Italian provinces at the NUTS 3 level, she determined that cultural heritage indirectly affects economic performance via its impact on artistic and scientific creativity. The empirical analysis reveals that this relationship is particularly evident in affluent, well-educated, and urban settings. Cerisola and Panzera (2022) conducted an analysis to explore the relationship between urban cultural engagement and regional output in cities rich in culture and creativity. Their research revealed a positive association between local cultural participation and economic productivity. Besides, Tubadji (2012) offers an insightful delineation of the culture-based development (CBD) concept, identifying culture as an encompassing socio-economic determinant. The CBD concept advances by delineating living culture and cultural heritage as the two components of cultural capital, which are interconnected in a path-dependent manner. Substantial positive results supporting the CBD concept, signifying that cultural capital positively influences economic development, have been demonstrated at the regional level for the European Union (Tubadji & Nijkamp, 2015a) and the United States (Tubadji et al., 2015), as well as for Germany (Tubadji, 2012) and Greece (Tubadji & Nijkamp, 2015b) specifically. Similarly, Kostakis et al. (2016) discerned a positive correlation between cultural heritage and regional growth, corroborating the hypothesis of culture-led growth within the context of the Greek economy. Backman and Nilsson (2018) discovered that the local provision of built heritage and cultural environments contributes significantly to human capital growth in Sweden, suggesting that such cultural heritage assets are vital place-based resources with the potential to enhance regional attractiveness and promote growth. Correa-Quezada et al. (1649) conducted an investigation to evaluate the impact of employment within the creative industries on regional economic expansion in Ecuador. Their empirical findings substantiated a significant correlation between creative employment and regional productivity and development. In contrast, Romão and Nijkamp (2018) analyzed economic progress, tourism, and territorial capital in European regions, concluding that cultural resources do not have a significant impact on economic growth.

In recent years, apart from examining the role of cultural heritage and tourism in economic development, scholars have begun to explore their contributions to achieving regional economic resilience. Within the framework of the SmartCulTour project, the connection between cultural tourism and economic resilience has been thoroughly established (Petrić et al., 2021) and empirically demonstrated using a sample of 35 European local administrative units. The primary conclusion drawn from this research is that cultural tourism bolsters regional resilience, with tourism dynamics playing a crucial role in the process. Furthermore, the study confirmed that an abundance of cultural resources and cultural enterprises enhances a region's capacity to withstand and recover from external economic shocks. More recently, Muštra et al. (2023) investigated the impact of tourism demand and cultural UNESCO sites on regional economic resilience among European Union countries, with their conclusions underscoring the significance of cultural heritage in maintaining regional economic resilience.

In the context of Croatia, Demonja (2013) notes that while cultural tourism is not a new concept in the country, there is limited publishing activity within the Croatian scientific and professional community concerning its effects, which remain inadequately evaluated. As same before mentioned authors explain, Croatian cultural tourism is seldom examined in academic terms, evaluations of Croatian culture and tourism resources are rare, and numerous problems persist within the realm of cultural tourism. The primary reasons include insufficient intersectoral cooperation between tourism and culture, a lack of research results and post-measure evaluations, and the general difficulty in obtaining limited official data from government institutions. Mikulić and Petrić (2014) explored the interplay between culture and tourism in the urban regeneration of Croatian cities. They found direct positive associations between strategies that encourage the establishment of cultural districts and related projects integrated into broader city and tourism development plans, predominantly reliant on small and medium-sized enterprises. Zadel and Bogdan (2013) examined the economic impacts of cultural tourism in Croatia and found its economic contribution to be relatively low. Demonja and Gredičak (2015) carried out a concise examination and critical evaluation of the impact of tourism and culture on Croatia's economic development. They concluded that the tourist valorization of cultural heritage constitutes a selective form of tourism, which could offer the Croatian economy a sustainable competitive edge. Lovrentjev (2015) introduced the concept of multiple effects on sustainable tourism development resulting from the incorporation of intangible cultural heritage into a destination's tourist offerings. The study concluded that benefits could be experienced by both tourists and the local community. Kordej-De Villa and Šulc (2021) conducted a detailed scrutiny of the management practices at cultural heritage sites in Croatia, specifically those acknowledged on the UNESCO World Heritage List. These sites face mounting complications due to the phenomenon of overtourism. The chosen case studies in Croatia underscored that the most common mode of heritage valorization is situated within the realm of tourism, wherein heritage is frequently associated with sustainable tourism. Further, Šimundić et al. (2022) carried out a thorough examination of seven strategies for urban agglomeration development to identify the prevailing discourses on cultural heritage within public documents formulated to procure EU funds in Croatia. The first notable discourse pertains to the insufficient incorporation of cultural heritage into the tourism provision, despite its inherent potential and accessibility. The second dominant discourse pertains to various socio-economic challenges in Croatia, which include limited entrepreneurial engagement, suboptimal public consciousness and interest towards cultural heritage, an inadequate understanding of the significance of heritage conservation and its contribution to national identity, and a deficient level of knowledge among the local populace and tourist coordinators pertaining to cultural management.

Despite the expanding literature on cultural heritage, tourism, and economic development, Maldonado-Erazo et al. (2022) observe that the scholarly mapping acquired in their study reveals a limited body of literature addressing the relationship between the utilization of cultural resources by tourism and regional development of a territory, encompassing both economic and social perspectives. Panzera (2022) draws a similar conclusion, emphasizing that although the interactions between cultural heritage, tourism, and economic development, are strongly advocated and widely acknowledged in public discourse, quantitatively validating and substantiating these links proves challenging, especially for intangible forms of cultural heritage. Indeed, as Dalle Nogare and Devesa (2023) underscore, the evidence from quantitative analysis is less definitive, which calls for novel methodologies to unravel the puzzle; one suggested approach, for instance, is spatial econometrics. This research seeks to bridge the gap in the existing literature by employing a spatial regression approach to explore the connections between the utilization of cultural resources and regional development. By focusing on both tangible and intangible cultural resources within Croatia, this study strives to deliver a holistic analysis, enhancing our understanding of the various factors that influence regional development in the country. Additionally, this research will significantly enrich the academic discourse by illuminating the distinct challenges and opportunities present in the Croatian context, an area that has been comparatively underrepresented in existing literature.

3   Research Methodology, Results, and Discussion

As outlined earlier, this paper examines the role of cultural tourism in the regional development of Croatian NUTS 3 regions. Consequently, it is essential to define regional development. The variable employed for this purpose is the regional development index provided by the Ministry of Regional Development and EU Funding (Ministry of Regional Development & EU Funding). The Development Index (DI) is a composite metric derived from the mean of multiple socio-economic indicators. Conceived to facilitate a consolidated method for gauging the progress of local and regional self-government units at the NUTS 3 level, the DI encompasses a variety of indicators: (i) unemployment rate, (ii) per capita income, (iii) income per capita from local/regional budgets, (iv) population fluctuation, (v) educational attainment rate, and (vi) aging index. The new model for calculating the DI is based on the expert basis (Denona Bogović et al., 2017). As articulated by Golob et al. (2018), the DI is a critical instrument for assessing the socioeconomic development levels and evaluating the advancement of local and regional self-government units while also categorizing assisted areas. Thus, it is evident that it is a key component in the regional policy framework of the Republic of Croatia The latest available DI, published in 2018 (Ministry of Regional Development & EU Funding, 2018), utilized the values of single indicators for the period of 2014–2016. The average value of the DI is 100, representing the national average; thus, units with an index above 100 are considered higher-developed regions.

The primary focus of this study centers on the variables of cultural heritage and tourism demand. In the majority of scholarly papers, this variable has been proxied using UNESCO material heritage (Muštra et al., 2023) due to the lack of comparable data for a diverse range of resources, encompassing material assets such as monuments and buildings, as well as intangible aspects like local traditions and knowledge (Romão & Nijkamp, 2018). Within the Horizon2020 SmartCulTour project, Petrić et al. (2020) proposed employing spatial indicators of cultural resources as relevant determinants of cultural heritage, acting as catalysts for cultural tourism development. These resources encompass: (i) the number of national monuments (MON), (ii) the number of World Heritage Sites (WHS), (iii) the number of intangible cultural heritage items on national lists (ICH), and (iv) the number of elements inscribed on UNESCO's Intangible Cultural Heritage Lists (ICHL). Furthermore, a composite Cultural Heritage Index (CHI) was computed using the Satty method, based on the methodology provided by Petrić et al. (Petrić et al., 2020, 2021) within the context of the aforementioned project. This process entailed the normalization, weighting, and aggregation of the previously mentioned indicators in accordance with their proposed methodology. A composite indicator can prove advantageous in this context, as it aggregates multiple dimensions of cultural heritage to assess its multidimensionality (Montalto et al., 2019; Neuts, 2022) and its role in economic development (Petrić et al., 2021). Consequently, the CHI serves as the primary indicator used in the subsequent analysis within the baseline model. Tourism plays a vital role in Croatia's economy. For example, the country recorded the highest proportion of tourism in GDP among EU member states at 24.8% in 2019 (2021). Additionally, tourism accounted for 23.2% of total employment, and international visitor expenditures constituted 37.7% of the nation's overall exports (Travel Tourism Economic Impact). The Tourism-Led Growth Hypothesis (TLGH), which posits that tourism drives overall economic growth (Kuliš et al., 2018; Šimundić & Kuliš, 2016), was confirmed at the regional NUTS 3 level for Croatia by Trinajstić et al. (2018). The tourism demand indicator (TOUR) used in this study is tourism density, defined as the total number of nights spent over a year in a tourist destination (region) per square kilometer of the destination's land area. Moreover, two control variables are incorporated into the model. One of them is gross value added (GVA) as a proxy for economic activity (Mikulić et al., 2016), defined as output (at basic prices) minus intermediate consumption (at purchaser prices). In this paper, the indicator utilized is GVA per capita at constant prices, ref. 2015. An additional control variable is trade openness (TRADE), defined as the share of exports plus imports over total regional GDP. International openness could positively contribute to regional economic development (Mikulić & Galić Nagyszombaty, 2015). For the following variables: tourism demand, GVA, and trade openness, the values used in the analysis are average values between 2014 and 2016, as the dependent variable, DI, utilized the values of single indicators for the period of 2014–2016. Single indicators of cultural heritage used to form the CHI are collected based on the inventory of the current state as of April

2023. However, this should not pose a problem for the analysis, as Panzera (2022) notes that due to the time-invariant nature of cultural heritage, it can be reasonably assumed that the number does not change significantly over the years. Table 1 summarizes all variables, associated labels, defined proxies, and corresponding data sources (ARDECO, 2023; CBS, 2023; Ministry of Culture & Media).

Consequently, a simple note of relation between dependent and independent variables can be written in the form of a non-spatial, cross-sectional linear regression model (OLS) as follows:

$$DI = \beta_1 CHI + \beta_2 TOUR + X\gamma + \varepsilon \tag{1}$$

where DI represents a vector of the regional development index for the 21 Croatian NUTS-3 regions; CHI denotes a vector of the cultural heritage index; β_1 refers to the coefficient of CHI; TOUR signifies a vector of tourism density; β_2 is the coefficient of TOUR; X is a matrix of the control variables (GVA and TRADE), and γ is a vector of coefficients for the control variables, including the constant term; ε is a vector of error terms.

In this paper, a spatial econometrics approach is employed to address the literature gaps identified by Panzera (2022) and Dalle Nogare and Devesa (2023). The concept of spatial spillovers holds a unique place within regional science as it provides a platform for empirical scrutiny of magnitude and significance, a feature not available in conventional econometric models that presume spillovers to be non-existent (Halleck Vega & Elhorst, 2015). Furthermore, spatial analysis enriches our comprehension of the intrinsic traits of various phenomena by including geographical elements, which

Table 1 Variables' definition, indicator, and sources

Variable	Label	Indicator	Source
Regional development	DI	Regional development index	Ministry of Regional Development and EU Funding
Cultural heritage	MON	Number of monuments in national lists	Ministry of Culture and Media
	WHS	Number of World Heritage Sites	
	ICH	Number of intangible cultural heritage in national lists	
	ICHL	Number of elements inscribed in the UNESCO Intangible Cultural Heritage Lists	
	CHI	Cultural Heritage Index	
Tourism demand	TOUR	Tourism density (total number of nights spent per square kilometer)	CBS
Economic activity	GVA	GVA per capita at constant prices, ref. 2015	ARDECO
Trade openness	TRADE	Sum of exports and imports as a share of GDP	CBS

can uncover obscured patterns and offer insights into spatial dependency and the interplay between variables across diverse locations (Kopczewska, 2020). Rüttenauer's (2022) research gives a thorough explanation of several spatial models designed to tackle spatial dependence issues. The Spatial Autoregressive (SAR) model employs a spatial weights matrix W and integrates a spatially lagged dependent variable. The Spatial Error Model (SEM) accommodates spatial dependence within error terms, while the Spatial Lag of X (SLX) model incorporates spatial lags of exogenous covariates. Advanced models, such as the Spatial Autoregressive Combined (SAC) model, Spatial Durbin Model (SDM), and Spatial Durbin Error Model (SDEM), provide more intricate analyses, and the General Nesting Spatial (GNS) model encapsulates all three spatial elements for a comprehensive analysis (Rüttenauer, 2022). This study employs general-to-specific approach (Elhorst, 2010; Mur & Angulo, 2009), beginning with the most complex model and later using the likelihood-ratio (LR) test to successively drop non-significant variables (Gallo et al., 2021; Herrera-Gómez, 2022). As highlighted by Burkey (2018), LeSage (2014) recommends running SDM for a global specification, and for a local structure, firstly running SDEM. Rodríguez-Pose and Muštra (2022) have noted that both methodologies present discernible empirical strengths and weaknesses. SDM model has the advantage of embracing global spillovers. This model's spillover effects are adaptable, enabling the SDM to identify both direct impacts (originating from the region under consideration) and indirect influences (stemming from spillovers in other regions), as elaborated by Le Sage (2014). Moreover, spatial autocorrelation for the dependent variable was tested using the Global Moran I's test in GeoDa (Anselin et al., 2010), which confirmed the significant presence of spatial autocorrelation in DI. Consequently, this study starts with the SDM and then tests possible nested models, namely SAR, SLX, SEM, and OLS (Burkey, 2018). Spatial models are estimated using a maximum likelihood estimator. The weight matrix employed is an inverse-distance contiguity matrix, which contains inverse distance for neighbors and 0 otherwise (StataCorp, 2017). Results are presented in Table 2.

As previously explained, the SDM model serves as the starting point. To select the appropriate model, LR tests are employed. As noted by Burkey (2018), many spatial econometricians favor the LR approach because any model can be tested to determine if a simpler, nested model may be more appropriate. The Likelihood Ratio (LR) test begins with a null hypothesis asserting that the restricted model is true. As presented in Table 2, the first step involves evaluating whether the SDM should be confined to one of the following models: SAR, SLX, or SEM. For both the SLX and SEM models, the null hypothesis is dismissed, leading to the preference of the SDM. However, a comparison between the SDM and SAR indicates the legitimacy of the imposed restrictions, thereby suggesting SAR as the fitting model. Subsequently, to choose between SAR and OLS, another LR test is administered, which corroborates SAR as the more suitable model specification. This deduction is further reinforced by the Akaike Information Criterion (AIC) assessment, where the SAR model registers the minimum AIC score among the tested models. Consequently, the chosen SAR model can be written as follows:

Table 2 Regression estimates for SDM, SAR, SLX, SEM, and OLS

Variable	SDM	SAR	SLX	SEM	OLS
CHI	10.44***	11.42***	11.52***	11.51***	11.33***
	(2.945)	(3.021)	(3.202)	(3.007)	(3.571)
TOUR	0.000994*	0.000997**	0.00127**	-0.0000371	0.000453
	(0.000562)	(0.000480)	(0.000604)	(0.000468)	(0.000522)
GVA	0.00153***	0.00145***	0.00119**	0.00233***	0.00177***
	(0.000489)	(0.000298)	(0.000511)	(0.000316)	(0.000328)
TRADE	0.00536	0.0449*	0.0142	0.0694***	0.0763***
	(0.0298)	(0.0230)	(0.0325)	(0.0199)	(0.0239)
const	83.15***	79.67***	82.69***	75.94***	79.04***
	(3.251)	(2.042)	(3.580)	(1.883)	(2.400)
W*CHI	18.12		-2.650		
	(23.34)		(23.36)		
W*TOUR	-0.00723*		-0.000490		
	(0.00436)		(0.00328)		
W*GVA	0.00267		-0.0000574		
	(0.00166)		(0.00115)		
W*TRADE	0.0943		0.112		
	(0.116)		(0.127)		
ρ	-0.228**	0.0553***			
	(0.108)	(0.0191)			
λ				-0.759***	
				(0.253)	
N	21	21	21	21	21
R^2	0.9275	0.9022	0.9149	0.8521	0.8627
LogLik	-42.810059	-46.319431	-44.815759	-48.296736	-49.832518
LR test (SDM)		7.02	4.01**	10.97**	
LR test (SAR)					7.03***
AIC	107.6201	106.6389	109.6315	110.5935	109.665
VIF					2.13

Standard errors in parentheses, * p < 0.1, ** p < 0.05, *** p < 0.01

$$DI = \rho WDI + \beta_1 CHI + \beta_2 TOUR + X\gamma + \varepsilon \qquad (2)$$

where ρ signifies the spatial autoregressive parameter, W represents an ($n \times n$) spatial weight matrix containing non-negative elements that demonstrate the spatial connections between a region and its adjacent areas. Furthermore, WDI is a vector corresponding to the spatially lagged dependent variable. To ascertain the absence of multicollinearity issues, the Variance Inflation Factor (VIF) was computed based on the

Table 3 SAR direct, indirect, and total effects of independent variables

Variable	Direct effects	Indirect effects	Total effects
CHI	11.42345*** (3.022023)	0.309433** (0.137814)	11.73288*** (3.107051)
TOUR	0.000998** (0.000481)	0.000027 (0.000019)	0.001025** (0.000498)
GVA	0.001452*** (0.000298)	0.0000393*** (0.0000133)	0.001492*** (0.000301)
TRADE	0.044936* (0.022984)	0.001217** (0.000566)	0.046153** (0.023405)

Standard errors in parentheses, * $p < 0.1$, ** $p < 0.05$, *** $p < 0.01$

OLS results. The analysis indicated no multicollinearity problems, with an average score of 2.13 and the highest score of 3.06 for the TOUR variable, both well below the desired threshold of 5. To further ensure there were no issues with heteroskedasticity, the SAR model was estimated using robust standard errors. Although not reported here, these results were consistent with the initial findings, confirming the absence of heteroskedasticity concerns.

Kopczewska (2020) highlights, following LeSage and Pace (2009), that models incorporating spatial lag of the dependent variable (Wy) encounter issues related to simultaneity, which constrain both the predictive capability and interpretation of coefficients in these models. In such models, the dependent variable y in location j influences y in location i (for $i \neq j$), and the reverse relationship holds true simultaneously. Consequently, in the final model, the focus shifts from interpreting β coefficients to examining direct and indirect impacts. Accordingly, Table 3 displays these effects for the preferred SAR model.

As observed from Table 3, there is a positive and statistically significant effect of cultural heritage endowment on regional development, encompassing direct (within the region), indirect (other, neighboring regions), and total effects (across Croatia). This corroborates the assertion by Camagni et al. (2020) that cultural heritage constitutes one of the multiple elements of "territorial capital," playing a crucial role in local (regional) development. Besides, this conclusion is congruent with and validated by findings at both the European Union level (Panzera, 2022) and the regional level for various specific country instances, such as Germany (Tubadji, 2012), Greece (Tubadji & Nijkamp, 2015b), and Italy (Cerisola, 2019). Moreover, tourism demand is another important variable explaining the regional development of Croatian NUTS 3 regions (Jurun & Pivac, 2011). Positive and statistically significant direct and total effects are produced. Although positive, the indirect effects of tourism demand are not statistically significant, indicating a lack of positive spillover effects of tourism on regional development. This may be attributed to Croatia's relatively smaller share of direct value added in internal tourism expenditures compared to most EU countries. Ivandić and Šutalo (2019) suggest that this situation indicates a potential for significant augmentation in the gross domestic value of tourism without an increase in physical tourism activities. Such a transformation could be achieved via alter-ations to the economic structure and the inter-relations of activities associated with tourism. The other two control variables, GVA and trade openness, exhibit statisti-cally significant and positive effects, implying that higher levels of economic activity and international openness enhance the development capacities of Croatian NUTS 3 regions (Đokić et al., 2016).

4 Conclusion

This study aimed to address the research gap concerning the role of tangible and intangible cultural resources in regional development in Croatia using a quanti-tative, spatial econometrics approach. In line with the framework established by the Horizon 2020 SmartCulTour project, a composite Cultural Heritage Index was created, encompassing UNESCO and national material and immaterial cultural assets. Utilizing the spatial autoregressive model, it was confirmed that cultural heritage constitutes a significant aspect of territorial capital, generating positive direct and indirect (spillover) effects on regional development in Croatian NUTS 3 regions. Moreover, the results verified the importance of tourism in regional development, with the highlight on the opportunities for enhancing positive spillover effects. This paper contributes to the literature by quantitatively demonstrating, through spatial econometric analysis, the connection between cultural heritage, tourism demand, and regional development in the context of Croatia. These findings provide valuable insights for policymakers seeking to foster sustainable cultural tourism activities in Croatia, potentially leading to a more regionally balanced tourism sector between the Adriatic and continental regions and reducing regional disparities. The impli-cations of these findings become particularly salient in the recovery stages of the COVID-19 pandemic. Efficient leveraging of cultural heritage, achieved through policies built on the foundation of local tangible and intangible assets, can catalyze local economic development (Camagni et al., 2020). This viewpoint is reinforced by the UNWTO, which acknowledges culture and tourism as crucial elements of post-pandemic recovery strategies. Opportunities presented by these sectors can stimu-late the creation of new partnerships, encourage diversification of tourism offerings, attract fresh audiences, and foster the development of novel skills. Collectively, these changes can facilitate a smoother global transition towards the new societal norms emerging post-pandemic (UNWTO). However, this research has certain limitations. It is based on a cross-sectional analysis, utilizing the latest available development index calculations, which were derived from averages for the period 2014–2016, without incorporating time series data. Future research could replicate this study by employing spatial panel data analysis. Alternative regional development proxy vari-ables could also be employed when new regional index calculations become available. Other potential directions for investigation may include exploring different cultural tourism variables, such as cultural infrastructure (e.g., museums), cultural business and employment, or investment in culture and government expenditure on culture.

Finally, this research could be expanded to other countries or extended to all EU NUTS 3 regions.

Acknowledgements The work of doctoral student Zvonimir Kuliš has been supported by the "Young Researchers' Career Development Project—Training of Doctoral Students" of the Croatian Science Foundation. Additionally, this work was supported by the European Union Horizon 2020 Research and Innovation Programme—SmartCulTour project, grant agreement number 870708. The author alone bears responsibility for the information, terminology, and opinions presented in this paper, and these may not necessarily align with the views of the funding organization.

References

Šimundić, B. (2017). The socio-economic determinants of tourism demand: The case of Push factors in an Emiive Region. In: Book of Proceedings, pp. 291–300. Varazdin Development and Entrepreneurship Agency, Melbourne.

Gunter, U., Smeral, E., & Zekan, B. (2022). Forecasting tourism in the EU after the COVID-19 Crisis. *Journal of Hospitality & Tourism Research. 10963480221125130.* https://doi.org/10.1177/10963480221125130.

Yang, Y., Zhang, C. X., & Rickly, J. M. (2021). A review of early COVID-19 research in tourism: Launching the annals of tourism research's curated collection on coronavirus and tourism1. *Annals of Tourism Research, 91,* 103313. https://doi.org/10.1016/j.annals.2021.103313

Directorate-General for Education, Y. (2019). Sustainable cultural tourism. Publications Office of the European Union, LU.

Directorate-General for Internal Market, I. (2022). Transition pathway for tourism. Publications Office of the European Union, LU.

Lykogianni, E., Mobilio, L., Procee, R., Airaghi, E., Kern, P., Le Gall, A., Krohn, C., & Vanhoutte, C.: Material cultural heritage as a strategic territorial development resource: Mapping impacts through a set of common European socio-economic indicators. ESPON EGTC, Luxembourg.

Neuts, B. (2022). Second policy report. Zenodo.

Neuts, B., Matteucci, X., Von Zumbusch, J., Calvi, L., & Moretti, S. (2021). First policy report.

Petrić, L., Mandić, A., Pivčević, S., Škrabić Perić, B., Hell, M., Šimundić, B., Muštra, V., Mikulić, D., & Grgić, J. (2020). Report on the most appropriate indicators related to the basic concepts

Petrić, L., Škrabić Perić, B., Hell, M., Kuliš, Z., Mandić, A., Pivčević, S., Šimundić, B., Muštra, V., Grgić, J., & Mikulić, D. (2021). Report outlining the SRT framework.

Russo, A., & Borg, J. V. D. (2006). European cultural resources and regional development: Pressure and opportunities from the European enlargement. ERSA conference papers.

Stoica, G. D., Andreiana, V.-A., Duica, M. C., Stefan, M.-C., Susanu, I. O., Coman, M. D., & Iancu, D. (2022). Perspectives for the development of sustainable cultural tourism. *Sustainability., 14,* 5678. https://doi.org/10.3390/su14095678

Cultural heritage in regional policy I Culture and Creativity. https://culture.ec.europa.eu/node/222.

Naramski, M., Szromek, A.R., Herman, K., & Polok, G. (2022). Assessment of the activities of European cultural heritage tourism sites during the COVID-19 pandemic. *Journal of Open Innovation: Technology, Market, and Complexity, 8,* 55. https://doi.org/10.3390/joitmc8010055.

Jelinčić, D. A., & Senkić, M. (2017). Creating a heritage tourism experience. The Power of the Senses. Etnološka tribina.

Kovačević, D. (2020). Economic impact of COVID-19 on the European tourism sector with special view on Croatian tourism. *ME, 11,* 1652–1670. https://doi.org/10.4236/me.2020.1110115

Šimundić, B., Škokić, V., & Čaušević, S. (2022). Cultural Heritage tourism in EU policy discourse. *Tourism Planning and Development in Eastern Europe*, 100–116. https://doi.org/10.1079/978 1800620353.0007.

Kordej-De Villa, Ž, & Šulc, I. (2021). Cultural Heritage cultural heritage, tourism and the UN sustainable development goals UN sustainable development goals (SDGs): The case of Croatia. In M. B. Andreucci, A. Marvuglia, M. Baltov, & P. Hansen (Eds.), *Rethinking sustainability towards a regenerative economy* (pp. 341–358). Springer International Publishing.

Fakultet za menadžment u turizmu i ugostiteljstvu, Blue Rock Consulting: Istraživanje stavova ispitanika s emitivnih tržišta. Fakultet za menadžment u turizmu i ugostiteljstvu & Blue Rock Consulting (2021).

Ministry of Tourism and Sport. (2022). Strategija razvoja održivog turizma do 2030. Godine. https://mint.gov.hr/strategija-razvoja-odrzivog-turizma-do-2030-godine/11411.

Demonja, D. (2013). Cultural tourism in Croatia after the implementation of the strategy of development of cultural tourism. *Turizam, 17*, 1–17. https://doi.org/10.5937/Turizam1301001D

Ministry of Culture and Media: Kulturna baština na UNESCO-ovim popisima. https://min-kulture.gov.hr/izdvojeno/kulturna-bastina/kulturna-bastina-na-unesco-ovim-popisima/17251.

Ministry of Culture and Media: Register of Cultural Property. https://min-kulture.gov.hr/register-of-cultural-property/16777.

Tomljenović, R. (2021). Regional action plan of Croatia - from Heritage preservation to its sustainable use. Institute for Tourism, Croatia.

Panzera, E. (2022). *Cultural heritage and territorial identity: synergies and development impact on European regions*. Springer International Publishing.

Richards, G. (2018). Cultural tourism: A review of recent research and trends. *Journal of Hospitality and Tourism Management., 36*, 12–21. https://doi.org/10.1016/j.jhtm.2018.03.005

Škrabić Perić, B., Šimundić, B., Muštra, V., & Vugdelija, M. (2021). The role of UNESCO cultural heritage and cultural sector in tourism development: The case of EU countries. *Sustainability., 13*, 5473. https://doi.org/10.3390/su13105473

UNWTO. (2018). Tourism and Culture Synergies. , Madrid

Timothy, D. J. (2021). Cultural Heritage and tourism. Channel View Publications.

Matteucci, X., & Von Zumbusch, J. (2020). Theoretical framework for cultural tourism in urban and regional destinations.

Csapo, J. (2012). The role and importance of cultural tourism in modern tourism industry. In: Kasimoglu, M. (ed.) Strategies for Tourism Industry - Micro and Macro Perspectives. InTech.

Romão, J. (2018). Tourism, territory and sustainable development. Springer, Singapore.

Gómez-Vega, M., Martín, J. C., & Picazo-Tadeo, A. J. (2021). Ranking world tourism competitiveness: A comparison of two composite indicators. In S. Suzuki, K. Kourtit, & P. Nijkamp (Eds.), *Tourism and regional science: New roads* (pp. 15–35). Springer.

Cellini, R., & Cuccia, T. (2016). UNESCO sites as public goods: Comparative experiences in Italy. *Rev. Econ. Contemp., 20*, 553–569. https://doi.org/10.1590/198055272037

Panzera, E., de Graaff, T., & de Groot, H. L. F. (2021). European cultural heritage and tourism flows: The magnetic role of superstar World Heritage Sites. *Papers in Regional Science, 100*, 101–122. https://doi.org/10.1111/pirs.12562

Romão, J. (2015). Culture or nature: A space-time analysis on the determinants of tourism demand in European regions. Spatial and Organizational Dynamics Discussion Papers.

Romão, J., Guerreiro, J. P. S. M., & Rodrigues, P. M. M. (2017). Territory and sustainable tourism development: A space-time analysis on European regions. REGION. 4, 1–17. https://doi.org/10.18335/region.v4i3.142.

Romão, J., & Neuts, B. (2017). Territorial capital, smart tourism specialization and sustainable regional development: Experiences from Europe. *Habitat International., 68*, 64–74. https://doi.org/10.1016/j.habitatint.2017.04.006

Camagni, R., Capello, R., Cerisola, S., & Panzera, E.: The cultural heritage - Territorial capital nexus: theory and empirics / Il nesso tra Patrimonio Culturale e Capitale Territoriale: teoria ed evidenza empirica. IL CAPITALE CULTURALE. Studies on the Value of Cultural Heritage, pp. 33–59. https://doi.org/10.13138/2039-2362/2547.

Cerisola, S. (2019). A new perspective on the cultural heritage–development nexus: The role of creativity. *Journal of Cultural Economics, 43*, 21–56. https://doi.org/10.1007/s10824-018-9328-2

Cerisola, S., & Panzera, E. (2022). Cultural participation in cultural and creative cities: Positive regional outcomes and potential congestion concerns. *Papers in Regional Science, 101*, 1245–1261. https://doi.org/10.1111/pirs.12709

Tubadji, A. (2012). Culture-based development: Empirical evidence for Germany. *International Journal of Social Economics, 39*, 690–703. https://doi.org/10.1108/03068291211245718

Tubadji, A., & Nijkamp, P. (2015a). Cultural gravity effects among migrants: a comparative analysis of the EU15. *Economic Geography, 91*, 343–380. https://doi.org/10.1111/ecge.12088

Tubadji, A., Osoba, B. J., & Nijkamp, P. (2015). Culture-based development in the USA: Culture as a factor for economic welfare and social well-being at a county level. *Journal of Cultural Economics, 39*, 277–303. https://doi.org/10.1007/s10824-014-9232-3

Tubadji, A., & Nijkamp, P. (2015b). Cultural impact on regional development: Application of a PLS-PM model to Greece. *The Annals of Regional Science, 54*, 687–720. https://doi.org/10.1007/s00168-015-0672-2

Kostakis, I., Lolos, S., & Doulgeraki, C. 1998–2016 (2016). Cultural Heritage led Growth: Regional evidence from Greece. https://mpra.ub.uni-muenchen.de/98443/.

Backman, M., & Nilsson, P. (2018). The role of cultural heritage in attracting skilled individuals. *Journal of Cultural Economics, 42*, 111–138. https://doi.org/10.1007/s10824-016-9289-2

Correa-Quezada, R., Álvarez-García, J., Del Río-Rama, M.D. la C., & Maldonado-Erazo, C. P. (2018). Role of creative industries as a regional growth factor. *Sustainability, 10*, 1649. https://doi.org/10.3390/su10051649.

Romão, J., & Nijkamp, P. (2018). Spatial impacts assessment of tourism and territorial capital: A modelling study on regional development in Europe. *International Journal of Tourism Research, 20*, 819–829. https://doi.org/10.1002/jtr.2234

Muštra, V., Perić, B. Š., & Pivčević, S. (2023). Cultural heritage sites, tourism and regional economic resilience. *Papers in Regional Science n/a*. https://doi.org/10.1111/pirs.12731

Mikulić, D., & Petrić, L. (2014). Can culture and tourism be the foothold of urban regeneration? A Croatian case study. *Tourism: An International Interdisciplinary Journal, 62*, 377–395.

Zadel, Z., & Bogdan, S. (2013). Economic impact of cultural tourism. *UTMS Journal of Economics., 4*, 355–366.

Demonja, D., & Gredičak, T. (2015). Tourism and culture in the function of local economic development. Podravina : časopis za geografska i povijesna multidisciplinarna istraživanja. 14, 0–0.

Lovrentjev, S. (2015). Intangible cultural heritage and tourism: comparing Croatia and the Czech republic. *Mediterranean Journal of Social Sciences, 6*, 522.

Maldonado-Erazo, C. P., del Río-Rama, M. de la C., Álvarez-García, J., & Flores-Mancheno, A. C. (2022). Use of natural and cultural resources by tourism as a strategy for regional development: bibliometric analysis. *Land, 11*, 1162. https://doi.org/10.3390/land11081162.

Dalle Nogare, C., & Devesa, M. (2023). Heritage, tourism and local development. https://journals.sagepub.com/pb-assets/Icons/TE-SF-Heritage%20tourism%20local%20development-167637 1690723.pdf.

Ministry of Regional Development and EU Funding: Indeks razvijenosti. https://razvoj.gov.hr/o-ministarstvu/djelokrug-1939/regionalni-razvoj/indeks-razvijenosti/112.

Denona Bogović, N., Drezgić, S., & Čegar, S.: Evaluacija postojećeg i prijedlog novog modela za izračun indeksa te izračun novog indeksa razvijenosti jedinica lokalne i područne samouprave u Republici Hrvatskoj.

Golob, M., Golob, M., & Doretić, J. (2018). Croatian development index and regional disparities in spatial distribution of EU funds for rural development. Zbornik radova Ekonomskog fakulteta Sveučilišta u Mostaru, pp. 40–58. https://doi.org/10.46458/27121097.2018.SI.40.

Ministry of Regional Development and EU Funding. (2018). Vrijednosti indeksa razvijenosti i pokazatelja za izračun indeksa razvijenosti. https://razvoj.gov.hr/o-ministarstvu/djelokrug-1939/regionalni-razvoj/indeks-razvijenosti/vrijednosti-indeksa-razvijenosti-i-pokazatelja-za-izracun-indeksa-razvijenosti-2018/3740.

Montalto, V., Tacao Moura, C. J., Langedijk, S., & Saisana, M. (2019). Culture counts: An empirical approach to measure the cultural and creative vitality of European cities. *Cities, 89*, 167–185. https://doi.org/10.1016/j.cities.2019.01.014

Travel and tourism GDP share by country EU 2021. https://www.statista.com/statistics/1228395/travel-and-tourism-share-of-gdp-in-the-eu-by-country/.

Travel & Tourism Economic Impact I World Travel & Tourism Council (WTTC) – Croatia. https://wttc.org/DesktopModules/MVC/FactSheets/pdf/704/96_20220613155343_Croatia2022_.pdf.

Kuliš, Z., Šimundić, B., & Pivčević, S. (2018). The analysis of tourism and economic growth relationship in central and eastern European countries. In A. Karasavvoglou, S. Goić, P. Polychronidou, & P. Delias (Eds.), *Economy, finance and business in southeastern and central Europe* (pp. 537–551). Springer International Publishing.

Šimundić, B., & Kuliš, Z. (2016). Tourism and economic growth in Mediterranean region: Dynamic panel data approach. *Acta Economica Et Turistica., 1*, 177–196.

Trinajstić, M., Baresa, S., & Bogdan, S. (2018). Regional economic growth and tourism: A panel data approach. *Journal of Economics, 9*, 145–155.

Mikulić, D., Bakarić, I. R., & Slijepčević, S. (2016). The economic impact of energy saving retrofits of residential and public buildings in Croatia. *Energy Policy, 96*, 630–644. https://doi.org/10.1016/j.enpol.2016.06.040

Mikulić, D., & Galić Nagyszombaty, A. (2015). Does international trade cause regional growth differentials in Croatia? *Zbornik Radova Ekonomskog Fakulteta u Rijeci: Časopis Za Ekonomsku Teoriju i Praksu., 33*, 81–102.

ARDECO. (2023). ARDECO database I Knowledge for policy. https://knowledge4policy.ec.europa.eu/territorial/ardeco-database_en#database.

CBS. (2023). Statistics in line. https://podaci.dzs.hr/en/statistics-in-line/.

Halleck Vega, S., & Elhorst, J. P. (2015). The SLX model. *Journal of Regional Science, 55*, 339–363. https://doi.org/10.1111/jors.12188

Kopczewska, K. (2020). *Applied spatial statistics and econometrics: data analysis in R.* Routledge.

Rüttenauer, T. (2022). Spatial regression models: a systematic comparison of different model specifications using Monte Carlo experiments. *Sociological Methods & Research, 51*, 728–759. https://doi.org/10.1177/0049124119882467

Elhorst, J. P. (2010). Applied spatial econometrics: Raising the bar. *Spatial Economic Analysis., 5*, 9–28. https://doi.org/10.1080/17421770903541772

Mur, J., & Angulo, A. (2009). Model selection strategies in a spatial setting: Some additional results. *Regional Science and Urban Economics., 39*, 200–213. https://doi.org/10.1016/j.regsciurbeco.2008.05.018

Herrera-Gómez, M. (2022). Spatial econometrics with Stata: Exploratory Spatial Data Analysis (ESDA), Spatial Models for Cross-Sectional Data, Spatial Models for Panel Data.

Le Gallo, J. (2021). Cross-section spatial regression models. In M. M. Fischer & P. Nijkamp (Eds.), *Handbook of regional science* (pp. 2117–2139). Springer.

Burkey, M. L. (2018). Spatial econometrics and GIS YouTube playlist. REGION. 5, R13–R18. https://doi.org/10.18335/region.v5i3.254.

LeSage, J. P. (2014). What regional scientists need to know about spatial econometrics. *The Review of Regional Studies, 44*, 13–32.

Rodríguez-Pose, A., & Muštra, V. (2022). The economic returns of decentralisation: Government quality and the role of space. *Environment and Planning A, 54*, 1604–1622. https://doi.org/10.1177/0308518X221118913

Anselin, L., Syabri, I., & Kho, Y. (2010). GeoDa: An introduction to spatial data analysis. In M. M. Fischer & A. Getis (Eds.), *Handbook of applied spatial analysis: software tools, methods and applications* (pp. 73–89). Springer.

StataCorp, L. L. C. (2017). *Stata spatial autoregressive models reference manual*. Stata press College Station.

LeSage, J., & Pace, R. K. (2009). *Introduction to spatial econometrics*. Taylor & Francis Group.

Jurun, E., & Pivac, S. (2011). Comparative regional GDP analysis: Case study of Croatia. *Cent Eur J Oper Res., 19*, 319–335. https://doi.org/10.1007/s10100-010-0163-6

Ivandić, N., & Šutalo, I. (2019). An integrated TSA and IO model for the estimation of the overall contribution of tourism: The example of Croatia. *Tourism: An International Interdisciplinary Journal. 67*, 389–404.

Đokić, I., Fröhlich, Z., & Rašić Bakarić, I. (2016). The impact of the economic crisis on regional disparities in Croatia. *Cambridge Journal of Regions, Economy and Society, 9*, 179–195. https://doi.org/10.1093/cjres/rsv030

UNWTO: Cultural tourism & COVID19 | UNWTO. https://www.unwto.org/cultural-tourism-covid-19.

Towards a Circular Cultural Tourism Impact Assessment Framework for Decision Support in Less-Known and Remote Destinations

Ludovica La Rocca, Francesca Buglione, Eugenio Muccio, Martina Bosone, Maria Cerreta, Pasquale De Toro, and Antonia Gravagnuolo

Abstract Recent environmental, climate and sustainability challenges are leading several sectors, including cultural tourism, to rethink their development model in a more sustainable and circular perspective, preserving fragile resources—including cultural resources—and regenerating natural capital. The assessment of the multidimensional impacts of cultural tourism strategies becomes an essential tool for designing specific positive impacts linked to the conservation, regeneration and valorisation of tangible and intangible cultural resources, together with natural resources, human and social capital. The Horizon 2020 Be.CULTOUR project developed a methodological and operational approach, based on a set of impact criteria and indicators, to guide the evaluation and monitoring process of cultural tourism strategies in less-known and remote cultural tourism destinations. The Be.CULTOUR multidimensional impact assessment framework was deemed to support the development and monitoring of strategic Action Plans for circular and human-centred cultural tourism, experimented in six European pilot heritage sites. The tool reconsiders the linearity of the Theory of Change, a collaborative and multistakeholder approach that is well suited to the conceptual framework of circular and human-centred cultural tourism, in order to move towards circular production and consumption models in the tourism sector, opening the way for the redesign of traditional decision-making processes. Thus, the proposed tool stimulates the construction of a dynamic and iterative evaluation process that falls within the framework of "circular" co-assessment.

Keywords Circular tourism · Sustainable impact design · Theory of Change · Multidimensional indicators

L. La Rocca · F. Buglione · E. Muccio · M. Cerreta · P. De Toro
University of Naples Federico II, Naples, Italy

M. Bosone · A. Gravagnuolo (✉)
National Research Council, Rome, Italy
e-mail: antonia.gravagnuolo@cnr.it

B. Neuts et al. (eds.), *Advances in Cultural Tourism Research*, Advances in Digital and Cultural Tourism Management, https://doi.org/10.1007/978-3-031-65537-1_8

1 Introduction

In recent decades, it became necessary to address unprecedented environmental, climate and sustainability challenges such as biodiversity loss, climate change, natural resource use and pollution, which are reflected also in the cultural tourism sector. According to the definition adopted by the UNWTO General Assembly, (UNDP, 2017), cultural tourism can be defined as "a type of tourism activity in which the visitor's essential motivation is to learn, discover, experience and consume the tangible and intangible cultural attractions/products of a tourist destination". These attractions/products refer to a set of distinctive material, intellectual, spiritual and emotional characteristics of a society including the arts and architecture, historical and cultural heritage, culinary heritage, literature, music, creative industries and living cultures with their lifestyles, value systems, beliefs and traditions. In order to achieve more sustainable cultural tourism models, approaches and tools emerged to promote the development of tourist destinations (WTO, 2004) and to assess the generation of positive impacts by integrating circular economy approaches in the tourism sector. The circular economy aims to transform the traditional "linear" economy based on a "take-make-dispose" process to become regenerative by minimising resource use and avoiding all kinds of waste (Dişli & Ankaralıgil, 2022). The basic principles of the circular economy (systemic thinking, optimisation, efficiency, collaboration, transparency, accountability, inclusiveness) can also be applied in the tourism sector, as diverse projects and initiatives are shown in the last few years. The promotion of circular economy principles in heritage rehabilitation and conservation initiatives is crucial for the sustainable continuity of this sector (Rodríguez, Flórido & Jacob, 2020). Due to its complexity, cultural tourism can have a significant impact on society, the environment and the economy. Indeed, the tourism sector is not only an economic activity that represents a fundamental driver of development, but a combination of culture, nature and historical heritage, which contributes to make each destination unique in terms of offer, distinctiveness, recognisability and competitive potential (Abouelmagd, 2023) In some cases, without the necessary balance and attention to each of these aspects, tourism can even damage or compromise the quality of life of local communities and can be a source of additional pressure on cultural and natural resources. For this reason, it is necessary to design new cultural tourism models, capable of generating well-being and contributing to the quality of ecosystems and human health, both locally and globally.

Circular tourism can be defined as a model capable of creating a virtuous production-consumption circle for achieving sustainability goals and providing services without wasting the planet's non-renewable resources, such as raw materials, water and energy (Girard & Nocca, 2017). Furthermore, circular tourism proposes a model in which each actor involved adopts an eco-friendly approach (Sgambati et al., 2021). By applying the principles of the circular economy, tourism and hospitality operators can accelerate the growth of their businesses and advance conceptually and practically to provide a more sustainable experience for all parties involved in these sectors (Van Rheede, 2012). Circular tourism refers to its ability to trigger and stimulate circular flows, with the aim of reconciling the tourism sector and sustainable resource management (Neves & Marques, 2022). It is not only "green" tourism, aimed at limiting the consumption and waste of non-renewable energy sources, but is concerned with recovery, reuse, redevelopment, valorisation and regeneration of cultural and natural resources.

At the European level, several projects and frameworks have been set up to encourage the production of impact-based tourism strategies, following the principles of sustainability, which provide the necessary dimensions, criteria and indicators to describe the phenomenon of sustainable tourism. In October 2022, the EU Tourism Dashboard (European Commission, 2022) was launched to improve access to statistics and indicators relevant to tourism policies at EU level and to help destinations and public authorities monitor their progress in the green and digital transition of the tourism sector. For this purpose, indicators were developed at national and regional level organised in four areas: (1) environmental impacts; (2) digitalisation; (3) socio-economic vulnerability; (4) basic tourism attributes. The Interreg MED "INCIRCLE" project (INCIRCLE, 2020), on the other hand, is particularly dedicated to the dissemination of circular economy principles in sustainable tourism planning. It aims to reduce pollution caused by tourism by introducing innovative technologies and processes, to preserve the quality and availability of natural resources, and to improve the quality of life of residents and tourists. It is structured around 4 core areas: mobility, energy, water and waste. The project defines guidelines to support decision-makers in the transition towards a more responsible and circular tourism.

The ETIS (European Commission, 2017) is a management, information and monitoring tool specifically designed for tourism destinations. It is conceived as a process of data collection and analysis at the local level with the overall objective of assessing the impact of tourism on a destination. The specific objective of the ETIS is to help improve the sustainable management of destinations. It aims to help destinations and stakeholders measure their sustainability management processes, enabling them to monitor their performance and progress over time. It contains 43 core indicators and a number of supplementary indicators. They allow for comparison over time and benchmarking between destinations. They refer to four main sections: Destination Management, Economic Value, Social and Cultural Impact, Environmental Impact.

In the wake of these reflections, the research presents a framework for the design and assessment of the impacts of sustainable, cultural, circular and responsible tourism initiatives, within the Horizon 2020 Be.CULTOUR project: "Beyond CULtural TOURism: heritage innovation networks as drivers of Europeanisation towards a human-centred and circular tourism economy". In particular, the Be.CULTOUR project expresses the objective of going beyond tourism through a long-term human-centred development perspective, enhancing cultural heritage and landscape. The proposed circular cultural tourism impact assessment framework can be a tool but also, and more importantly, a process to support destination managers and planners in orienting their strategies in the direction of sustainability and circularity, adopting a human-centred approach based on needs' assessment and identification of stakeholders' priorities, desires, aspirations.

This contribution presents in Sect. 2, the theoretical base of the Theory of Change as a useful tool for the assessment and co-design of circular cultural tourism strategies; in Sect. 3, the results of the definition of the assessment framework based on the Theory of Change and interaction with local stakeholders, with the proposed framework for the assessment of circular cultural tourism coherent strategies supported by a related set of suggested criteria as base for identifying suitable indicators; in Sect. 4, the discussion of the results achieved and the next steps of the ongoing research.

2 Materials and Methods

The Horizon 2020 project Be.CULTOUR: Beyond Cultural Tourism defined a methodological approach to assess the impacts of sustainable and circular cultural tourism through multidimensional quantitative and qualitative indicators.

The impact assessment framework was developed first on a theoretical base according to scientific literature, previous experiences and discussion with cultural tourism policy and practice stakeholders in six European pilot heritage sites: the Cultural Park of the Rio Martin in Aragon region, Teruel province in Spain; the historic small cities and natural areas in the Vulture-Alto Bradano area in Basilicata region in Italy; the rural cultural landscape of Larnaca in Cyprus; two historic industrial and rural villages in Västra Götaland region in Sweden; three historic rural villages in the region of Vojvodina in Serbia,; and finally a series of twenty heritage sites including religious buildings, fortresses, and civic buildings historically linked by the personality of Stephan the Great, which form a cultural route at the cross-border of North-East Romania and Moldova. These six pilot heritage sites have been selected to represent diverse European settings, less-known and remote destinations which are particularly rich in tangible and intangible heritage, as well as natural heritage sites, often located nearby more consolidated destinations, such as Matera in Basilicata and Novi Sad in Serbia, both European Capitals of Culture, but also the beaches of Cyprus, the pilgrimage route of Santiago crossing Aragon region in Spain, etc. The rationale behind the choice of the six pilot heritage sites was thus to represent less-known, remote rural and natural areas with a high potential for sustainable cultural tourism but currently less attractive and accessible to visitors.

To identify relevant and complete criteria and indicators which can support decision-making and monitoring of results in the pilot areas of the project, a series of non-structured interviews and focus groups were conducted with local representatives of the sites, exploring their priorities and preferences with regard to diverse circularity dimensions and criteria. The framework here proposed results from both theoretical studies and reflections, and interaction with pilots.

The impact assessment tool developed in Be.CULTOUR project has a twofold aim: it represents an orientation tool for decision-making in less known destinations, enabling understanding of circularity and sustainability objectives by stakeholders and decision-makers; on the other hand, multidimensional criteria and indicators can be used for monitoring progress and assessing impacts in more advanced stages and already well-established experiences. For this reason, the tool was discussed also with additional destination managers out of the six pilot areas, to assess the usability and adaptability to specific impact assessment needs. This paper presents the theoretical and methodological process that led to the definition of the impact assessment framework, while the testing phase is currently ongoing and will be presented at a later stage.

2.1 Defining a Theory of Change for Circular Cultural Tourism Destinations

Among the impact methods that are able to capture social, cultural and environmental returns over time, the Be.CULTOUR project adopted the Theory of Change (ToC). ToC is an impact assessment tool that belongs to the family of process-based approaches, which is focused on the analysis of the value production process. The application of the ToC allows one to reflect qualitatively on the different steps that lead to the impact objective that the organisation aims to help achieve through the specific action or project (Bengo et al., 2016). Defining a ToC supports ensuring that inputs and activities lead to tangible results that contribute to the required change (Venturi, 2022).

ToC can be considered both a theory and a practice, a process and a product and can be both a planning and problem-framing tool and a monitoring and evaluation tool (Vogel, 2012). ToC is a participatory process in which different stakeholders articulate their long-term objectives in the course of a planning process and identify the conditions they believe must be unfolded for these objectives to be achieved (Mackenzie & Blamey, 2007). These conditions are schematised into the changes they want to achieve and are organised graphically in a hierarchical structure which reads from left to right. Developing a ToC allows to understand what long-term change needs to be achieved and what are the best short- and medium-term pre-conditions to achieve it (Allen et al., 2017). The Theory of Change is based on a fluid dialogue and communication between stakeholders, that is, those interested in the change that the programme intends to trigger. Active participation covers all the different phases of the project cycle: from the analysis of the context, to the identification of the desired long-term change, as well as the formulation of hypotheses on how this change might be achieved and the definition of the sequence of events that would make it happen, the identification of available resources, the choice of the most appropriate activities and methodologies, the definition and measurement of indicators, the implementation, monitoring and evaluation of the change and of the project itself. The participatory process can be constructed through one or more participatory workshops, the details of which vary depending on the context and its complexity, the organisational competencies, and the impact to be generated (Stein & Valters, 2012a, b).

Research applies ToC to the tourism sector in order to understand how change is achieved following the implementation of tourism strategies in such a way that development programmes can better exploit the territory's potential, reducing risks (Twining-Ward et al., 2018) and more effectively orienting strategies towards achieving sustainability goals. In addition, this tool encourages the construction of a dynamic, collaborative and iterative evaluation process, which belongs to the framework of the "circular" co-assessment (Gravagnuolo et al., 2021a, b) according to which change processes are no longer seen as linear, but as patterns characterised by iterative feedback loops that need to be understood to support monitoring, evaluation and mutual learning (Limata, 2017). Based on these assumptions, the research redefined the ordinary structure of the social impact value chain by confronting the need for impact evaluation of the Be.CULTOUR project's strategic Action Plans in the pilot areas of experimentation. The intention was to define a methodological approach and, at the same time, an operational tool that provides a reinterpretation of the impact value chain by assimilating the resources and flows within a circular urban/territorial metabolism and the logical structure and attributes of the theory of change.

3 Results

In order to obtain the operational and methodological framework for the assessment of the impacts of circular cultural tourism strategies of strategic Action Plans within the Be.CULTOUR project, the ToC approach was adapted by designing an operational framework and a dashboard of functional criteria and indicators for the assessment of impacts. The tool works as a support system for decision-makers for the design and monitoring of sustainable, responsible and circular cultural tourism impact strategies (Be.CULTOUR impact assessment framework, Fig. 1). The assessment framework proposed does not necessarily foresee a digital application for its use, being developed as a co-creation and co-evaluation tool which can be employed using specific canvases within workshops and focus groups.

The assessment process is based on a set of relevant dimensions, criteria and indicators and consists of three main phases arranged in the following sequential order:

1. Impact design, which is based on the analysis of current urban metabolism context and identification of specific challenges to be addressed;
2. Impact simulation, which represents an intermediate stage between the impact design part and the impact assessment;
3. Impact measurement and evaluation, starting from input and activating strategies to address the specific challenges identified.

Phase 1. Impact design: Following the sequence of the impact value chain (from right to left), the first phase is divided into several procedural steps. The first step consists of defining the impact objectives (Outcomes) that are the changes in the long

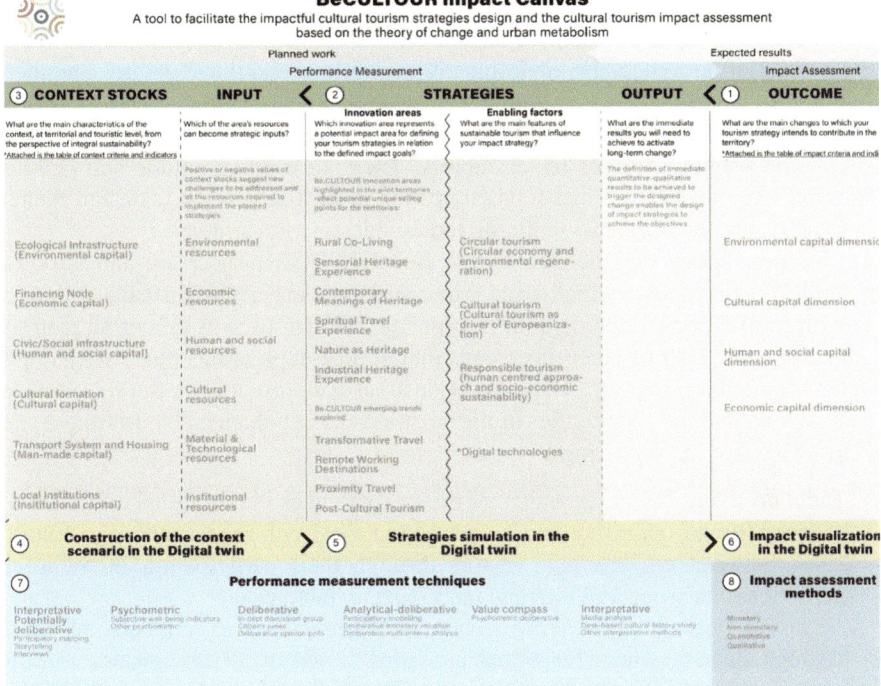

Fig. 1 Be.CULTOUR impact assessment framework based on the theory of change

term to be achieved through the activation of strategies related to the tourism sector. They can be direct (as a direct consequence of the activated product or service) or indirect (indirect effects on the life of the beneficiary and other persons), as well as expected or not expected, thus not initially foreseen by the intervention. Outcomes represent a part of change attributed exclusively to the activities implemented by the organisation, as a measure of outcomes net of unavoidable changes, those that would have occurred even without the project.

The second step concerns the definition of Outputs, that are, the results to be achieved in the short term necessary to trigger the change objectives. Outputs represent the immediate and controllable results of activities. They are measured through indicators that estimate the performance, quantity or quality of the goods and services of the tourism strategy to generate social change.

For the third step, the model drives and stimulates the planner's creativity in defining the activities necessary to achieve the objectives (Strategies), suggesting factors that guarantee the construction of sustainable tourism strategies, also in light of the most recent European guidelines. Strategies are actions, processes and programmes to be activated to generate improvements and changes in the beneficiaries' lives and territorial transformations. In this sense, the research identifies in activities those enabling factors, deriving from processes and strategies, that constitute the driving force of change. Planned actions impact positively or negatively on the context of reference, the environment, the society, and the economy, and therefore require careful reflection and design from a human-centred and sustainability perspective. For this reason, the Be.CULTOUR project suggests some areas of innovation and enabling factors for circularity. They are useful to guide and facilitate stakeholders and decision-makers participating in the ToC process to design changes in the direction of circularity-defining tourism destination strategies.

The innovation areas defined by the Be.CULTOUR project are understood as potential impact areas in which to place tourism strategies in relation to the objectives. The innovation areas include both the specific tourism aspects emerging from the pilot areas and a set of emerging trends that will be explored as potentially impact sectors for cultural tourism. The innovation areas are promoted by the six-pilot case and are linked to the specificities of the territories to be enhanced by drafting Action Plans. They are the following:

- Rural co-living promotes authentic rural experiences in traditional cultural landscapes through homestay and hospitality in rural villages, stimulating relationships between citizens and visitors through their participation in traditional activities such as agricultural and landscape maintenance.
- Sensorial heritage experience encourages immersive experiences of places through didactic and educational activities aimed at all age groups to come into deeper contact with local culture and traditions through the expressions of intangible heritage using the five senses.
- Contemporary meanings of heritage, through artistic creation, the aim is to generate emotional experiences for citizens and visitors by developing new forms of heritage use such as gamification and virtual travel experience, creative storytelling and augmented ways of enjoying cultural heritage such as augmented reality and hybrid digital-physical immersive experience.
- Spiritual travel experience includes pilgrimage routes, spiritual retreats and other different ways to regenerate and preserve religious heritage sites, promoting the value of religious heritage.
- Nature as heritage includes nature as cultural heritage by exploring the meanings and values of natural areas, their "genius loci" through ecotourism experiences, trekking, sports, active tourism and the promotion of local biodiversity, such as native species of flora and fauna.
- Industrial heritage experience promotes innovative ways to create an audience for industrial heritage sites through adaptive reuse.

The emerging trends are: Transformative travel, which focuses on learning and educational experiences, self-reflection, self-discovery and integrating the visitor's travel experiences; Remote working destinations, based on the possibility of working from home; Proximity travel, that is a practice of travelling close to one's everyday environment. Citizens rediscover nearby cultural and natural sites, becoming "tourists at home"; Post-cultural tourism, exploring different forms of alternative travel that aim to discover authentic places that are not included in conventional cultural tourist itineraries.

The enabling factors of circularity, on the other hand, are understood as the main drivers of change capable of influencing the impact strategy and are subdivided into circular tourism (circular economy and environmental regeneration), cultural tourism experience (cultural tourism as a driver of Europeanisation), responsible tourism (human-centred approach and socio-economic sustainability).

The fourth step is the analysis of the resources needed to trigger change. The suggested resource stocks were identified from an expanded declination of the dimensions of sustainability (Forte et al., 2019) compared to that of the canonical dimensions of sustainability, due to the need to catalogue a considerable amount of multidimensional information by identifying the following categories: ecological infrastructure (environmental capital), financial node (economic capital), civic/social infrastructure (human and social capital), cultural education (cultural capital), transport system and housing (anthropic capital), local institutions (institutional capital).

Phase 2. Impact simulation. The second phase is dedicated to the simulation of the designed impact through the construction of the context scenario in a Geographic Information System or spatial modelling. This simulation is useful to visualise the designed impacts in three-dimensional space, which can facilitate a better understanding of the impacts by means of the digital model, in order to value the effects of the designed strategies and choose the preferred scenarios.

Phase 3. Impact measurement and evaluation. The third step produces the evaluation of expected impacts, for which the model suggests performance measurement techniques and impact assessment methods, encouraging decision-makers to use collaborative and multistakeholder techniques, supporting a circular and human-centred approach. To assess the impacts of sustainable tourism, the Be.CULTOUR project proposes a set of 35 criteria and 147 indicators retrieved from existing literature sources and adapted to the circular cultural tourism framework (Table 1). The main criteria for assessing the performance of circular cultural tourism are identified in relation to the four main dimensions of capital: cultural capital, environmental capital, social and human capital, and economic capital. The outcomes indicators measure change and, therefore, the effectiveness of the intervention in terms of the change generated in the communities and territories concerned. They are quantitative and qualitative and constitute a base monitoring indicator set from which to draw when identifying the specific indicators useful for a specific territory, according to the strategic actions identified by stakeholders through the ToC process. In this sense, a flexible, adaptive and adaptable indicators dashboard is intended, which can be integrated and used through collaborative processes aimed at implementing and redefining the indicator set over time.

Table 1 Circular cultural tourism key dimensions and criteria

Dimension	Criteria
Cultural capital	Preservation of cultural heritage resources authenticity and integrity Sense of ownership and community care of cultural heritage Appreciation of cultural heritage Underused heritage regeneration Cultural vibrancy Landscape beauty enhancement
Environmental capital	Energy self-sufficiency Freshwater efficiency Wastes reduction GHG emissions reduction Climate change mitigation Soil regeneration Air quality enhancement Natural sites enhancement
Social and Human capital	Community well-being Community empowerment Inclusion and human rights Network density Youths engagement Quality of life Safety Skills enhancement Visitors satisfaction Transformative travel experience
Economic capital	Jobs creation Entrepreneurship Innovation ecosystem enhancement Local economy enhancement Destination development Sustainable destination management Digitalisation Tourism seasonality Overcrowding Gentrification effects

4   Discussion and Conclusions

The methodological proposal for the impact assessment of tourism strategies, in the experimental framework of the Horizon 2020 Be.CULTOUR project, represented a useful design and monitoring tool for circular tourism destinations, for decision-makers, managers and stakeholders involved in the design of impact strategies and the monitoring of changes achieved, adopting the Theory of Change approach. Be.CULTOUR intended to develop an evaluation framework capable of including cultural resources and cultural tourism flows as an integral part of the urban/territorial metabolism of cities and regions, applicable to heritage sites. It intends to reconsider the linearity of the Theory of Change in favour of a circular orientation, based on dynamic and evolutionary evaluation theories (Gravagnuolo et al., 2021a, b). This keystone in the development of theory moves away from traditional value chains and towards circular production and consumption models, paving the way for the redefinition of traditional decision-making processes in the tourism sector through more circular approaches and the adoption of theoretical and practical circularity-oriented models by all actors involved.

The impact assessment framework can support stakeholders in the application of place-based and human-centred tourism strategies that are truly sustainable and capable of limiting potential negative impacts of tourism. While many decision-support tools are based on a "black-box" software approach, the approach adopted in Be.CULTOUR privileges interaction and discussion between stakeholders, exploiting the opportunity of co-designing cultural tourism strategies for developing enhanced collaboration capacity, trust, shared vision and mutual understanding, enabling shared reflection, discussion and co-evaluation taking into account diverse points of view, motivations and objectives. To operationalise the proposed framework enabling participatory co-evaluation processes in which non-experts can easily understand and visualise possible impacts of diverse strategies, it can be particularly useful to experiment with the simulation of the designed strategy which could be supported by a digital simulation environment, such as a digital twin, modelled starting from the analysis of context data and indicators that give back the status quo and possible future changes as a result of the expected impacts. In this way, a digital twin could effectively support decision-making processes allowing the simulation and visualisation of impacts, enabling more effective co-assessment and co-design processes leading to the choice of preferred scenarios. The dashboard of criteria and indicators proposed represents a possible support framework for destination managers and stakeholders to stimulate and guide the design of sustainable and circular cultural tourism strategies and at the same time to facilitate the process of selecting key indicators for monitoring and evaluating their strategic action plans.

Next research efforts should be focused on the implementation, testing and validation of criteria and indicators to support *ex-ante, in itinere* and *ex-post* evaluations. The pilot heritage sites of the Be.CULTOUR project represent a test bed for the assessment framework proposed, which will support the co-evaluation of local strategies for circular cultural tourism and stakeholders' engagement in the definition of shared directions/objectives and eventual adjustments over time, in a circular co-evaluation process—in line with previously experimented approaches in the Horizon 2020 CLIC project. Moreover, the additional "mirror" heritage sites included in the Be.CULTOUR community will be engaged as more advanced practices towards sustainable and circular cultural tourism, well-established destinations which are currently struggling for identifying a longer-term model of innovative, creative and sustainable cultural tourism that can benefit local communities and stakeholders, as well as providing authentic and culturally rich experiences to visitors. The orientation criteria and indicators included in the Be.CULTOUR framework will be thus tested and validated in the next phases of the research, collecting relevant feedback and adjusting to specific contexts, assessing the feasibility and replicability of the specific evaluation tools and methods identified, with the aim of generating a usable methodology and tool to support European destination becoming circular, human-centred and integrally sustainable.

Acknowledgements A.G. developed the overall research concept and assessment criteria, introduction and research questions, identification of pilot case studies, coordination of the research, discussion and conclusions, as well as funding acquisition. L.LR., M.C., F.B., M.B. and A.G. specifically developed the methodology based on ToC. All co-authors co-developed the theoretical study, literature review, results section and conclusions.

Funding This research was funded under the framework of Horizon 2020 research project Be.CULTOUR "Beyond cultural tourism". This project has received funding from the European Union's Horizon 2020 research and innovation programme under grant agreement Number 101004627.

References

Allen, W., Cruz, J., & Warburton, B. (2017). How decision support systems can benefit from a theory of change approach. *Environmental Management. Jun;59*(6), 956–965. https://doi.org/10.1007/s00267-017-0839-y. Epub 2017 Mar 9. PMID: 28280913.

Bengo, I., Arena, M., Azzone, G., & Calderini, M. (2016). Indicators and metrics for social business: A review of current approaches. *Journal of Social Entrepreneurship.*

Blamey, A., & Mackenzie, M. (2007). Theories of change and realistic evaluation: Peas in a Pod or Apples and Oranges? *Evaluation, 13*(4), 439–455. https://doi.org/10.1177/1356389007082129

Dişli, G., & Ankaralıgil, B. (2023). Circular economy in the heritage conservation sector: An analysis of circularity degree in existing buildings. *Sustainable Energy Technologies and Assessments, 56,* 103126. ISSN 2213-1388, https://doi.org/10.1016/j.seta.2023.103126.

Doaa Abouelmagd. (2023). Sustainable urbanism and cultural tourism, the case of the Sphinx Avenue, Luxor. *Alexandria Engineering Journal, 71,* 239-261. ISSN 1110-0168, https://doi.org/10.1016/j.aej.2023.03.041.

European Commission. (2022). EU Tourism Dashboard. Retrieved from https://tourism-dashboard.ec.europa.eu/?lng=en&ctx=tourism.

European Commission. (2017). The European tourism indicator system: ETIS toolkit for sustainable destination management. Retrieved from https://data.europa.eu/doi/https://doi.org/10.2873/983087.

Forte, B., Cerreta, M., & De Toro, P. (2019). The human sustainable city: Challenges and perspectives from the habitat agenda. *The Human Sustainable City: Challenges and Perspectives from the Habitat Agenda.* https://doi.org/10.4324/9781315198569

Fusco Girard, L., & Nocca, F. (2017). From linear to circular tourism, Aestimum [Preprint]. Retrieved from https://doi.org/10.13128/Aestimum-21081.

Gravagnuolo, A., Bosone, M., & Fusco Girard, L. (2021). Methodologies for impact assessment of cultural heritage adaptive reuse. Deliverable D2.5 Horizon 2020 CLIC project.

Gravagnuolo, A., Bosone, M., & Fusco Girard, L. (2021). Deliverable D2.5 – Methodologies for impact assessment of cultural heritage adaptive reuse. Retrieved from https://www.clicproject.eu/wp-content/uploads/2022/01/D2.5-Methodologies-for-impact-assessment-of-cultural-heritage-adaptive-reuse.pdf.

INCIRCLE project. (2020). Measuring tourism as a sustainable and circular economic sector. The INCIRCLE model Deliverable 3.3.1 INCIRCLE set of circular tourism indicators.

Limata, P. (2017). Assessing social impact through theory of change in voluntourism, in 20th Excellence in Services International Conference.

Neves, S. A., & Marques, A. C. (2022). Drivers and barriers in the transition from a linear economy to a circular economy. *Journal of Cleaner Production, 341,* 130865. ISSN 0959-6526. https://doi.org/10.1016/j.jclepro.2022.130865.

Rheede, A., & Blomme, R. (2012). Sustainable practices in hospitality: A research framework. *Advances in Hospitality and Leisure, 8,* 257–271. https://doi.org/10.1108/S1745-3542(2012)000 0008018

Rodríguez, C., Florido, C., & Jacob, M. (2020). Circular economy contributions to the tourism sector: A critical literature review. *Sustainability, 12*(11), 4338. Retrieved from https://doi.org/10.3390/su12114338.

Sgambati, M., Acampora, A., Martucci, O., & Lucchetti, M. C. (2021). The integration of circular economy in the tourism industry: A framework for the implementation of circular hotels. In Advances in Global Services and Retail Management. Cobanoglu, C., Della Corte, V., Eds., University of South Florida M3 Center Publishing: Tampa, FL, USA, pp. 1–10, ISBN 978-1-955833-03-5.

Stein, D., & Valters, C. (2012). Understanding "Theory of Change" in international development: a review of existing knowledge. In: Paper Prepared for the Asia Foundation and the Justice and Security Research Programme at the London School of Economics and Political Science.

Stein, D., & Valters, C. (2012). Understanding theory of change in international development. (JSRP and TAF collaborative project) (JSRP Paper 1). Justice and Security Research Programme, International Development Department, London School of Economics and Political Science, London, UK.

Twining-Ward, L., Messerli, H., Sharma, A., & Villascusa Cerezo, J. M., (2018). Tourism theory of change. Tourism for Development Knowledge Series; World Bank, Washington, DC. http://hdl.handle.net/10986/35459.

UNDP. (2017). Tourism and the sustainable development goals. Journey to 2030. World Tourism Organization (UNWTO). https://doi.org/10.18111/9789284419401.

Venturi, P., De Benedictis, L., & Miccolis S. (2022). Società benefit. Promuovere senso e valore nel perimetro offerto dalla normativa, AICCON, Short Paper 26/2022.

Vogel, I. (2012). Review of the use of 'Theory of Change' in international development. Retrieved from https://www.theoryofchange.org/pdf/DFID_ToC_Review_VogelV7.pdf.

WTO. (2004). Indicators of sustainable development for tourism destinations a guidebook (English version). World Tourism Organization (UNWTO). https://doi.org/10.18111/9789284407262.

Golden Rules for Sustainable Cultural Tourism Development: Findings of the EU SPOT Project

Milada Šťastná⬤ and Antonín Vaishar⬤

Abstract Amongst the objectives of the H2020 SPOT project (Social and Innovative Platform On cultural Tourism and its potential towards deepening Europeanisation), there was the intention to explore the use of cultural tourism as a vehicle for improving the social and economic fabric of disadvantaged rural areas. Through 15 Case Studies (including a small number of over-touristed areas for comparison), partners 'clustered' examples to establish common themes around which to describe the good practice. The detailed analysis demonstrated that each cultural tourism target is unique. It may be that there is an attraction of cultural tourism despite there isn't a 'brand' but each site has its own special features. Following extensive dialogue with stakeholders and the collation of relevant statistical data in each area, being inspired by the work on Regional Development carried out by the European Research Centre in its work on Smart Specialisation Strategies, SPOT teams described the key factors which need to be addressed in progressing Cultural Tourism in new locations or in capitalising on existing examples of Cultural Tourism. The factors are explored in detail and the relationship between them is identified by the local stakeholder's observations; examples of successful interventions are quoted from our extensive database of Case Study findings. The importance of stakeholder engagement is described and the support which can be given by the academic communities is highlighted. The framework of European, national, regional and local policy approaches is analysed in general terms and observations are made on the organisational structures which support (or impede!) cultural tourism activity. Whilst SPOT argues that each example of Cultural Tourism is unique, it is still able to draw conclusions regarding priorities at each level (EU/national/regional/local) which need to be addressed. The approach is holistic—single-issue intervention is not considered effective. The overall approach encourages sustainability; sustainability in economic terms, sustainability in social and community relationships, sustainability in resources, environmental point of view and finally in the use of cultural tourism activity to promote community empowerment, reduce conflicts and provide a dynamic future for disadvantaged areas.

M. Šťastná (✉) · A. Vaishar
Mendel University in Brno, Zemědělská 1, 61300 Brno, Czechia
e-mail: milada.stastna@mendelu.cz

© The Author(s) 2025

B. Neuts et al. (eds.), *Advances in Cultural Tourism Research*, Advances in Digital and Cultural Tourism Management, https://doi.org/10.1007/978-3-031-65537-1_9

Keywords Cultural tourism · Regional development · Sustainability · Europe ·
Recommendations · Golden rules

1 Introduction

Tourism is one of the fastest-growing sectors of the economy, despite the damage
it has suffered as a result of the measures against the spread of COVID-19. It is
in line with the current transition of developed countries from a material to a post-
material society, or from production to consumption. The European Union, individual
countries and regions have high expectations regarding the development of tourism,
among other things, in the sense of replacing job opportunities lost by production.

Tourism represents a richly structured category. Different regions have different
bases for certain forms of tourism (mountains, sea, important historical buildings or
objects). However, the prerequisites for the development of cultural tourism can be
found (or created) in almost every place. In addition, cultural tourism brings not only
recreation and physical recovery, but also knowledge of foreign regions, customs
and people. This broadens the cultural horizons of both, tourists and residents. In
this sense, they are not only economic but also social categories.

Development can be understood in a quantitative sense—more products, higher
VAT and more inhabitants. However, recently, attention is turning (especially in rural
and less developed areas) to qualitative indicators of development. In this sense, we
can speak more about the contribution of cultural tourism to regional sustainability
in all three pillars: economic, social and environmental.

The article is one of the summarising outputs of the SPOT research project of
the HORIZON Europe program, which ran between 2020 and 2022. The consortium
included research institutions from 15 countries. Such a large consortium allowed
gaining knowledge about rural and partly urban tourism, in the countries of Northern,
Central and Southern Europe and in Israel, including the post-communist part of
Europe. The article presents possible strategic, political and practical measures/
recommendations to strengthen the role of cultural tourism in local, regional and
European development. Its goal is to generalise the main findings of the SPOT
project in the form of golden rules towards the support of sustainable cultural
tourism, not only as an economic sector but also as a tool of cultural development
and Europeanisation.

2 Cultural Tourism and Regional Development

The linkage between culture and tourism is not new (Richards, 2020). The peculiarity
lies in the fact that it is at the same time a combination of the economic sector and the
cultural development of tourists and local residents. The economic nature of tourism
is growth-oriented and emphasises income and employment opportunities (e.g. Pablo

Romero and Molina, 2013). According to Mei Pung, Gnoth and del Chiappa (2020), contextual stimuli can lead tourists to reflectively interpret the experience and acquire skills, values and knowledge, with consequences on attitude, habits and behaviour.

Cultural tourism in the narrowest sense is often considered as visiting cultural monuments, cultural facilities or cultural events. This approach theoretically makes it possible to divide destinations into cultural and other destinations. According to our approach, cultural tourism is connected with a cognitive function. From this point of view, it is not the destination that matters, but the purpose of travel. Kalvet et al. (2020) define cultural tourism as a type of tourism activity in which the visitor's essential motivation is to learn, discover, experience and consume the tangible and intangible cultural attractions/products in a tourist destination.

Cultural tourism can therefore be carried out in almost any place. It becomes part of the locality and regional identity (Abram and Waldren, 1997). Practically, every place has its history, traditions and peculiarities. The most famous ones form a network of tangible and intangible UNESCO World Heritage. However, there is a whole system of lower-level cultural heritage and, in addition, a large number of hitherto unknown attractions. It's just a matter of discovering, emphasising, or completing these aspects. The active participation of tourists in organising their trips is increasing. A new branch of creative tourism is emerging (Duxbury et al., 2021). Cultural tourism has many different forms. Without claim to completeness, one can name visits to traditional cultural institutions, namely museums, galleries, historical monuments, participation in cultural events such as concerts, theatre performances, folklore events, culinary and wine tourism, wandering in the footsteps of cultural events, cultural personalities and the like. Exploring nature and open-air museums is also a part of educational tourism. Games based on cognitive tourism are being developed, for example, geocaching (Pisula et al., 2023).

Cultural tourism has a number of similar demands as tourism in general, for example, infrastructure or information security requirements. However, at the same time, it has certain specificities, for example, the structure of visitors with a higher proportion of seniors or young families (McKarcher, 2020), not so pronounced seasonality compared to types of tourism dependent on the weather. Of course, cultural tourism is intertwined with other types of tourism (sports, recreation, entertainment) and also with other types of services that are not directly focused on tourism.

The main reason to develop cultural tourism is its potential benefit for different levels of development. On the one hand, it can be developed in the sense of growth, on the other one, it can be seen mainly in relation to less developed regions, which prefers issues of regional cohesion, namely the reduction of differences compared to other (more developed) regions. Another understanding can conceptualise regional development as regional sustainability. Individual concepts of regional development, therefore, choose different indicators for analysis. Durovic and Lovrentjev (2014) attempted to design such indicators.

3   Case Studies

Methodologically, the contribution is based on the generalisation of findings from 15 case studies in 15 countries (Fig. 1). Results are based on research done using questionnaire surveys, interviews and analysis of data and geographical contexts. Examples of good practices were identified and collected. The research was conducted during the period of the COVID-19 pandemic. Restrictions during the pandemic greatly limited the possibilities of face-to-face research; therefore, a large part of the interviews and questionnaires were carried out online, which particularly limited the possibilities of non-verbal communication. On the other hand, the added value of the research was the primary response of individual tourism actors to the pandemic and anti-pandemic measures (Vaishar and Šťastná, 2022).

The findings from the empirical research were widely analysed and discussed at workshops, organised especially in the last third of the project. Work workshops were dedicated to individual topics. They took place in groups and their conclusions were discussed in plenary. Recommendations for management could then be identified.

Here comes a brief specification of selected case studies. One of the case study regions was Art Nouveau in Barcelona as an example of urban cultural tourism with the risk of congestion. The Carpathians and their foothills in the Buzau region of Romania are an example of a geopark with landscape attractions and folk culture. The Cyclades archipelago in Greece includes both overcrowded and tourist-underappreciated islands. The Ida-Viruma region in Estonia is an example of

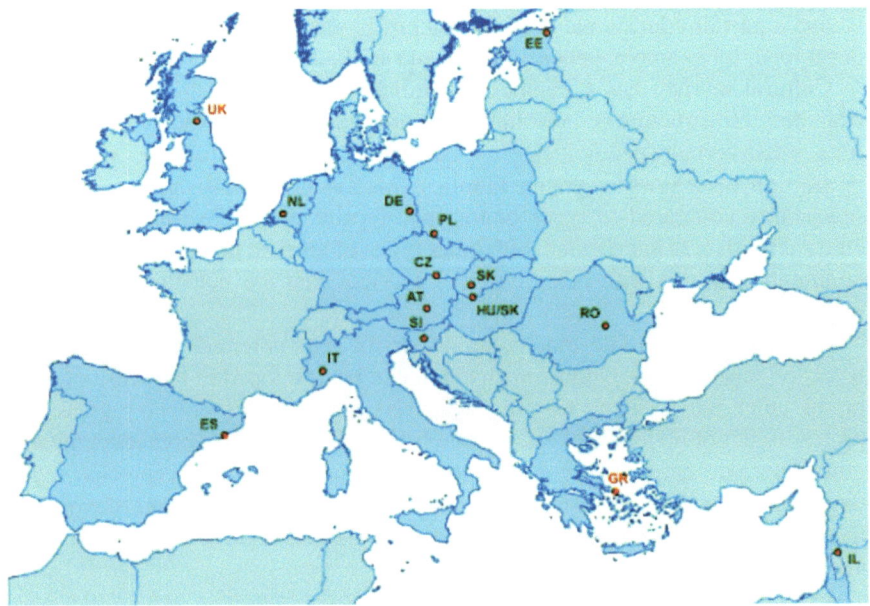

Fig. 1 Case study areas. 2022 *Source* van Elburg et al. ()

an originally industrial region turning into a cultural tourism region. The Kinderdijk area in the Netherlands is an important landscape of windmills and water canals.

Komárom/Komárno represents an example of cross-border tourism between Hungary and Slovakia while Germany's Lieberose/Oberspreewald region includes a specific landscape whose wildness has been preserved thanks to the military area. Ljubljana, the capital of Slovenia, is an example of urban cultural tourism. Lower Silesia in Poland is known as a land of palaces and gardens. The Scottish case studies focused on media tourism.

Nitra in Slovakia plays an important role as a centre of historical and religious tourism. Southern Piedmont is a complex of historical sites and cultural actors, highlighted by the culture of wine. Wine culture is also used by rural cultural tourism destinations in South Moravia in the Czech Republic. The Styrian Iron Route uses the traditions of iron mining and processing for the development of cultural tourism. The Beit Shean Valley in Israel combines archaeological and historical sites with the present.

Thus, cultural tourism has been empirically investigated in areas of various types, in the countries of northern, central, western and southern Europe, in cities and in the countryside. Among the main attractions were historical sites, cultural events, wine, nature, and technical monuments. Although the case studies were very different, certain general characteristics could be found. This made it possible to formulate conclusions for policy practice.

The importance of stakeholder's engagement is described and the support which can be given by the academic communities is highlighted. The framework of national, regional and local policy approaches is analysed in general terms and observations are made on the organisational structures which support (or impede!) cultural tourism activity. Whilst SPOT argues that each example of Cultural Tourism is unique, it is able to draw conclusions about priorities at each level (EU/national/regional/local) which need to be addressed. The approach is holistic—single-issue intervention is not considered effective. The SPOT project resulted (besides others) in Eight Golden Rules for policy actors at a different level.

These rules have been developed from an analysis of strategy, policy and practice in each of SPOT's 15 Case Studies. The results of the analysis have been shared with around 200 stakeholders from the public, private, voluntary and community sectors. The Golden Rules structure reflects the regional development model set out by the European Research Centre in its work on Smart Specialisation Strategies. An Assessment Wheel has been used to assist in identifying priorities and further details in each area and can be found in SPOT project reports such as Summary Report on Stakeholder Involvement and Policy Guidelines and Briefings.

4 Eight Golden Rules

Rule 1 Policy Formulation Formal policies at national, regional and local levels so far as they relate to Cultural Tourism will probably show relevant political priorities and will almost certainly point the way to funding opportunities and the potential for influencing those policies. These policies should contain visions, strategies and implementation rules for the implementation of cultural tourism at different geographical levels. They should also address the mutual competencies of the departments of tourism, culture, the environment, and possibly others. Horizontal and vertical linkages of policies, including cross-border cooperation, are also important.

Rule 2 Local Engagement/Local Benefit Successful Cultural Tourism activities tend to have strong local community support. To start a process of engaging local residents and businesses, it is necessary to be clear about the likely benefits (and dis-benefits) of any development. Unlike some other forms of tourism, where tourists can operate almost without contact with local residents, the development of cultural tourism directly requires the involvement of local residents, for whom it also brings their own cultural development. There are also other benefits for localities, especially direct financial benefits, creation of job opportunities, contracts for local entrepreneurs and the like. At the same time, it is necessary to minimise the possible negative manifestations of the development of (cultural) tourism, such as excessive traffic by strangers, noise, car traffic congestion, waste, etc.

Rule 3 Shared Vision to assemble the necessary finance, permissions, support from all economic and social sectors and motivation, a Shared Vision should be developed. There will be contrary forces, but the consultative processes involved in developing a Vision will pay off in terms of identifying any ameliorative measures. A locus (organisation or individual) will be needed to lead the work, along with a putative timescale. One promising option may be the initiation of the creation of destination management based on cooperatives or non-governmental associations with the participation of public administration, entrepreneurs and various associations. Their task would be to coordinate cultural tourism in individual destinations and offer these destinations as one package of experiences and products. Funding may initially be a problem, as the relationship between input and effort may be indirect and take time.

Rule 4 Sustainable Development Sustainability should be built into all aspects of the programme; this will be of benefit to local residents, sustainability measures can be an educational tool and may be attractive to potential visitors. In theory, sustainability has three pillars: economic, social and environmental. Sustainability should be evaluated in the context of regional development in a qualitative sense; inter-sectoral conflicts that could disrupt any of the three pillars should be satisfactorily resolved. However, it also makes sense to talk about the sustainability of cultural tourism as such, when excessive intensity (over-tourism) could destroy or seriously damage the very attractions of cultural tourism; so that the respective destination could lose its appeal.

Rule 5 Innovation Any development will be innovative; be aware of the level of innovation required to distribute benefits and impacts responsibly and ensure that any necessary training, investment, etc. are put in place. Recently, innovations in the tourism industry are mainly associated with digitalisation and online products. However, innovation can also consist in finding or creating new products, targeting other target groups of tourists, creation of new marketing structures, creating new collaborations, and the like. The usual innovative procedure mainly consists of an idea, development and implementation.

Rule 6 Infrastructure/Policy Mix Infrastructure may need to be in place in advance of market demand, meaning resources to develop transport, accommodation, sanitation, etc. have to be identified; the phasing of the different elements of implementation will need to be considered, as will the impact on local communities. Infrastructure is one of the fundamental prerequisites for the development of cultural tourism. It should correspond to the target groups of tourists. It is a purpose-built infrastructure, focused mainly on the needs of tourists, but also a general infrastructure of the destination, which can be used both by tourists and local residents. Improving infrastructure in relation to tourism development can also bring benefits to local residents and offset some of the inconveniences caused by tourism. In doing so, it is necessary to proceed sensitively, especially if the attraction of cultural tourism is historical heritage. In such a case, the construction of modern infrastructure could disturb the character of the cultural heritage.

Rule 7 Implementation Having decided what to do—policy and vision—who will deliver it? Check implementation structures and particularly liaison arrangements between public and private sectors. It is necessary to ensure support or at least acceptance of the accepted idea from local residents, cooperation of interested stakeholders, financial coverage, and responsible person or institution. Conditions and relationships between interested parties may change during implementation. It is necessary to maintain their motivation.

Rule 8 Monitoring and Evaluation Create processes for recording progress, in particular, and ensure the measures being used identify Cultural Tourism metrics specifically. Ensure data is shared between all stakeholders. Statistical data on the number of overnight stays or attendance at selected attractions can be used for monitoring. Sample surveys or visitor censuses can also be carried out using devices. However, these data do not cover the whole of cultural tourism and especially its qualitative aspect. This can be monitored using sociological methods—questionnaires, interviews, and monitoring of satisfaction indicators on social networks.

5   Europeanisation

In addition to the contribution of cultural tourism to regional and local development, from a Pan-European point of view, the importance of cultural tourism for Europeanisation is visible. Cultural tourism contributes to intercultural understanding within Europe through the discovery of different types of cultural heritage. The current focus on the development of cultural tourism does not fully appreciate this fact yet. At least there are significant differences between individual countries, and regions, accepted: Europeanisation is understood in a vertical sense as a political framework for harmonising top-down strategies or in a horizontal sense as emerging autonomous similarities creating place-based identities grounded in similarities in culture. Culture deals with people's habits, beliefs, and views. Generally, cultural tourism fosters Europeanisation by emphasising distinctive cultural values—often featuring characteristic landscapes—that are typical for Europe. Europeanisation can be a responsible strategy for promoting both cultural diversity and European identity as reflected in the landscape.

The following recommendations for stakeholders on the European level have been adopted:

- Focus more on horizontal Europeanisation and less on vertical Europeanisation.
- Create policies to promote individual cultural tourism. It increases diversity, prevents exclusion and encourages horizontal Europeanisation.
- Approach cultural tourism and Europeanisation as a process of emancipation and recognise them as forms of democratisation and management of cultural resources.
- Involve tourists actively in planning, creating and doing their trips.
- Implement cultural tourism at local and regional levels and align this with European regional development policy.
- Identify EU financial support for the development of cultural tourism (multilevel financing or cofinancing).

Acknowledgements This project has received funding from the European Union's Horizon 2020 programme for research and innovation under grant agreement no. 870644.

References

Abram, S., & Waldren, J. D. (1997). Introduction: tourists and tourism—identifying with people and places. In Abram, S., Macleod, D., & Waldren, J. D. (eds.) Tourists and Tourism: Identifying with People and Places, not paged. Routledge, Abingdon-on-Thames. https://doi.org/10.4324/9781003136002.

Durovic, M., & Lovrentjev, S. (2014). Indicators of sustainability in cultural tourism. *The Macrotheme Review, 3*(7), 180–189.

Duxbury, N., Bakas, F. E., Vinagre de Castro, T., & Silva, S. (2021). Creative tourism development models towards sustainable and regenerative tourism. *Sustainability 13*(2), 2. https://doi.org/10.3390/su13010002.

Elburg, E. van, Pleijte, M., Pedroli, B., Donders, J., & Rip, F. (2022). Report on the results of surveys for tourists, residents and entrepreneurs in the case studies [D1.4 report]. Wageningen Research.

Kalvet, T., Olesk, M., Tiits, M., & Raun, J. (2020). Innovative tools for tourism and cultural tourism impact assessment. *Sustainability, 12*, 7470. https://doi.org/10.3390/su12187470

McKarcher, B. (2020). Cultural tourism market: A perspective paper. *Tourism Review, 75*(1), 126–129. https://doi.org/10.1108/TR0320190096

Mei Pung, J., Gnoth, J., & del Chiappa, G. (2020). Tourist transformation: Towards a conceptual model. *Annals of Tourism Research, 81,* 102885. https://doi.org/10.1016/j.annals.2020.102885

Pablo-Romero, M. P., & Molina, J.A. (2013). Tourism and economic growth: A review of empirical literature. *Tourism Management Perspectives, 8,* 28–41. https://doi.org/10.1016/j.tmp.2013.05.006.

Pisula, E., Florek, M., & Homski, K. Marketing communication via geocaching—When and how it can be effective for place? *Journal of Outdoor Recreation and Tourism 42,* 100622. https://doi.org/10.1016/j.jort.2023.100622.

Richards, G. (2020). Culture and tourism: Natural partners or reluctant bedfellows? A perspective paper". *Tourism Review, 75*(1), 232–234. https://doi.org/10.1108/TR-04-2019-0139

Vaishar, A., & Šťastná, M. (2022). Impact of the COVID-19 pandemic on rural tourism in Czechia. *Preliminary Considerations. Current Issues in Tourism, 25*(2), 187–191. https://doi.org/10.1080/13683500.2020.1839027

.

New Data Methods and Digital Tools

The Holistic, Digital Cultural Heritage Documentation of the Fikardou Traditional Village in Cyprus

Marinos Ioannidesⓘ**, Orestis Rizopoulos**ⓘ**, Drew Baker**ⓘ**,
Elena Karittevli**ⓘ**, Maria Hadjiathanasiou**ⓘ**, Panayiota Samara**ⓘ**,
Ioannis Panayi**ⓘ**, Marina Mateou**ⓘ**, Iliana Koulafeti**ⓘ**,
Marios Koundouris**ⓘ**, Kyriakos Efstathiou, George Savva**ⓘ**,
and Elina Argyridou**ⓘ

Abstract This paper focusses on the case study of Fikardou Village (Cyprus), a UNESCO World Heritage Tentative List monument, highlighting its unique cultural value by referencing historical evidence identified during our research. Our contribution investigates Fikardou's cultural offerings by presenting and analysing the major

M. Ioannides (✉) · O. Rizopoulos · D. Baker · E. Karittevli · M. Hadjiathanasiou · P. Samara ·
I. Panayi · M. Mateou · I. Koulafcti · M. Koundouris · K. Efstathiou · G. Savva · E. Argyridou
Department of Electrical Engineering, Computer Engineering and Informatics, Cyprus University
of Technology, UNESCO Chair on Digital Cultural Heritage, Arch. Kyprianou 31, 3036 Limassol,
CY, Cyprus
e-mail: marinos.ioannides@cut.ac.cy

O. Rizopoulos
e-mail: orestis.rizopoulos@cut.ac.cy

D. Baker
e-mail: drew.baker@cut.ac.cy

E. Karittevli
e-mail: elena.karittevli@cut.ac.cy

M. Hadjiathanasiou
e-mail: m.hadjiathanasiou@cut.ac.cy

P. Samara
e-mail: panayiota.samara@cut.ac.cy

I. Panayi
e-mail: ioannis.panagi@cut.ac.cy

M. Mateou
e-mail: marina.mateou@cut.ac.cy

M. Koundouris
e-mail: marios.koundouris@cut.ac.cy

K. Efstathiou
e-mail: kyriakos.efstathiou@cut.ac.cy

B. Neuts et al. (eds.), *Advances in Cultural Tourism Research*, Advances in Digital and
Cultural Tourism Management, https://doi.org/10.1007/978-3-031-65537-1_10

outcomes of three H2020 EU-funded projects (TExTOUR, MNEMOSYNE, IMPAC-TOUR) that include Fikardou as a major component in their research programme. By elaborating on selected successful outputs such as policy interventions, new cultural tourism trends, advances in visitor management systems, and new business and/or governance models that arise from this specific case study, we argue for the advances that have been achieved in the cultural tourism sector in Cyprus, as exemplified through the experience of Fikardou Village as a developing cultural tourist destination exploring and embracing digital technology as a force multiplier in achieving its aims.

Keywords Holistic documentation · Digital Fikardou Village · Digital cultural heritage · Cultural tourism · Cultural strategies

1   Introduction

Fikardou Village is a traditional Cypriot village with rich cultural and natural heritage assets but a complex and sometimes competing set of economic, social and environmental challenges involving national, international, and local stakeholders that must be carefully balanced if the village is to capitalize on its memory and heritage resources as a sustainable cultural tourist destination. Views of Fikardou Village can be seen in Fig. 1.

Located on the southeastern slopes of the Troodos Mountain range, about thirty kilometres (30 km) southwest of the capital city of Nicosia, on the Eastern Mediterranean island of Cyprus, the origins of the village suggest its existence at least as far back as the fifteenth century. The use of the genitive case in the village's name

Fig. 1   The traditional Cypriot village of Fikardou © UNESCO Chair on Digital Cultural Heritage

G. Savva
e-mail: georgesavva@windowslive.com

E. Argyridou
e-mail: elina.argyridou@cut.ac.cy

suggests that it probably once belonged to one Tomazo Phicardo, notary to King James II during Frankish rule in Cyprus, as a feudal fief (George Jeffrey, 1918). The village is considered a genuine example of eighteenth- and nineteenth-century Cypriot folk architecture with some modifications belonging to the first decades of the twentieth century (Hegoumenidou & Floridou, 1987). In the mid-twentieth century, however, the trends of urbanization and rural abandonment led to a dramatic population decline, causing economic depression in the village, which left many properties deserted and at risk of becoming derelict. Due to its uniqueness the village was put under the supervision of the Republic of Cyprus Department of Antiquities in 1978, being listed as an "Ancient Monument" in its entirety, and a "Controlled Area" was established around the settlement to control any contemporary development in its immediate surroundings (Philokyprou & Limbouri-Kozakou, 2015). In 1984, the Department of Antiquities undertook a wide programme to revitalize the entire village, restoring collapsing houses and improving the image and infrastructure of Fikardou. Owners of private dwellings received generous state subsidies for the restoration and rehabilitation works they made. Aiming at high-quality protection and management of the heritage components that constitute its uniqueness the village was included on the UNESCO World Heritage Tentative List[1] in 2002.

2 Fikardou—The Challenge of Multimodal Heritage Use

2.1 Fikardou as a UNESCO World Heritage Tentative List Site

The entire village of Fikardou has been placed on the UNESCO World Heritage Tentative List[2] (UNESCO-WHTL), an inventory of those properties which each State Party intends to consider for nomination for inscription. States Parties are encouraged to nominate national properties that they believe to be of "exceptional universal value" in terms of their cultural and/or natural heritage but must comply to *The UNESCO Operational Guidelines for the Implementation of the World Heritage Convention criteria for the assessment of Outstanding Universal Value,*[3] and satisfy at least one of the ten selection criteria.

Fikardou was nominated by the Republic of Cyprus Department of Antiquities under the Ministry of Communications and Works. It describes Fikardou as an "excellent example of a traditional mountain settlement, which has preserved its eighteenth- and nineteenth-century physiognomy and architecture, as well as its natural environment", echoing the UNESCO sentiment "The main aesthetic quality is the integrity

---

[1] The rural settlement of Fikardou, Tentative Lists, UNESCO World Heritage Convention.

[2] https://whc.unesco.org/en/tentativelists/1673/.

[3] https://whc.unesco.org/en/guidelines/.

and authenticity of the village, in complete harmony with its environment". Fikardou Village embodies four of the ten section criteria as follows:

- to exhibit an important interchange of human values, over a span of time or within a cultural area of the world, on developments in architecture or technology, monumental arts, town-planning, or landscape design;
- to bear a unique or at least exceptional testimony to a cultural tradition or to a civilization which is living or which has disappeared;
- to be an outstanding example of a type of building, architectural or technological ensemble or landscape which illustrates (a) significant stage(s) in human history;
- to be an outstanding example of a traditional human settlement, land-use, or sea-use which is representative of a culture (or cultures), or human interaction with the environment especially when it has become vulnerable under the impact of irreversible change;

2.2 Fikardou as a Cultural Heritage Resource

Due to its cultural, historical, and aesthetic value, the village has been the case study of academic papers, publications, and European projects. The village is one of the few examples left of a traditional settlement in Cyprus which has remained unspoiled over time and preserved elements and architectural features that demonstrate the traditional Cypriot way of life.

The architecture of the village is a representative example of Cypriot rural settlements during the eighteenth and nineteenth centuries (Philokyprou & Limbouri-Kozakou, 2015). The structures are small, unique and simple, constructed with local materials such as solid "iron" stone (*sieropetra*), pebbles, limestone slabs and mudbricks for the walls, and olive wood for the roof. Pine shingles and locally made tiles are the main components of sloping roofs, however most dwellings have flat roofs (known as *doma*), serving domestic functions notably the drying of grapes, pulses, and other products. Houses usually have two floors; the upper floor where the family would traditionally have lived, while the ground floor rooms were used for stabling animals and storing agricultural products.

At the northern edge of the village, two of the most important domestic structures can be found, the House of Katsinioros and the House of Achilleas Demetri, so named for their last owners. George Jeffrey (1918) wrote about them in 1918: "The House of Achilleas Demetris is also a representative example of 19th architecture in Cyprus, but it differs from the other houses in terms of construction, due to the incorporation of huge stones within the wall". Because of their architectural value, both houses are listed as "Ancient Monument Schedule A", meaning that they are state property and both were restored by the Department of Antiquities between 1984 and 1986 with a grant from the A.G. Leventis Foundation.[4] The two buildings subsequently became

---

[4] https://www.leventisfoundation.org/.

Fig. 2 Images of the Houses of Achilleas Dimitri (left) and Katsinioros (right) © Department of Antiquities

part of the Local Rural Museum project and received the Europa Nostra International Award recognizing outstanding heritage conservation initiatives (PIO, 1987).

Traditional monuments of Fikardou Village, like the House of Katsinioros and the House of Achilleas Dimitri, can be seen in Fig. 2.

Other notable buildings include a large winepress (*linos*) and the Church of Apostles Peter and Paul. The wine press was still operational until the second half of the twentieth century as a community cooperative, both the pressing mechanism and the large clay jars used to store wine are still preserved. The church built between the seventeenth and eighteenth centuries is a small, single-aisle church with a wooden slopping roof and walls built with local stones and a bell tower to the northeastern corner.

Although Fikardou is currently a quasi-abandoned settlement with only a handful of remaining permanent residents, the village has become a significant tourist attraction. While the cultural and natural heritage of the village and its surroundings are the predominant factors for tourism, Fikardou is more than an open-air museum. Contributing to the touristic offering is the active participation of Fikardou in the recent popularity and growth of organized traditional festivals promoting both local and national cultural heritage. For example, most recently Fikardou was awarded the best Christmas Village 2022–23 by the Cyprus Hospitality Awards of the Deputy Ministry of Tourism, a highly competitive and prestigious award.

2.3 Fikardou as a Cultural Tourist Destination

According to the United Nations World Tourism Organization,[5] cultural tourism is "movements of persons for essentially cultural motivations such as study tours, performing arts and cultural tours, travel to festivals and other cultural events, visits to sites and monuments, travel to study nature, folklore or art, and pilgrimages".

---

[5] https://www.unwto.org/.

Although tourism has great potential to promote a destination, attract visitors to study and learn about its cultural heritage and increase local revenue, some local communities and heritage experts are sceptical about tourism and possible negative impacts due to overcrowding, noise pollution and other nuisances, nature destruction, cultural appropriation, littering, and loss of authenticity, the very things that Fikardou wishes to guard against.

The IMPACTOUR project addresses sustainable cultural tourism as "integrated management of cultural heritage and tourism activities in conjunction with the local community creating social, environmental, and economic benefits for all stakeholders, to achieve tangible and intangible cultural heritage conservation and sustainable tourism development". To this extent, cultural tourism is about managing cultural heritage and tourism in an integrated way, working with local communities to create benefits for everyone involved. To ensure that both cultural heritage and the local community benefit from the channelling of tourism to the site, it is essential to include local stakeholders and communities in the decision-making processes. The goal is to integrate sustainable cultural heritage, tourism activities, and local communities, resulting in a greener environment, a healthier economy, and happier people. Finding the proper balance between the economic, social, and political aspects of tourism has been gaining importance.

3   e-Fikardou—Implementing a Digital Cultural Strategy

3.1   e-Fikardou—Creating the Platform

Managing and maintaining the demands of protecting heritage assets while promoting and supporting tourism, requires cooperation and constant dialogue with local communities, national and international agencies and, of course, tourists themselves, is essential if all parties are to benefit from cultural tourism. The TExTOUR project aims to establish pioneering, sustainable cultural tourism strategies to improve deprived areas in Europe and beyond. It further seeks to recognize difficulties, establish cooperation between regions and countries, and integrate the generated knowledge into a platform. The TExTOUR project team at CUT is working on a collaboration with Fikardou (one of the eight pilot sites in the project) to create a digital platform for the village. Named e*Fikardou.eu*,[6] the platform showcases applications presenting Fikardou's tangible and intangible cultural heritage, allowing the would-be visitor to plan their visit and be informed of its significance as a UNESCO-WHTL, seasonal events and responsible tourism. The platform includes 3D models, 360° Tours, Virtual Reality (VR) Tours, a Virtual Gastronomy Lab, e-books, images, and storytelling. Notably, the platform features a 3D model of the entire digitized village, its monuments and historical objects. Furthermore, it embodies the holistic

---

[6] https://efikardou.eu/.

digital documentation and archiving of the village's intangible cultural heritage, its related data, metadata, and paradata—the "Information about human processes of understanding and interpretation of data objects" (Denard, 2009).

Considering the different types of user needs, the team organized several workshops to produce valuable results and choose actions to be implemented. The team invited stakeholders, interested parties, and locals to participate and share their thoughts. A standout element of these workshops was that people who would have otherwise been passive "end-users" were offered the opportunity to be actively engaged in the decision-making process. This upgrade from end-users to decision-makers has been crucial in allowing the stakeholders to shape the development of the e-Fikardou platform, most notably for the local community, allowing them to decide the scale and form of impact on the local economy and market. Given that, currently, the Fikardou community generates zero revenue from tourism, it is a new opportunity for the village to decide what kind of incentives to offer in order to attract the desired types of visitors, investors, and businesses, and to what degree they wish to engage in economic ventures. It also presents an opportunity for Fikardou to reach out to its diaspora and invite them to return and bring life back to the village.

One of Fikardou's prime cultural elements is the harmony of the village with its natural environment and the advancement of the village must be approached strategically in order to protect this asset. The actions chosen in the framework of TExTOUR project in collaborating in the Fikardou pilot supported this requirement and formed the basis for developing the e-Fikardou platform. The e-Fikardou platform serves as a vessel for collected data and generated knowledge designed to offer a unique, integrated experience (and at the same time to educate users) and engagement with Fikardou's tangible and intangible cultural heritage. Moreover, the platform supports policymakers and practitioners in assessing cultural tourism strategies, services, and facilities as the sector develops within the village.

The platform incorporates educational content, an interactive e-book (Fig. 3), and a downloadable application from the Fikardou e-Gastronomy Lab (Fig. 4). The virtual gastronomy lab has been developed under the guidance and cooperation of the creators of the Cyprus Food Museum which is the first of its kind worldwide. Additionally, the platform includes VR Tours of the entire digitized village with the ability to access fully digitized points of interest (POIs) (Fig. 5). Additionally, the creation of the BIM (building information modelling) model is in progress (Fig. 6). Also, the 360° Tour application links the various location points from the digitization laser scan results and ultimately allows the user to navigate through the village from point to point, as can be seen Fig. 7. The 360° Tour is also compatible with the VR experience.

Among others, the e-Fikardou platform includes the following characteristics:

- **Shareability**: By integrating links and downloadable apps within the e-platform content and creating a platform readable in multiple formats with multilingual menus.
- **Functionality**: Integrating the generated knowledge into the platform to boost cultural tourism and support policymakers and practitioners.

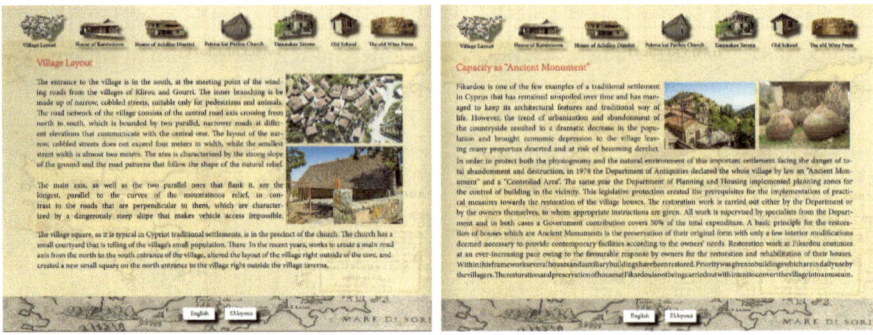

Fig. 3 Images of the interactive e-book © UNESCO Chair on digital cultural heritage

Fig. 4 Screenshots of the virtual gastronomy lab at the house of Katsinioros © UNESCO Chair on digital cultural heritage

Fig. 5 3D dense point cloud from drone photogrammetry © UNESCO chair on digital cultural heritage

Fig. 6 Creation of the BIM model using as base the point cloud of terrestrial laser scanner and drone © UNESCO chair on digital cultural heritage

Fig. 7. 360° Tour images from the inner layout of the village © UNESCO chair on digital cultural heritage

- **Usability**: By incorporating User Interface (UI)/User Experience (UX) components. The user is guided by recognizable icons and titles, with a practical and easily readable menu interface.
- **Accessibility**: By offering the opportunity to people who cannot travel to the site and to people with disabilities to experience Fikardou through a faithful Virtual Tour designed in collaboration with the Office of the Commissioner for Administration and the Protection of Human Rights (in its capacity as the competent authority for the protection and inclusion of persons with disabilities).

3.2 e-Fikardou—Holistic Heritage Digitization and Documentation

The process of holistic digitization and documentation of the movable and immovable tangible cultural heritages of Fikardou Village is crucial for the protection, preservation and renovation of the village and is based on the research outputs of the EU Study VIGIE2020/654 (Commission, 2022). Additionally, the 3D digitization process can significantly improve the accessibility of the unique cultural heritage of the village for research, innovation, education, and enjoyment. Digitized 3D cultural heritage tangible objects can be used in several ways such as.

- High-quality 3D scans and records can be used by archaeologists and engineers in conservation, protection, and conditional/structural assessment.
- Data of medium quality for 3D printing are extensively used in the creative industry sectors such as the games industry, XR applications, and education.
- Low- and/or high-resolution 3D structures are delivered through online platforms, repositories, and infrastructures to facilitate the work of scholars, archaeologists, museologists, historians, architects, engineers, multidisciplinary researchers/experts, and students.

The Study lays out clear guidelines and best practice in how to conduct a digitization campaign for cultural heritage and considers the wider implications of quality, complexity, and stakeholder requirements that are vital if the created "digital twin" is to be of maximum use and impact across multiple use cases as a trusted and authentic representation of cultural heritage assets. This is the fundamental principle behind the holistic documentation of cultural heritage and the MNEMOSYNE methodology.

3.3   e-Fikardou—Taxonomy of Holistic Documentation

Fikardou Village's monuments and environment as well as its embedded intangible aspects and features were examined using the MNEMOSYNE project methodology for the holistic documentation and digitization of tangible cultural heritage. The project developed an integrated taxonomy for the tangible cultural heritage assets of the village supporting the representation of movable/immovable heritage, the complexity of heritage assets and the embedded nature of intangible heritage assets within the context of the Fikardou study. The proposed taxonomy divides heritage into tangible and intangible components, with a focus on creating a class for tangible heritage. By dividing these two categories, it will be possible to determine where intangible heritage can be recognized, how it interacts with tangible heritage, and how this detailed information can be integrated into this system.

In its most basic form tangible cultural assets can fall into one of two categories, namely, movable or immovable (Fig. 8). Classifications beyond this simple division, however, become more complex as definitions become refined and progressive classification is a major challenge. The subcategories are distinguished by various difficulties and levels of complexity that have been recognized and handled in various ways. Although there may be an overlap between the categories—even at the movable/immovable classification level—they should be considered separately before expanding the wider knowledge system that is available for each object, monument, and site of Fikardou.

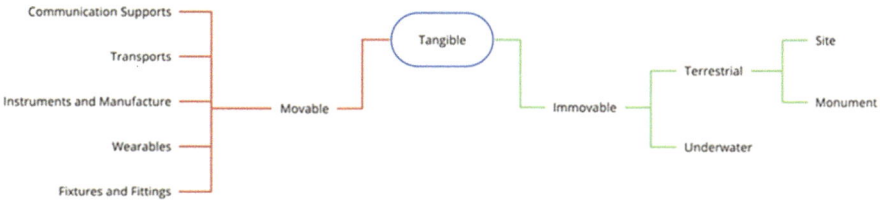

Fig. 8 Classification of tangible heritage class into the movable and immovable cultural heritages of Fikardou village

The following standards are used to categorize movable objects:

- *function* which refers to an asset's technical capabilities;
- *form* which refers to the typological categories of an asset;
- *subject type* which describes a particular use or purpose of an asset that distinguishes it from another physical form with similar physical characteristics;
- *material/technique* which refers to the physical characteristics of the asset relating to its creation or manufacture, including its material(s) and production technique(s), where those are discernible;
- *location or context* which serves as a crucial connecting point between tangible and intangible heritages, as well as the heritage of both movable and immovable objects, and emphasizes documenting the asset's temporal and physical provenance;
- *state and condition* which covers the asset's entire lifecycle, pre- and post-depositional.

Furthermore, monuments can be classified according to:

1. *feature* depending on the spatial–temporal variables, rooted in the general environment;
2. *significance* intended as the main function attached to the monument and how it related to the human social economic context (e.g. storage, cultic, etc.);
3. (3a) *components* partitioned into two categories, namely, space, which can be delimited (indoor) or not (outdoor) (3b) *built elements* referring to the parts composing a specific structure depending on the segmentation of the space they provide.

The village can be categorized by using a general taxonomic system based on The Getty Vocabularies,[7] within the classes of "Tangible", "Immovable", "Terrestrial", "Site", "Function", and "Residential", to "villages" the indicative type for Fikardou as a cultural heritage asset (Fig. 9). Furthermore, the data and information needed to record the tangible facet of this cultural heritage asset are represented in classes such as "Elements" and "Materials". The "Elements" taxonomy of the village includes the historical monuments of the village such as the church, winepress, museum, and

---

[7] https://www.getty.edu/research/tools/vocabularies/aat/index.html.

Fig. 9 Conceptualization of holistic documentation regarding Fikardou Village

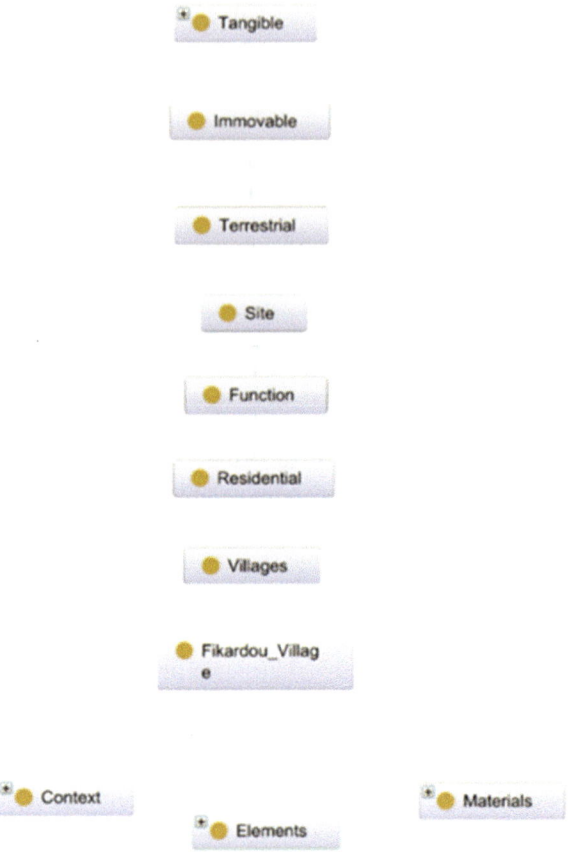

traditional houses. Finally, "Materials" taxonomy refers to the physical characteristics of the asset relating to its creation and manufacture, including its materials and production technique, where those are discernible.

The intangible information of the asset is recorded in the class "Context", which includes general and historical information about Fikardou Village.

Subsequent branches can be added to the class tree increasing the complexity of the representation but deepening the understanding and interrelationships between the components of the assets. Further details of these taxonomies for Fikardou Village are available for the Fikardou case study from the MNEMOSYNE project.[8]

---

[8] https://erachair-dch.eu/case-studies/.

3.4   e-Fikardou—Creation of a User Classification

As noted previously a vital component to implementing the cultural strategies chosen to support Fikardou was the inclusion of parties at all levels of investment in developing the village as a cultural heritage asset, from UNESCO to the Department of Antiquities to residents of Fikardou and the wider community diaspora. The MNEMOSYNE methodology considers all stakeholders, or asset users, to be part of the documentation process classifying and categorizing these them based on their needs and backgrounds. This is in part supported by the taxonomy which can be used to assist in identifying missing stakeholders and engaging them with the project dialogue.

The first step of this classification is to define interdisciplinary user groups, their members, and identify users' knowledge of cultural heritage. The main criteria by which users are displayed are informational needs (general, educational, trade visitors), expertise (domain expertise and technical expertise), and motivations (curiosity, work, planning visits, pleasure, captive, and non-captive learning). These categories distinguish previously identified groups and provide a way to introduce specific categories of users whose contribution is frequently underestimated or not considered at all (e.g. the hobbyist).

Figure 10 shows the four main identified categories, based on their area of expertise and knowledge with corresponding subcategories. We note that experts are also involved as users. The four main categories are.

Fig. 10 The multidisciplinary community of experts and users involved in the documentation and knowledge of Fikardou Village

- *experts* with domain and technical expertise in this particular area, e.g. historians, geographers, and geologists;
- *case study experts* with empirical knowledge and studies of this domain, e.g. curators, archaeologists, architects, surveyors, civil engineers, and IT specialists;
- *non-experts* who are motivated by this particular area, e.g. students, tourists, guides, policymakers, decision-makers, the general public, the tourist industry, and creative industries;
- *case study users* who are involved in the use and reuse part of the process, e.g. educators and multimedia experts.

3.5   e-Fikardou—Data Acquisition and Digitization Pipelines

While the documentation process, taxonomy and user classification are vital in defining the problem domain (what needs to be digitized, who are the stakeholders, how will the results be used, etc.), it does not inherently address the practicalities of data acquisition actualization. EU Study VIGIE2020/654 (European Commission, 2020) establishes best practice in data acquisition both in terms of planning a digitization campaign and in the recording of paradata as part of the holistic documentation and digitization process. The MNEMOSYNE method implements these guidelines allowing the objective measurement for the confidence and credibility in produced data, metadata, and paradata described by the fundamental parameters of Complexity and Quality.

The complexity of 3D data acquisition is determined by multiple factors that can be evaluated and assigned a confidence weighting; for example, software and hardware are evaluated based on reliability, operability, compatibility, maintainability, security, etc. A more specific evaluation can be undertaken as necessary, in the case of hardware based on license availability (i.e. frequencies, interferences with other systems), the precision of multisensory systems under different environmental conditions, the usability (i.e. communication, transfer of data, battery life, available storage), the efficiency (i.e. speed of data and accuracy), and sensor integration. These groupings and subcategories, including their rationale and evaluation criteria, can be found within the Study (European Commission, 2022).

Figure 11 shows the resulting general radial chart for the evaluation of the complexity of digitizing Fikardou Village, with categories highlighted to indicate the expected effort and estimated impact of these factors and contribution to complexity from each subcategory within a particular group.

The MNEMOSYNE methodology aligns itself with the position expressed by the Expert Group on Digital Cultural Heritage and Europeana (European Commission, 2022) that "Quality in 3D digitisation of cultural heritage is not only about capture accuracy and resolution, but also about other key aspects such as historical accuracy, range of data and metadata generated and collected, and fitness for purpose". The

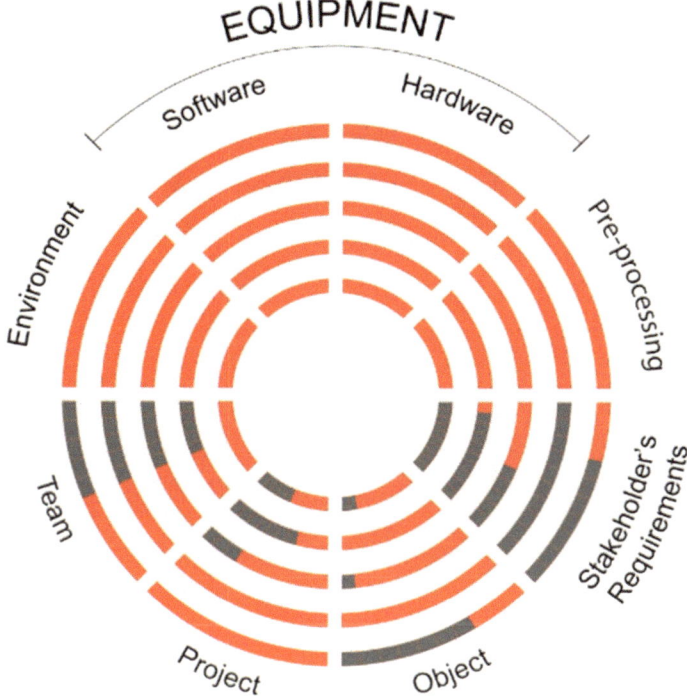

Fig. 11 Radial chart describing the complexity parameters for Fikardou Village

methodology therefore records the wider aspects of quality in regard to the documentation of the project, not in the fidelity of 3D data output (although it may be indicative of high-fidelity results).

In a similar approach to the quantification of complexity, the quality parameters' documentation types are grouped according to recording type/task with subcategories for specific parameter weighting. For example, when considering the recording of Materials this is broken down into individual parameters like yield, fatigue, tensile or toughness. These parameters in turn may be directly or indirectly, singly or collectively, engaged with the overall quality of the digitization process in response to the complexity imposed by the properties of the concerned material(s), i.e. chemical composition, moisture, corrosion, carbonation, resistance, and porosity which refer to the layers of the material parameter. These groupings and subcategories, including their rationale and evaluation criteria, can be found within the Study (European Commission, 2022).

The resulting quality of the digitization for Fikardou is described in Fig. 12.

The 3D digitization process necessarily varies according to the heritage asset under consideration (as described through the taxonomy), the processes and methods utilized during the acquisition (the complexity parameters), the physical disposition of the asset (the quality parameters) and the potential uses or purposes of the produced

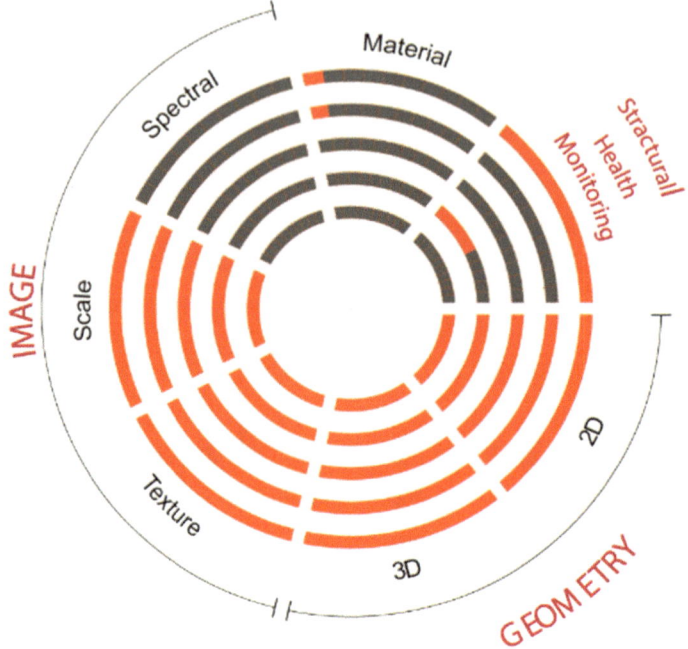

Fig. 12 Radial chart describing the quality parameters for Fikardou Village

material (identified during the user classification). Taking all of these into consideration, if the criteria set by the parameters are achieved, the confidence in the results of a digitization campaign and the resulting data capture's fidelity as a faithful and complete record of a cultural heritage asset is increased within the given (and known) constraints.

In the case of Fikardou Village, having holistically considered the digital documentation of the site provided a ground truth on which to base confident, informed and appropriate decision-making (based on the strategies/actions developed in the IMPACTOUR and TExTOUR projects) in collaboration and engaging with all stakeholders at the appropriate level, and ultimately the realization of the e-Fikardou platform, its content and digital cultural tourism offering.

4 Conclusion and Future Plans

This paper has presented the case study of Fikardou Village, a UNESCO Tentative List monument, as a successful example of cultural tourism advancement. The three European projects that include Fikardou in their work plan have decidedly set the pace for opening new routes in experiencing tourism in Cyprus. Nevertheless, already plans are in place to further the objectives of each one of the projects and to establish new lines of inquiry. Specifically, in the context of the TExTOUR project, the CUT team aims to digitize the cycling and walking routes and experiences in and around the village recording and mapping of the routes for accessible tourist activities.

Figure 13 shows the first stage of the mapping process in KML format and integrated into Google Earth. When all stages of the process are completed, the results will be fully integrated into a geoinformatics platform with applications for cyclists, hikers, and visitors. Moreover, such athletic excursions can be combined with experiencing the surrounding nature or a visit to the village to experience its traditions and gastronomy through touristic scenarios and available workshops. The village seeks to capitalize on this and establish a Cycling/Hiking Centre to organize and host sports events, to create local accommodation for visitors, as well as introduce modest commercial activity through bike rentals.

As part of the wider commitment to revitalize the village and stimulate the local economy, the CUT team, in collaboration with the Department of Antiquities and the Community Council of Fikardou, has been working on creating incentives for renovating the buildings to attract former residents back to the village or to rent them to new people who wish to enjoy the lifestyle that Fikardou now offers. Alternatively, given the increased tourist activity in the village, there is interest in how buildings may serve visitors as shops run by local owners or as potential rentals. The next step

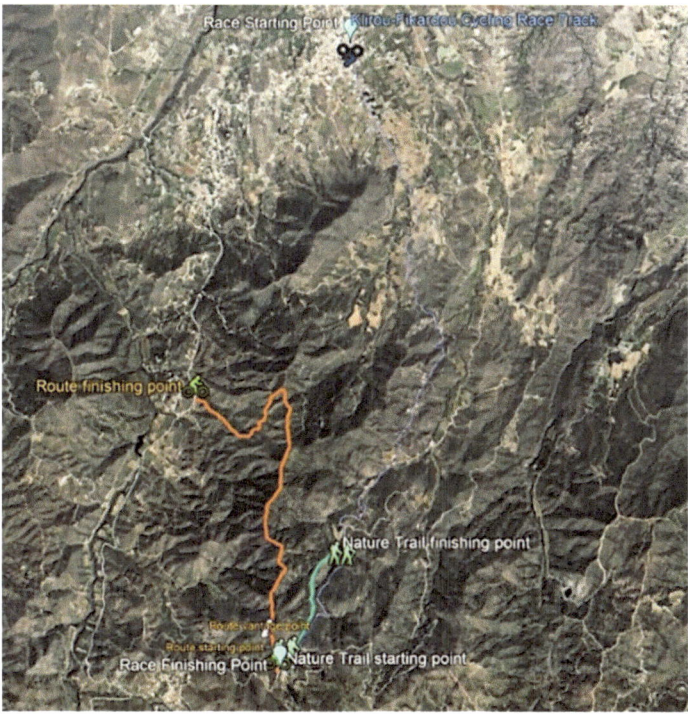

Fig. 13 Fikardou-Kalo Chorio cycling/hiking routes mapping KML

is to organize a pan-community gathering, bringing together village residents and property owners who may not reside in Fikardou, to inform them of these incentives and opportunities.

Finally, the project co-designs pioneering and sustainable cultural tourism strategies to improve deprived areas in Europe and beyond. This framework contains provisions for the creation of a roadmap of cooperation around cultural heritage and tourism between Fikardou, Cyprus and Anfeh, Lebanon.[9] Anfeh and Fikardou share important similarities; both are placed on the Tentative List of the UNESCO World Heritage, and both present a harmonious relationship between the built and the natural environment, enabling a perspective of the cultural landscape. A milestone of this cooperation has been the signing of a Memorandum of Understanding (MoU) between the municipalities of the two cultural sites. This MoU signifies a remarkable partnership between an EU and a non-EU member for regional development and sets a new precedent for furthering cultural diplomacy in the Eastern Mediterranean and the Middle East, allowing for the interaction of peoples, the exchange of language, religion, ideas, arts, and societal structures, thus forming and/or strengthening relations between divergent groups. The Levantine Basin has always been an epicentre of interaction, not only regarding trade in goods, but importantly, regarding the exchange of ideas, values, traditions, and other aspects of culture or identity, whether to strengthen relationships, enhance socio-cultural cooperation, promote national interests and beyond. Hence, the cooperation between Fikardou and Anfeh re-establishes long-standing traditions and shared history of the region.

The goal is to design and set up a roadmap for the development of long-term sustainable cooperation between the two regions, including the local communities, as well as local and regional policymakers and stakeholders. Resources from the two sites include local agriculture and gastronomy, art and crafts, literature and music, and underwater, urban, and natural sites of historical, religious, and archaeological significance. This aims to introduce local tourism exchange, widening of regional professional networks, knowledge exchange, commerce and trade on local products.

Acknowledgements *IMPACTOUR* has received funding from the European Union's Horizon 2020 research and innovation programme under grant agreement no. 870747.

MNEMOSYNE project has received funding from the European Union's H2020 Framework. Programme for research and innovation under Grant agreement no. 810857

TEXTOUR has received funding from the European Union's Horizon 2020 research and innovation programme under grant agreement no.101004687

EU VIGIE2020/654 Study at the request of and financed by the European Commission, Directorate-General of Communications Networks, Content & Technology VIGIE 2020/654.

Special thanks to the excellent cooperation with the Community Council of Fikardou and the Cyprus Department of Antiquities which is responsible for the management of the archaeological heritage of Cyprus. The settlement of Fikardou has been under the supervision of the Department since 1978, as an "Ancient Monument" in its entirety, and within a "Controlled Area".

---

[9] Anfef, Lebanon.

References

Denard, H. (ed). (2009). *The London Charter for the Computer-Based Visualisation of Cultural Heritage.* London, [Online]. Retrieved from https://www.london-charter.org/.

E. Commission. (2022). Directorate General for Communications Networks, and Technology, *Study on quality in 3D digitisation of tangible cultural heritage: mapping parameters, formats, standards, benchmarks, methodologies, and guidelines: executive summary.* Publications Office of the European Union. https://doi.org/10.2759/581678.

European Commission, Expert Group on Digital Cultural Heritage and Europeana. (2020). *Basic principles and tips for 3D digitisation of tangible cultural heritage for cultural heritage professionals and institutions and other custodians of cultural heritage.* Luxembourg [Online]. Retrieved from https://ec.europa.eu/newsroom/dae/document.cfm?doc_id=69201.

George Jeffrey, F. S. A. (1918). A description of the historic monuments of Cyprus. Studies in the archeology and architecture of the Island. Nicosia: Governing Printing Office, Nicosia, Cyprus [Online]. Retrieved from http://www.archive.org/details/cu31924028551319.

Hegoumenidou, F., & Floridou, A. (1987). *Phikardou: A traditional village in Cyprus.* Nicosia: Chr. Nicolaou and Sons Ltd, A.G. Leventis Foundation, Dept. of Antiquities.

Philokyprou, M., & Limbouri-Kozakou, E. (2015). An overview of the restoration of monuments and listed buildings in Cyprus from antiquity until the twenty-first century. *Studies in Conservation, 60*(4), 267–277. https://doi.org/10.1179/2047058414Y.0000000136

PIO. (1987). Houses in Fikardou Village are selected for Europa Nostra's certificate of value. Press and Information Office, 3.

Methodology and Application of 3D Visualization in Sustainable Cultural Tourism Planning

Karima Kourtit⬤, Peter Nijkamp⬤, Henk Scholten, and Yneke van Iersel

Abstract This paper addresses the global imperative of implementing sustainable initiatives in contemporary industrial and service sectors, with a focus on the tourism industry's quest for resilience and recovery post the COVID-19 pandemic. To foster balanced tourism development, the necessity for evidence-based information at local and regional levels is emphasized, highlighting the demand for transparent planning support tools within the sector. Alongside traditional statistical monitoring tools like Tourist Satellite Accounts, the increasing popularity of digital tools, including local tourism dashboards, e-booking systems, and interactive tourist guidance devices, is noted. Noteworthy is the prospect of applying digital twins, an emerging visualization technique in spatial planning, to local and regional sustainable cultural tourism planning. This paper explores the scope and utility of digital twins, drawing on principles from geoscience and geodesign, to create 3D visualizations of spatial tourist realities. The urban architecture of these visualizations is outlined, demonstrating their use through an empirical illustration of digital twins for the Parkstad region in Limburg, the Netherlands. The 3D images depict the tourism area across various cultural-historical periods, presenting a multi-layer representation of 'cultural-historical epochs', starting from the Roman period. This innovative approach contributes to digital sustainable cultural tourism planning by offering a data-based perspective on spatial realities and historical epochs, providing a valuable tool for the industry's planning and decision-making processes.

Keywords Cultural tourism · Sustainability · Circularity · Digital twin · Cultural-historical epochs

K. Kourtit (✉) · P. Nijkamp
Open University, The Netherlands, Valkenburgerweg 177, 6419 AT Heerlen, Netherlands
e-mail: karima.kourtit@ou.nl

H. Scholten
VU University, The Netherlands, De Boelelaan 1105, 1081 HV Amsterdam, Netherlands
e-mail: henk.scholten@geodan.nl

H. Scholten · Y. van Iersel
Geodan Amsterdam, The Netherlands, President Kennedylaan 1, 1079 MB Amsterdam, Netherlands
e-mail: yneke.van.iersel@geodan.nl

© The Author(s) 2025   173
B. Neuts et al. (eds.), *Advances in Cultural Tourism Research*, Advances in Digital and Cultural Tourism Management, https://doi.org/10.1007/978-3-031-65537-1_11

1 Aims and Scope

Over the past decades the tourism sector has shown—both locally and globally—a rapid structural rise. It has become one of the most important industries in the world, as a result of the rise in leisure time, decline in transportation costs, globalization and logistic accessibility, local scale advantages from mass tourism, and a rise in global tourism participation by visitors from emerging economies (Yang & Wong, 2021; The World Tourism Organization 2021, 2022). More recently, digital technology has become one of the accelerators of worldwide tourism, e.g. through the use of e-booking systems, digital information systems on literally all places on our planet, social media and electronic platform access and use, etc. (Lau, 2020). Tourism has turned from a rather low-tech physical mobility activity for visitors to a high-tech information-driven and data-based industrial sector (Daldanise, 2016; Kourtit et al., 2022). It has the typical features of an advanced Industry 4.0 sector.

Nevertheless, modern tourism has also many shadow sides. Environmental decay is one of the obvious consequences of tourism in destination places, e.g. noise, waste, air and water pollution, etc. But there are also other negative externalities, like local crowding effects and loss of local identity and authenticity (Gössling, 2020; Lu et al., 2022; Song et al., 2022). Examples like Venice and Barcelona illustrate that tourism is not an undisputed activity that only serves the local economy in a positive way. Is there a possibility to turn tourism into an economic activity that would lead to environmentally benign, climate-neutral or circular outcomes for tourist destinations? And can digital technology provide tools to pave the road to sustainable results at local or regional level that are supported by the locals and at the same time avoid or mitigate insider versus outsider conflicts? The challenges involved are multi-faceted and complex, and call for evidence-based creative responses (Angrisano et al., 2016; Hampton, 2005). The Be.CULTOUR project—as part of the EU Horizon programme—seeks to develop a co-creation approach, with many partner institutions from all over Europe, in order to provide informed strategies and policy lessons for cultural tourism in a circular economy context, based on modern research tools. In this context, digital data handling capacity is a sine qua non for an effective sustainability- and circularity-oriented policy approach.

The present paper aims to demonstrate the potential of three-dimensional (3D) visualization methods in local cultural tourism planning, with a particular emphasis on the use of 'digital twins' as spatial imaging tools for providing policy-makers and planners with appropriate and evidence-based information for acquiring an integrated perspective on sustainable cultural tourism planning. The paper is organized as follows. After this introductory Sect. 1, we will introduce in Sect. 2 some evidence on the need for appropriate visualization methods, by referring to critical tourist issues in a particular case study, viz. the Heerlen/Parkstad region in the Southern part of the province Limburg in the Netherlands. Then, Sect. 3 is devoted to the analytical and planning potential of geoscience and geodesign in a digital world. Section 4 provides a concise overview of digital planning support (DPS) tools that highlight the relevance of digital twins in cultural tourism planning. This culminates then in the presentation of an empirical illustration of digital twins for urban circularity for the Parkstad region, South-Limburg, in Sect. 5. The final section provides some concluding remarks.

2 Culture and Tourism: A Complex Nexus

Culture is a broad economic sector that comprises inter alia art, history, architecture, entertainment, performing arts, creative professions, and so forth (Alberti & Giusti, 2012; Coccossis & Nijkamp, 1995; Nijkamp & Kourtit, 2023). It has both a material and spiritual component. It forms a representation or mapping of societal trends and mindful developments that combine the past with the present. It goes without saying that tourism is all over the world attracted by rich local or regional cultural amenities, as is witnessed by cities like Venice, Paris, Amsterdam, Boston, Cape Town, Mumbai, or Shanghai. This also holds for smaller cities like Leeuwarden in the Netherlands, Bruges in Belgium, Delphi in Greece, or Bandung in Indonesia. Tourism is of course an economic asset which may generate many financial resources for the host area. However, in the age of mass tourism, an uncontrolled influx of visitors may lead to countervailing crowding effects that erode the cultural and ecological assets which form exactly the basis of tourism (see a sketch of the tourism paradox in Fig. 1).

There is an abundant literature on the paradoxical developments in tourism (Fusco Girard & Nijkamp, 2009; Greffe, 2004; McManus & Carruthers, 2014). Studies include inter alia crowding effects, environmental decay, decline in quality of life of residents in destination places, etc. (e.g. Gössling et al., 2020; Hall et al., 2020; Song et al., 2022; Yang & Wong, 2021). In this context, it should be noted that cultural-historical heritage is not just a static asset from the past, but a dynamic phenomenon comprising influences from different periods ('*cultural-historical epochs*'). This will

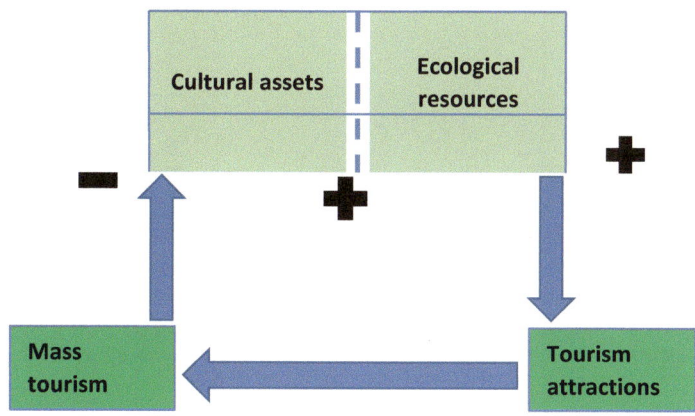

Fig. 1 The tourism paradox

be illustrated here for the case of South-Limburg in the Netherlands, an attractive and rich cultural-historical and vulnerable ecological area near the German and Belgian border. It is for Dutch people a peripheral region, but it has a good accessibility for Germans (nearby Aachen) and Belgians (nearby Liege, and not very far from Brussels). It is also for Dutch tourists one of the most attractive natural areas to visit, with a wealth of cultural-historical and ecological resources dating even back to the Roman period (Nijkamp & Kourtit, 2023).

The historical, political and cultural time frame of South-Limburg can be subdivided into five distinct cultural-historical epochs (Visit Zuid Limburg, 2022):

1. the Roman period; 750 BC–500 AC ('*Carrefour of the Romans*');
2. the Medieval period; 500 AC till the seventeenth century ('*Knights and Bandits*');
3. the coal mine era; modern time till 1970s ('*Golden Mining*');
4. the intermediate era; break-down period end of last century ('*Dramatic Transition*');
5. the modern era; beginning twenty-first century ('*New Revival*').

Each of these epochs is part of the 'great story' of this region and has left behind important characteristic footprints ('icons'). So, for each of these five epochs, one can draw a map that presents the location of cultural-historical landmarks in the area at hand. By using an overlay approach to each of these five maps, one may obtain a comprehensive map of the entire region containing the cultural-historical assets in an integrated way (see Fig. 2).

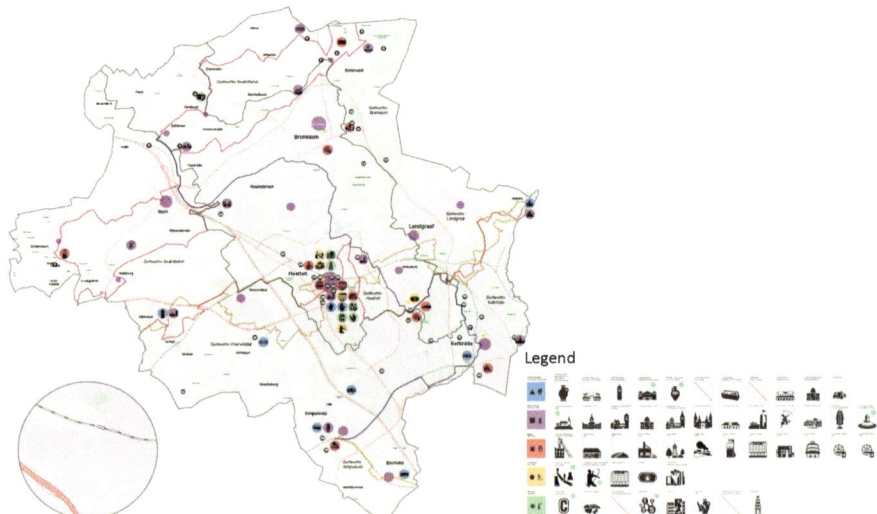

Fig. 2 An integrated representation of the cultural-historical assets across the entire region in the form of a comprehensive map. *Source* The Story of Parkstad, and its implementation within the Customer Journey Model, a presentation by Anya Niewierra, General Director Visit Zuid Limburg, on 8 September 2022 (pp. 27)

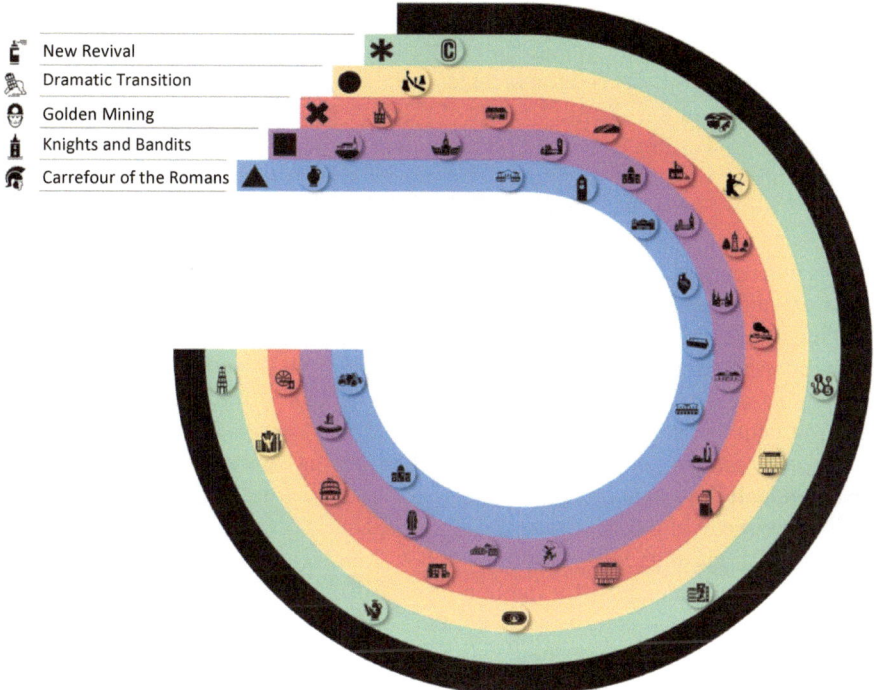

Fig. 3 Sketch of the cultural-historical epochs in South-Limburg. *Source* The Story of Parkstad, and its implementation within the Customer Journey Model, a presentation by Anya Niewierra, General Director Visit Zuid Limburg, on 8 September 2022 (pp.27)

In an image form, the cultural-historical evolution of South-Limburg can also be visualized systematically from a synthetic multi-faceted time perspective (see Fig. 3).

In goes without saying that the visitors to South-Limburg have different motives: nature, culture, history, shopping, entertainment, etc. Especially in the summer season, clearly overcrowded places can be observed, which reduces the tourist attractiveness of this area and leads also to dissatisfaction among the local residents. Tourism policy is therefore a delicate search for a balance between conflicting interests. To find such a balance, detailed user-friendly information of tourist attractions, tourist pressure, and negative externalities is needed. To that end, the use of digital support tools is a necessity. This will be discussed in Sect. 3.

3   Benefits of Geoscience and Geodesign Methods

Over the past decades we have witnessed an enormous interest in the development and application of geoscience and geodesign approaches. This development was stimulated by (i) the 'quantitative revolution in geography' which started in the 1970s and which heralded a new period in geographical analysis and (ii) the need for a proper visualization of complex spatial data systems, characterized by multi-dimensional features and multi-scalar geographical information. Geographic Information Systems (GIS) were one of the clear exponents of this new development and have provided a wealth of applications in spatial planning all over the world.

The above-described revolutionary trends in geoscience were, in particular, induced by the quantitative and modelling orientation in the spatial sciences; the combination of spatial data systems and advanced spatial visualization techniques led to a great popularity of geoscience in modern spatial analytics and in urban or regional planning in many policy fields.

Geodesign was the next step in geoscience, as it enabled researchers to link spatial data representations to spatial design issues, ranging from municipal planning tasks to urbanization challenges (including housing stocks, infrastructural facilities, or environmental provisions). Consequently, these new toolboxes formed the beginning of a new planning tradition in the field of urban and regional policy and management. And gradually this new orientation has also entered the domain of tourism planning (Albuquerque et al., 2018; Brown & Weber, 2012; Liritzis et al., 2015; Melenchuk, 2021; Valjarević et al., 2017).

The tourist sector forms a mutually interwoven amalgam of supply conditions and visitors' demand or responses. On the supply side, we may distinguish several core tourist facilities, in particular, cultural amenities (e.g. museums, historical quarters), tourist assets (e.g. hotels), urban ambiance (e.g. historical-cultural atmosphere), and environmental quality (e.g. green areas and nature). On the demand side, we may identify volumes of tourist visits, tourist expenditures, crowding effects, space–time profiles/concentrations of tourists, etc. The combination of this bi-polar tourist constellation forms the data base pattern that is needed for a mapping of the local tourist sector (see Fig. 4).

Such a mapping needs both a data metrics approach and a 2D—but preferably a 3D—geoscience image approach. One of the modern techniques for mapping the space–time complexity of spatial systems—in this case, a local tourist system—is a digital twin. Digital twinning has in recent years become a fashionable geoscience approach. Examples can be found inter alia in Scholten (2017), Micheli et al. (2018), Craglia et al. (2021), Ivanov and Dolgui (2021). This approach is gradually also

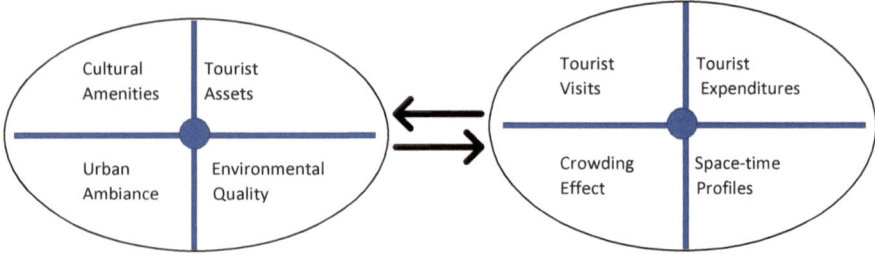

Fig. 4 The supply–demand nexus of local tourism

finding useful applications in the tourist sector and will briefly be introduced in Sect. 4 of this study.

4 Digital Planning Support Tools and Digital Twins in Cultural Tourism

Local tourist planning presupposes tailor-made information on the supply and demand profiles of the characteristics of tourist areas, including core touristic amenities, attractiveness conditions, bottlenecks on the supply and demand sides (e.g. contextual constraints due to physical geography), and strength-weakness conditions at local or regional level (Niccolucci et al., 2022; Singh et al., 2022). In addition, general conditions on sustainability development (e.g. fulfilments of the 17 SDGs), urban circularity conditions, and climate-neutrality objectives are to be considered as well, taking into account a differentiation of objectives due to multiple stakeholder groups.

A wide variety of evidence-based digital planning support (DPS) tools has been developed in the past decades. Examples are digital scoreboards; interactive user-oriented dashboards; community-based geodesign tools; 3D visualization techniques and maps; and, more recently, digital twins. Digital twins may be seen as a virtual 3D mapping of a real-world constellation of a multi-faceted and complex physical phenomenon, with space–time components based on an array of systematically organized micro-based or meso-based data. They do not only offer a static picture of characteristic features of the urban space on the basis of a collection of multi-scalar data, but incorporate also an array of time-varying digital data sources (ranging from cadastral data to GPS data). Consequently, a digital twin is much more than a 3D atlas: it is systematically and thematically organized and is able to meet the users' requirements by its interactive nature and its 3D simulation capacity (e.g. in the form of virtual museums, historical experience centres, and metaversal digital cultural heritage).

It goes without saying that the modern ICT sector—and in particular digital technology—provides unprecedented opportunities for cultural tourism as well as for the cultural and creative sector in Europe and elsewhere. It will not only benefit the tourism industry and the cultural economy at macro- or meso-level, but will also enrich cultural awareness among the citizens and local stakeholders and NGOs. The cultural tourism ecosystems nurtured by tailor-made DPS tools have the capacity to foment innovativeness and creativity in the current age of sustainability initiatives, including Green Deal objectives and the New European Bauhaus programmes. We will now present in Sect. 5 a pedagogical example of the use of a data-driven digital twin exercise for the Parkstad region in South-Limburg.

5   A Digital Twin Prototype for South-Limburg

Cultural heritage is a broad concept that comprises a wide range of historical urban and regional assets that reflect a rich past and are still memorable in present times (see, e.g. Angrisano et al., 2016). Historical landscapes and cityscapes are part of cultural heritage (UNESCO 2011). Cultural heritage contains a wealth of intrinsic and use functions (e.g. economic, social, creative, financial, environmental, iconic, historical, aesthetic, cultural, etc.) related to both the built environment and natural areas (see, e.g. Throsby, 2001; Kourtit & Nijkamp, 2022). An important question pertains to the key factors (X-Factors) that drive societal well-being in the context of cultural tourism and historical-cultural heritage. This calls for an impact assessment and market potential analysis of sustainable, inclusive, and circular cultural tourism through the use of multi-dimensional quantitative and qualitative indicators, systematically organized in the decomposition scheme with measurable key performance indicators (KPIs). To that end, a digital data toolbox using as a frame of reference a digital twin approach is very helpful, as this may also generate the necessary data of spatial digital planning support (DPS) tools like an interactive user-oriented dashboard for sustainable cultural tourism at urban and regional levels (see Fig. 5). This decomposed data structure can be represented in an integrated data warehouse from a multi-scalar perspective (see Fig. 6), where the symbol XXQ in the centre represents the highest possible level of urban quality or well-being from the perspective of cultural tourism performance. It is clear that Fig. 6 comprises all multi-scalar data that are needed for constructing a digital twin for the area concerned in South-Limburg.

The empirical focus in the present study will be on a prototype design of a digital twin for sustainable and circular development of the city of Heerlen, the touristic centre of the Parkstad region in South-Limburg. To undertake this endeavour, an extensive data base collection (based on municipal statistics, cadastral data, place-specific tourist data, relevant land-use data, etc.) had to be organized. A necessary condition for building up a reliable 3D thematic image of a given area is to specify precisely the points of interest and to get precise data on the coordinates of this site.

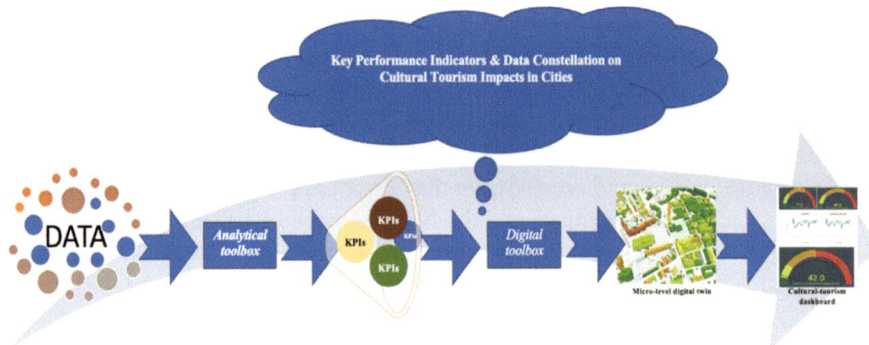

Fig. 5 A cascade of hierarchical data use and monitoring

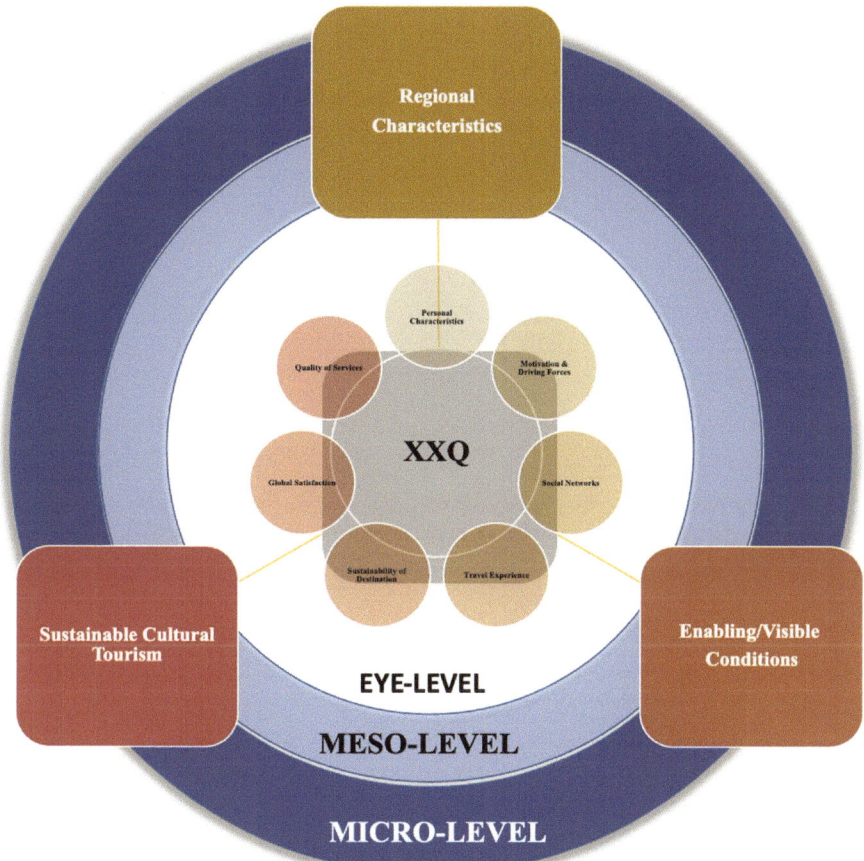

Fig. 6 Integrated data warehouse for sustainable and circular performance of cultural tourism

This is certainly a sine qua non for a reliable and quantitative representation of spatial phenomena in relation to cultural tourism and sustainable urban development.

As an illustrative introduction to the spatially varying tourist amenities in the city of Heerlen, we present here a GIS map of all hospitality provisions (including hotels, restaurants, (snack)bars, café's) in the city (see Fig. 7). The centre of the city and the main axes appear to be popular locations of these visitors' facilities.

The next step is to present a few prototypes of digital twins for the central part of the city of Heerlen. We demonstrate now the first results from an empirical proof-of-concept experiment on Heerlen by zooming in on two KPIs, viz. (i) the spatial sustainability/circularity dimension of the housing stock (measured in terms of its energy efficiency, as a proxy for favourable conditions of the built environment) and (ii) the density and spatial spread of urban green in relation to the construction year of the buildings, as a proxy for attractive quality of life of neighbourhoods in the

Legend
- 🟣 55102 OR 55201 OR 55101 OR 5530 OR 55202 OR 5590
- 🟢 56101 OR 5590
- 🔴 56101 OR 56102
- ⚫ 56102
- 🟢 56102
- 🔴 56102 OR 5630
- 🟡 5630
- 🟢 5630 OR 85522 OR 85521 OR 5914
- 🔵 91011 OR 85522 OR 90042 OR 90041
- 🔴 9103 OR 91011 OR 91022 OR 92001 OR 91012 OR 93211 OR 93299 OR 91019 OR 92009 OR 91042 OR 91021 OR 91041
- 🔴 93299 OR 94911
- 🟣 94911 OR 9604

Fig. 7 Location of hospitality amenities in the centre of Heerlen

city. The detailed spatial 3D images of these KPIs for the centre of the city can be found in the prototype digital twins presented in Figs. 8 and 9, respectively.

Figure 8 shows a 3D map of the spatial distribution of energy labels for individual buildings (ranging from highly energy-efficient outcomes in the central part of the city to extremely inefficient outcomes elsewhere). In general, there appears to be an enormous spread of the ecological energy (and circularity) performance in the urban area of Heerlen, while it is noteworthy that the density of trees appears to be rather irregular. This reveals an interesting finding in comparison to Fig. 7: tourist attractions like hospitality amenities and shopping areas are positioned in areas with a relatively high energy performance.

Figure 9 shows another interesting digital twin feature of the city. The construction years of the buildings in the inner city display a great variation, with only a few buildings constructed in the past decades. This finding illustrates once more that generally the attractiveness of the inner city is not balanced from the perspective of tourist visits.

Fig. 8 Prototype digital twin of Heerlen for energy efficiency of buildings at micro-scale (based on energy labels of houses and presence of trees)

Fig. 9 Prototype digital twin of Heerlen for age of buildings at micro-scale (based on year of construction and presence of trees)

Clearly, many more digital twins on the attractiveness characteristics of the city might be created, e.g. cultural amenities, entertainment places, synergies among tourist attractions, and accessibility for visitors. Our digital twin experiment offers only a prototype of the actual potential of geoscience techniques and needs much more detail in future research. In addition, an analysis of the interaction between different thematic digital twins is an interesting challenge.

6 Conclusion

The present study has to be seen against the background of the UN SDGs and the New Urban Agenda. It aimed to position cultural tourism in the context of sustainable, inclusive, and circular urban development. Tourism may be a major resource for the urban economy and culture, while urban attractiveness may act as a major magnet for enhancing the cultural development potential of cities and regions. But negative externalities involved (e.g. environmental decay, crowding) overshadow the benefits of tourism. And therefore, effective planning for balanced tourism is pertinent. In this context, advanced digital planning support (DPS) tools are needed, in particular, sustainability dashboards and digital twins. This study has presented in a concise form the principles of modern geoscience techniques, with a particular focus on the potential offered by digital twins.

The empirical illustration in the present paper focussed on a vulnerable tourist area in the southern part of the Netherlands, viz. the Heerlen/Parkstad region. It has brought to light that systematic data collection—in particular, in the form of a data warehouse that is systematically and hierarchically decomposed into relevant KPIs—is a prerequisite for evidence-based balanced tourism policy.

Digital twins can generate ample 3D insights into the fragility and development potential of urban tourist areas, provided the underlying database is up to date. Such digital twins can also be instrumental for mapping citizens' interests regarding tourists' spatial choices in cities with a wealth of cultural-touristic amenities. And finally, they may support an interactive design of urban liveability scenarios, displayed in an attractive and citizen-oriented visible way.

Acknowledgements Peter Nijkamp and Karima Kourtit acknowledge the grant from the European Union's Horizon 2020 research and innovation programme under grant agreement no. 101004627.

References

Alberti, F. G., & Giusti, J. D. (2012). Cultural heritage, tourism and regional competitiveness: The motor valley Cluster. *City, Culture and Society, 3*(4), 261–273.

Albuquerque, H., Costa, C., & Martins, F. (2018). The use of geographical information systems for tourism marketing purposes in Aveiro Region (Portugal). *Tourism Management Perspectives, 26*, 172–178.

Angrisano, M., Biancamano, P.F., Bosone, M., Carone, P., Daldanise, G., De Rosa, F., Franciosa, A., Iodice, S., Gravagnuolo., A, Nocca, F., Onesti, A., Panaro, S., Ragozino, S., Sannicandro, V., Fusco Girard, F. (2016). Towards operationalizing UNESCO recommendations on '*Historic Urban Landscape*'; a Position Paper, *Aestimum, 69*, 165–190.

Brown, G., & Weber, D. (2012). Using public participation GIS (PPGIS) on the Geoweb to monitor tourism development preferences. *Journal of Sustainable Tourism, 21*(2), 192–211.

Craglia, M., Scholten, H. J., Micheli, M., Hradec, J., Calzada, I., Luitjens, S., Ponti, M., & Boter, J. (2021). *Digitranscope: The Governance of Digitally-transformed Society*; EUR 30590 EN; Publications Office of the European Union: Luxembourg. ISBN 978-92-76-30229-2. https://doi.org/10.2760/503546, JRC123362.

Coccossis, H., & Nijkamp, P. (eds.). (1995). *Sustainable Tourism Development*. Aldershot, Avebury, UK.

Daldanise, G. (2016). Innovative strategies of urban heritage management for sustainable local development. *Procedia-Social and Behavioral Sciences, 223*, 101–107.

Fusco Girard, L., & Nijkamp, P. (Eds.). (2009). *Cultural tourism and sustainable local development.* Ashgate.

Gössling, S. (2020). Risks, resilience, and pathways to sustainable aviation: A COVID-19 perspective. *Journal of Air Transport Management, 89*, 1–4. https://doi.org/10.1016/j.jairtraman.2020.101933

Gössling, S., Scott, D., & Hall, C. M. (2020). Pandemics, tourism and global change: A rapid assessment of COVID-19. *Journal of Sustainable Tourism, 29*(1), 1–20. https://doi.org/10.1080/09669582.2020.1758708

Greffe, X. (2004). Is heritage an asset or a liability? *Journal of Cultural Heritage, 5*(3), 301–330.

Hall, C. M., Scott, D., & Gössling, S. (2020). Pandemics, transformations and tourism: Be careful what you wish for. *Tourism Geographies, 22*(3), 577–598. https://doi.org/10.1080/14616688.2020.1759131

Hampton, M. P. (2005). Heritage, local communities and economic development. *Annals of Tourism Research, 32*, 735–759.

Ivanov, D., & Dolgui, A. A. (2021). Digital supply chain twin for managing the disruption risks and resilience in the Era of industry 4.0, *Production Planning & Control, 32*, 775–788.

Kourtit, K., & Nijkamp, P. (2022). Creative actors and historical-cultural assets in urban regions. *Regional Studies*. https://doi.org/DOI.ORG/10.1080/00343404.2018.1541077.

Kourtit, K., & Nijkamp, P. (2023). Culture and tourism: A sustainability Dilemma?, *Liber Amicorum in Honour of Harry Geerlings* (J. Vroomans, B. Kuipers, and J.H.R. van Duin (eds.)), Erasmus School of Social and Behavioural Sciences.

Kourtit, K., Nijkamp, P., Östh, J., & Türk, U. (2022). Airbnb and COVID-19: Space time vulnerability effects in six world-cities. *Tourism Management, 93*, 104569. https://doi.org/10.1016/j.tourman.2022.104569.

Lau, A. (2020). New technologies used in COVID-19 for business survival: Insights from the hotel sector in China. *Information Technology and Tourism, 22*(4), 497–504. https://doi.org/10.1007/s40558-020-00193-z

Liritzis, I., Al-Otaibi, F. M., Volonakis, P., & Drivaliari, A. (2015). Digital technologies and trends in cultural heritage. *Mediterranean Archaeology and Archaeometry, 15*(3), 313–332.

Lu, J., Xiao, X., Xu, Z., Wang, C., Zhang, M., & Zhou, Y. (2022). The potential of virtual tourism in the recovery of tourism industry during the COVID-19 pandemic. *Current Issues in Tourism, 25*(3), 441–457. https://doi.org/10.1080/13683500.2021.1959526

McManus, C., & Carruthers, C. (2014). Cultural quarters and urban regeneration—The case of cathedral quarter Belfast. *International Journal of Cultural Policy, 20*(1), 78–98.

Micheli, M., Blakemore, M., Ponti, M., Scholten, H., & Craglia, M. (eds.). (2018). The governance of data in a digitally transformed european society. In *Second Workshop of the DigiTranScope Project*.

Melenchuk, A. (2021). Inclusive local digital participation in Georgia, Moldova, and Ukraine. *Policy Paper, German Marshall Fund of the United States*.

Niccolucci, F., Felicetti, A., & Hermon, S. (2022). Populating the data space for cultural heritage with heritage digital twins. *Data, 7*, 105.

Nijkamp, P. (2012). Economic valuation of cultural heritage. In G. Licciardi & R. Amirtahmasebi (eds.), *The Economics of Uniqueness*, World Bank, Washington, DC.

Scholten, H. (2017). Geocraft as a means to support the development of smart cities, getting the people of the place involved - youth included -. *Quality Innovation Prosperity, 21*(1), 119–150. https://doi.org/10.12776/qip.v21i1.784.

Singh, M., Srivastava, R., Fuenmayor, E., Kuts, V., Qiao, Y., Murray, N., & Devine, D. (2022). Applications of digital twin across industries: A review. *Applied Sciences, 12*, 5727.

Song, X., Gu, H., Li, Y., & Ye, W. (2022). A systematic review of trust in sharing accommodation: progress and prospects from the multistakeholder perspective. *International Journal of Contemporary Hospitality Management*, 1–35. https://doi.org/10.1108/IJCHM-12-2021-1555.

The World Tourism Organization (UNWTO). (2021). *UNWTO Tourism Recovery Tracker*. Retrieved 25 April, 2023, from www.unwto.org/unwto-tourism-recovery-tracker.

The World Tourism Organization (UNWTO). (2022). *International Tourism Back to 60% of Pre-pandemic Levels in January-July 2022*. Retrieved 25 April, 2023, from www.unwto.org/taxonomy/term/347.

Throsby, D. (2001). *Economics and culture*. Cambridge University Press.

UNESCO. (2011). *Recommendation on the Historic Urban Landscape*. Retrieved from www.whc.unesco.org.

Valjarević, A., Vukoičić, D., & Valjarević, D. (2017). Evaluation of the tourist potential and natural attractivity of the Lukovska Spa. *Tourism Management Perspectives, 22*, 7–16.

Yang, F. X., & Wong, I. A. (2021). The social crisis aftermath: Tourist wellbeing during the COVID-19 outbreak. *Journal of Sustainable Tourism, 29*(6), 859–878. https://doi.org/10.1080/09669582.2020.1843047

Identifying Cultural Tourists via Computational Text Analysis and Association Rule Mining

Bart Neuts⊙

Abstract Cultural tourism has evolved into a mass market phenomenon that contributes a sizeable portion to international tourist arrivals in Europe. Yet, exact estimates of cultural tourists are hard to come by, due both to a lack of standardized conceptualization, and a difficulty in operationalization. Mostly, estimates are based on visitor surveys, which are expensive to conduct, infrequent, and often do not allow an in-depth analysis of the phenomenon. This paper proposes an alternative analytical methodology, scraping user-generated content and applying computational text analysis and association rule mining on visitor reviews in order to establish both centrality of cultural travel motives and improve understanding of cultural tourism typologies via analysing topical associations within the reviews. The methodology is tested on 2507 reviews for the historical centre of the city of Ghent, Belgium. The results show estimates that are comparable in size to visitor survey statistics, while lending additional information on relative importance of cultural travel motivations.

Keywords Cultural tourism · Typologies · Computational text analysis · Association rule mining · User-generated content

1 Introduction

According to a frequently reported statistic, 40% of all European tourists are considered culturally motivated (United Nations World Tourism Organization, 2018). This proportion is based on a survey of UNWTO Member States, where each nation estimated the market size for cultural tourism. However, it should be noted that different nations employed various estimation techniques; 32% of the surveyed countries based their estimate on information about cultural participation, 30% on information about cultural motivations, 15% on both, and another 25% on various other metrics.

Not only is measurement of the phenomenon difficult and non-standardized, the definition of what constitutes a cultural tourist is in itself not clarified. Richards (2018)

B. Neuts (✉)
KU Leuven, Celestijnenlaan 200E, 3001 Heverlee, Belgium
e-mail: bart.neuts@kuleuven.be

© The Author(s) 2025
B. Neuts et al. (eds.), *Advances in Cultural Tourism Research*, Advances in Digital and Cultural Tourism Management, https://doi.org/10.1007/978-3-031-65537-1_12

mentions how cultural tourism has only become an academically established field of study, and being recognized as an emerging niche form of international tourism, since the 1980s. In the past 40 years, coinciding with the exponential growth in arrivals, cultural tourism has rapidly gained mass market appeal, in itself being fragmented into niche activities and motivations, often distinguished by (i) the types of landscape in which the activity is performed (e.g., natural, rural, cultural, urban/built), (ii) the main motivation (e.g., ecotourism, heritage tourism, urban tourism), and/or (iii) the main attraction(s) being visited (including both tangible and intangible elements). Hughes (2000), therefore, rightly concludes that cultural tourism is now often used as an umbrella term that covers a variety of activities, motivation, and types of cultural resource the visitor connects with. This can lead to an erosion of the concept, with nearly every visitor adhering to at least part of the cultural tourism phenomenon.

Therefore, some studies and definitions consider relative centrality and strength of culture and heritage as a travel motive to be an important antecedent for characterizing tourists, typically classifying about 11% (Association for Tourism & Leisure Education & Research, 2021) to 15% (Lord, 1999) as primarily or strongly motivated cultural tourists. Matteucci and Von Zumbusch (2020) state that due to the cultural tourism market fragmentation, besides considering degree of engagement, it might be more relevant to study visitor experiences and the meanings ascribed to cultural tourism activities. McKercher et al. (2002) specifically propose such behavioural segmentation, based on identifying homogenous visitor segments through on-site activity analysis. Gnoth and Matteucci (2014) provide contemporary experiential goals that are comparable to Cohen's (1979) earlier works, namely: experience as pure pleasure, as rediscovery, as existentially authentic exploration, and as knowledge seeking. All of these visitor types might be, to some extent, cultural tourists, but their prior expectations, on-site behaviour, engagement with local products and activities, and post-trip reflections will differ significantly. From a destination perspective, being able to frame cultural tourism through a more diverse and fragmented lens and acknowledging the various behavioural and experiential visitor types is important in order to ensure proper supply–demand links.

We can therefore conclude that (i) while the number of cultural tourists in total international arrivals is no doubt significant, it is challenging to acquire more or less accurate estimates, and (ii) beyond market size estimates, destinations need to be advised on behavioural and experiential typologies within the general label of cultural tourism. The most common practices for acquiring such information are either structural visitor data (e.g., in the form of entrance tickets sold at cultural venues), visitor surveys, qualitative interview methods, or, less frequently, other digital alternatives. While the first of these types of data—structural official data—can be reliable and consistent, it is only capable of capturing site-specific visits and does not allow to study visitation patterns between different attractions in a region, nor does it allow understanding of underlying visitor motivations. The method therefore fails to identify behavioural and experiential typologies. Visitor surveys are more flexible and have the potential to incorporate estimates of the market share of cultural tourism, as well as extent of motivation, different attractions being visited within a single trip, underlying behavioural and experiential typologies, and satisfaction.

However, such visitor surveys are costly and therefore only undertaken infrequently in a limited number of well-visited destinations, thus not allowing for a continuous evaluation. Qualitative studies adopting more in-depth interview methods, direct observations or visitor diaries, equally allow for more in-depth analysis of visitor motivations within cultural tourism destinations, but—apart from suffering from the same prohibitive costs associated with such fieldwork—fail in quantification efforts. Finally, some more contemporary studies have experimented with digital tracking technologies and visitor-employed photography. While such studies can potentially provide rich data in terms of visitor flows and the tourist gaze, it can be challenging to uncover behavioural and experiential typologies. While many advances have been made in the use of positioning data via a variety of methodologies (e.g., mobile apps, GPS trackers, RFID tags, mobile phone data, Wi-Fi or Bluetooth sensors, infrared or heat sensors, object recognition), they typically either require relatively large investments, are mostly limited to measuring quantities, and/or could lead to ethical concerns (Galí-Espelt, 2012).

In this paper, we therefore experiment with analysing user-generated content as an alternative. By adopting a methodology that focuses on linguistic data, we hope to be able to better understand travel motivations, cultural propensity to travel, and general market size. Via a combination of web scraping of open access user content, computational text analysis, and association rule mining, we aim to generate a better understanding of the various visitor typologies, while proposing a method that is economically affordable, effective, and sustainable (in terms of continuity) by using openly accessible data and open source software. The methodology is tested on user reviews of the historical city of Ghent (Belgium).

2 Methodology

2.1 Case Study Overview: Ghent

Ghent is the third largest city in Belgium and has a long and rich history, being one of the largest and richest cities of Northern Europe in the late Middle Ages. Many significant buildings of this period remain intact to this day and are well-preserved and renovated. The city has three beguinages and a belfry that are part of the UNESCO World Heritage Sites recognitions. Other significant cultural heritage attractions are the twelfth-century Gravensteen castle, the Graslei (old medieval harbour), and the Saint Bavo Cathedral, holding the famous fifteenth-century Ghent Altarpiece of the brothers Van Eyck: the Adoration of the Mystic Lamb. Similar to Bruges, the city is also characterised by the picturesque waterways crossing the inner city, starting with the Scheldt River.

The city is marketed as one of the five Flemish art cities, along with Bruges, Antwerp, Mechelen, and Leuven. In 2019 the city received 689,019 tourist arrivals (of which 65.1% were foreigners), for 869,901 overnight stays, and an average trip duration of 1.26 nights for overnight tourists and 7.47 h for day visitors. It was the third most visited destination in Flanders, behind Bruges and Antwerp. The type of international leisure visitors attracted to Flanders can be considered of slightly more affluent backgrounds due to the general cost of living—similar to other Western European countries—leading to a relatively low ranking of Belgium on price competitiveness in the Travel & Tourism Report of the World Economic Forum (2023). At rank 117 in 2019, Belgium was comparable in this sense to Japan, the United States, Austria, New Zealand, Finland, Germany, and the Netherlands. Visitor surveys conducted in 2018 as part of the Flemish art cities research, give insight into important visitor characteristics. On average, overnight leisure tourists were 43 years of age, with the largest contingent (38%) being between 18 and 34 years old. Only 12% of surveyed visitors were above 65. The majority of tourists were highly educated with tertiary degrees (65%). A small minority (6%) visited Ghent as part of a package tour. The survey further collected information on visitor motives, with the local heritage being a main motive for 33% of tourists in Ghent. 22% mentioned the city's rich history, while 9% mentioned its artists, museums and art-related attractions, 3% mentioned other cultural attractions, and 7% mentioned cultural events. Since visitors could choose up to three main motivations, there will likely be an overlap in these categories though. Apart from pre-trip motivations, tourists were also asked about their on-site activities while in the city. In Ghent, 55% of tourists had visited monuments, churches and/or museums, 22% followed guided tours or boat rides along the canals, and 7% participated in events or concerts (Vlaanderen, 2018).

2.2 Data Collection, Data Characteristics, and Analytical Procedures

Data were collected for the period 2012–2019, allowing for a modest longitudinal approach and avoiding the break in data due to the COVID-19 pandemic and subsequent lockdowns of 2020 and 2021. The study is based on secondary, user-generated online data, which has the advantage of being readily available, cheap and available across time periods, unlike survey data which is often expensive to collect, time-consuming and typically only represents a specific moment in time. On the other hand, the collected sample can exhibit patterns of self-selection bias, which cannot be managed to the same extent as in primary research. This is particularly true in terms of language groups, age groups, educational levels, and potentially spending patterns (Presi et al., 2014; Xiang et al., 2017).

Online user-generated data were scraped from the Tripadvisor webpage on Ghent City Centre (https://www.tripadvisor.com/Attraction_Review-g188666-d4185801-Reviews-Ghent_City_Center-Ghent_East_Flanders_Province.html) on 7 December

2019. A total of 2507 English-speaking reviews were scraped, using the RSelenium[1] and rvest[2] packages and retrieving the dynamic contents of the webpage via Document Object Model parsing.

Of the total sample, 13.4% of reviews were from the 2012–2014 period (6 in 2012, 79 in 2013, 251 in 2015), 60.3% from the 2015–2017 period (521 in 2015, 549 in 2016, 442 in 2017), 25.5% from the 2018–2019 period (386 in 2018, 252 in 2019) and the remaining 0.8% (21) had an unknown date. Only 435 reviews listed data on their travel company, with the majority of those (46.2%) travelling as a coupe, followed by travelling with friends (21.1%), family (16.6%) and solo (9.2%). Travelling for business purposes was less common in the collected sample (6.9%). Out of the 2507 reviews, the vast amount were positive with 5-star (76.4%) and 4-star reviews (20.3%) encompassing the near-complete sample. Only 3.3% of reviews were more negative (2.5% of 3-star, 0.6% of 2-star, and 0.2% of 1-star reviews).

In order to identify visitor origin, R countrycode (Arel-Bundock et al., 2018) was used in order to clean the non-formatted structure of the Tripadvisor location variable. This led to a limited data loss due to faults in user-generated strings and allowed for the nationality identification of 2022 reviews. Unsurprisingly, given the linguistic choices made during the scraping process, Great Britain (33.1%) and the United States (15.7%) dominated the reviews, followed by Belgium (11.7%), the Netherlands (4.9%), Australia (3.7%), Canada (2.7%) and India (2.2%). These countries accounted for nearly three quarters of the total. It needs to be acknowledged that significant differences exist between our sample and the population of international tourists in Ghent.

The computational text analysis we follow is based on the creation of a dictionary object, followed by an automated frequency analysis, rather than a fully unsupervised machine learning approach such as Latent Dirichlet Allocation (see e.g., (2021)). This entails an a priori selection of dictionary elements. To this extent, a random sample of 150 reviews was drawn—50 from the period 2012 to 2015, 50 from the period 2016 to 2017, and 50 from 2018 to 2019. This sample formed the basis for a traditional qualitative thematic analysis, following the recommended steps of Braun and Clarke (2006), namely: data familiarization, outlining of initial codes, identification of final codes, definition of tentative themes, finalization of themes, and identification of categories. The computational text analysis focused on frequencies in a bag-of-words text analysis, preparing the scraped data as suggested by Welbers et al. (2017) in terms of basic string operations such as tag, whitespace, punctuation and stopword removal, and lowercase transformation. Normalization stemming was also adopted to convert inflected forms into base forms. The resulting document-term matrix (DTM) was analysed via the quanteda-package in R (Benoit et al., 2018), based on a constructed dictionary that followed from the qualitative thematic analysis.

---

[1] The RSelenium package allows for web browser automation to mimic the behaviour of native users. More information can be found at https://cran.r-project.org/web/packages/RSelenium/.

[2] The rvest package helps to harvest web pages and download and manipulate HTML and XML. More information can be found at https://cran.r-project.org/web/packages/rvest/.

Next, association rule mining via the R package arules (Hahsler & Grün, 2005) was used as a data mining technique to help discover relationships between word categories. The procedure aims to observe patterns, correlations, or associations between non-numeric data, rather than focusing on a single-item analysis. Association rules are commonly used in market basket analysis in order to identify items that are commonly bought together. The dependency between objects is based on an antecedent and a consequent—i.e., the items more commonly consumed together with the items in the antecedent. There are three main metrics that support association rule mining: lift, support, and confidence. Support is the probability that a particular combination of items is present in the transaction database and can simply be calculated as the count of each itemset, divided by the total number of transactions. For example, if the total sample consists of 5 tourists and 4 out of 5 tourists visited Gravensteen, then the support count for Gravensteen would be 0.8 (=4/5). If 2 out of 5 tourists visited both Gravensteen and the Saint Bavo Cathedral, then the support for this itemset would be 0.4 (=2/5). So clearly individual items will always have more support than multi-item item sets. In order to simplify the analysis, commonly a minimum support standard is defined, excluding all item sets that do not reach this minimum probability (Benoit et al., 2018).

As a second metric, Confidence is defined on the level of an association rule and, given the example of an association rule $\alpha \rightarrow \beta$ is calculated as: $P(\alpha,\beta) / P(\alpha)$. Reusing the previous example, if the antecedent is visiting Gravensteen (Support = 0.8), and the consequent is visiting Saint Bavo Cathedral, then the union of item sets in antecedent and consequent is {Gravensteen, Saint Bavo Cathedral}, with a support of 0.4. The confidence of the association rule between Gravensteen and Saint Bavo Cathedral is then equal to 0.4/0.8 = 0.5. Finally, the lift metric defines the strength of an association rule and is calculated as the ratio of the observed support versus expected support under the hypothesis that antecedent and consequent item sets are independent. Given an association rule $\alpha \rightarrow \beta$, this can be written as: $P(\alpha,\beta) / [P(\alpha)P(\beta)]$. Continuing the previous example, if support for Saint Bavo Cathedral would be 0.6, the lift for the association rule Gravensteen $\rightarrow$ Saint Bavo Cathedral would then be 0.4 / (0.8 * 0.6) = 0.83. The lift metric has some interesting analytical characteristics. If an association rule has a lift less than one, antecedent and consequent items could be considered substitutes, with increase in frequency of the one, leading to a decrease in frequency of the other. If the lift is greater than one, items are considered dependent on each other, while a lift of exactly one would mean that both items are independent (Goh & Ang, 2007).

3 Results and Discussion

The qualitative thematic analysis of the random sample of 150 reviews identified relevant codes from frequent words and sentences, related to visitor experience to the historic city centre of Ghent. The analysis revealed a number of relevant categories—each with a unique set of keywords. The vast majority of analysed reviews included multiple categories across themes, for example:

> Ghent is a beautiful small city, with magnificent old buildings. Linger at the 'Graslei', etc.… watch the magnificent old monuments of the former glorious city. Visit the Castle of the Counts, etc.…When you have done walking around, take a boattrip. It takes around 45 min. They show you all the important sites to see, and at the main time they tell you about the history of the city. Ghent has also many shops. So, when you are done sightseeing… go shopping in one of the many stores Ghent has. (R2018).

This review was coded as including aspects of 'History', 'General architecture', 'Landmarks: castle', 'River/Canals', 'Shopping', contributing dictionary elements to these categories. While many reviews are relative complex and extensive, there are also simple examples with limited information being represented, for instance, the following review was only assigned one category, 'General atmosphere':

> This place is so small and beautiful. I mean i felt as if i were in a fairy tale movie. This is a must stop. You won't need more than two days but it is totally worth it. (R1347).

From the 150 reviews, four main themes were distilled: (i) Culture: combining reviews that highlight the historical nature of the city, its general and specific historical landmarks, and the (art) museums, (ii) Atmosphere/sightseeing: relaying a more general sense of aesthetics of the city, as well as relating to review elements on the walkability (as a sightseeing activity), and the rivers, canals, boat cruises and carriage rides, (iii) Tourism services: including codes on restaurants, bars, general food and drinks, shopping, festivals and events, accommodations, tourist information offices, price-related opinions, transportation options within and to/from Ghent, and the sense of touristification—or lack thereof—in the visitor economy, and (iv) Social dimension: covering review elements on the local population, as well as perceptions of crowdedness of the city centre. Table 1 provides an overview of all categories within each theme and the associated dictionary elements that were identified and will serve the computational text analysis of the complete database.

In order to apply the codes identified via the qualitative analysis on the complete dataset of 2507 reviews, dictionary elements within the same categories were binarized, meaning that if a review included multiple codes within a specific category (e.g., 'restaurant', 'food', 'bar'), the category would only be counted once per review. This ensured that each category had a maximum score of 100%. As can be seen from Fig. 1, the five most mentioned categories were 'General atmosphere' (59.6% of reviews), 'Walkability' (39.7%), 'Food & drinks' (37.9%), 'History' (37.1%), and 'River/Canals' (36.8%). Notably, while the thematic cultural categories are important, there is a marked difference between the number of reviews mentioning more general sentiments of beauty, atmosphere and the historical nature of the city, and

Table 1 Themes, categories, and associated dictionary items

Themes and categories	Dictionary elements
Theme 1. Culture	
History	history*, old, medieval, centur*, authentic, untouched, heritage, preserve*
General architecture	building*, michael*, michiel*, picturesque, architecture, facade*, park*, scenery, cobblestone*, surrounding, gothic, roman*, graslei, patershol, korenlei, monuments, square, harbo*
Landmarks: cathedrals	cathedral*, church*, monestar*, nicholas, niklaas*, bavo, baaf*
Landmarks: castle	gravensteen, castle*, fortress
Landmarks: other	belfry, belfort, tower, stadhuis, lakenhalle, slaughterhouse, post, guild, cloth
Museums/art	musea, museum*, painting*, alter, lamb, eyck
Theme 2. Atmosphere/sightseeing	
General atmosphere	beaut*, atmospher*, fairy*, quaint, impressive, vibe*, vibrant, photo*, appeal*, lively, charm*, cozy, cosy, gorgeous, ambiance, scenic, love*, relaxed, alive
Walkability	walk*, stroll*, foot, wander*, compact, footpath*, car free, pedestrian, auto free, closed to traffic
River/canals	boat*, canal*, cruise*, waterway*, river*, water
Carriages	carriage*, horse*
Theme 3. Tourism services	
Food & drinks	terrace*, eat, restaurant*, food, drink*, bar, bars, waffle*, chocolate*, eateries, café*, cafe*, beer*, wine, fries, bite, pancake*, cake*, cuisine, pub, pubs, noses, brewery
Shopping	shop*, galleries, store*, vintage, antique*
Festivals/events	christmas, xmas, festival, theater, music, comedy, festivities, feesten
Hospitality industry	staff, hotel, hostel, tourist office
Price	pricey, overpriced, cheap, expensive
Connectivity/accessibility	accessible, connected, train, bus, tram, motorway, public transport
Touristification	authentic, inauthentic, tourist trap, overrun
Theme 4. Social dimension	
Locals	kind, divers*, friendly, welcoming, helpful, smiling
Crowding	crowd*, uncrowded, overcrowd*, calm, queues, busy, busier, masses, quiet, packed, laid back, lots of tourists, tourist trail

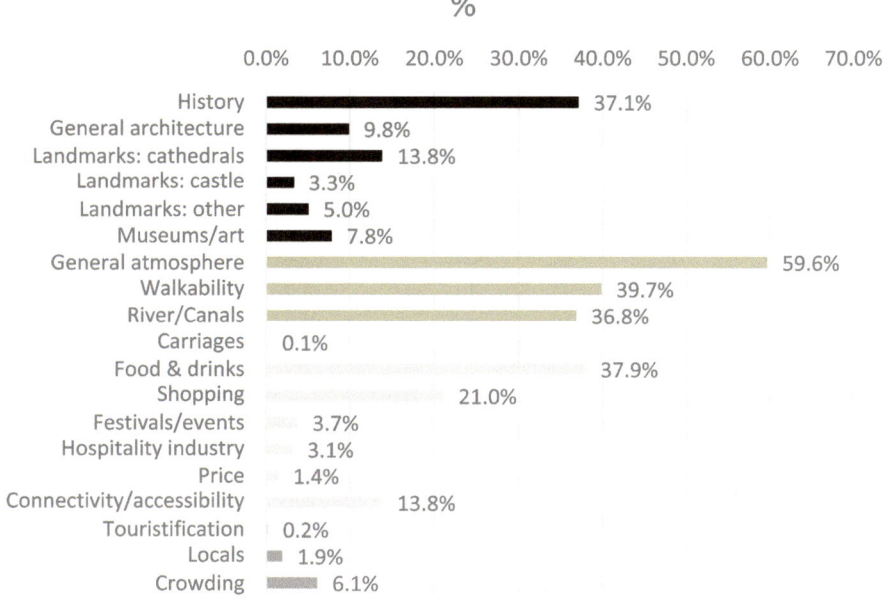

Fig. 1 Frequencies of categories within n = 2507 reviews

reviews mentioning more specific cultural heritage attractions such as Saint Bavo's Cathedral, Van Eyck's Adoration of the Mystic Lamb, or the Gravensteen castle. These data might be a first indication of the categorization of tourists as purposeful, sightseeing, serendipitous, and incidental cultural tourists (McKercher, 2002). At first glance, it would seem that a majority of tourists in Ghent fall in the category of sightseeing or serendipitous cultural tourists, with a smaller group being more strongly culturally motivated.

However, at this point in the analysis, the categories are still treated independently of each other while there is likely to be overlap in reviewers who mentioned both individual cultural landmarks, general atmosphere, general history, etc. Similarly, from the above figure we could not conclude that the 37.9% of reviews mentioning 'Food & drinks' are not culturally motivated. In order to further develop the conclusions, we therefore need to look at combinations of categories, which will help in identifying significant tourism segments based on user-generated text. Through association rule mining we can move beyond identifying relevance of single codes and identify relevance of itemgroups. We set a minimum support metric of 0.05; meaning that item sets should at least have a 5% likelihood of appearing, and a minimum confidence level of 0.5, meaning that given a particular antecedent, the consequent has a likelihood of 50%. This results in the creation of 39 rules via an apriori algorithm which are included in Table 2.

Table 2 Item association rules

Rule	Antecedent	Consequent	Support	Confidence	Lift	Count
1	Waterways, shopping	Food and drink	0.052	0.621	1.640	131
2*	landmarks.cathedral, atmosphere	Waterways	0.052	0.583	1.585	130
3	Atmosphere, connectivity	Walkability	0.053	0.624	1.572	133
4	Walkability, shopping	Food and drink	0.054	0.584	1.542	136
5	Atmosphere, shopping	Food and drink	0.077	0.578	1.527	193
6	Connectivity	Walkability	0.081	0.586	1.474	202
7*	History, atmosphere, walkability	Waterways	0.058	0.541	1.471	145
8	Atmosphere, walkability, food and drink	Waterways	0.053	0.538	1.463	134
9*	Landmarks.cathedral	Waterways	0.073	0.528	1.434	182
10	Shopping	Food and drink	0.113	0.540	1.426	284
11*	Landmarks.cathedral	History	0.071	0.519	1.400	179
12	Walkability, food and drink	Waterways	0.082	0.511	1.390	205
13*	History, atmosphere, waterways	Walkability	0.058	0.549	1.382	145
14*	History, walkability	Waterways	0.083	0.504	1.369	208
15*	Atmosphere, walkability, waterways	History	0.058	0.507	1.368	145
16*	History, waterways	Walkability	0.083	0.515	1.296	208

(continued)

Table 2 (continued)

Rule	Antecedent	Consequent	Support	Confidence	Lift	Count
17	Atmosphere, waterways, food and drink	Walkability	0.053	0.511	1.287	134
18*	Landmarks.cathedral, waterways	Atmosphere	0.052	0.714	1.199	130
19	Waterways, shopping	Atmosphere	0.059	0.706	1.185	149
20*	History, walkability, waterways	Atmosphere	0.058	0.697	1.170	145
21*	History, shopping	Atmosphere	0.057	0.691	1.159	143
22	Food and drink, shopping	Atmosphere	0.077	0.680	1.140	193
23	Walkability, connectivity	Atmosphere	0.053	0.658	1.105	133
24	Walkability, waterways, food and drink	Atmosphere	0.053	0.654	1.097	134
25*	History, waterways	Atmosphere	0.105	0.653	1.097	264
26	Walkability, shopping	Atmosphere	0.061	0.652	1.095	152
27	Walkability, waterways	Atmosphere	0.114	0.651	1.093	286
28*	Gen.architecture	Atmosphere	0.064	0.650	1.091	160
29*	History, walkability	Atmosphere	0.107	0.649	1.089	268
30	Waterways	Atmosphere	0.238	0.646	1.085	596
31*	Landmarks.cathedral	Atmosphere	0.089	0.646	1.085	223
32	Shopping	Atmosphere	0.133	0.635	1.066	334
33	Waterways, food and drink	Atmosphere	0.105	0.633	1.062	262
34*	History	Atmosphere	0.231	0.623	1.046	579
35	Walkability, food and drink	Atmosphere	0.099	0.621	1.042	249
36	Connectivity	Atmosphere	0.085	0.617	1.036	213
37*	History, food and drink	Atmosphere	0.091	0.617	1.035	227
38	Food and drink	Atmosphere	0.231	0.610	1.024	579
39	Walkability	Atmosphere	0.239	0.602	1.011	600

Of the 39 rules, 17 (identified in Table 2 by *) could be related to cultural tourism motivations. All lift statistics are above one, meaning that there is at least a positive association between the antecedents and consequences in these rules. The most common of these was rule 34, the combination of 'history' and 'atmosphere' elements in reviews, present in 579 out of 2507 reviews (=23.1%). Within this rule, a few more specific subsets in the antecedents can further be identified, namely rule 37 ('history' + 'food and drink', in 9.1% of reviews), rule 29 ('history' + 'walkability', in 10.7% of reviews), rule 25 ('history' + 'waterways', in 10.5% of reviews), rule 21 ('history' + 'shopping', in 5.7% of reviews), and rule 20 ('history' + 'walkability' + 'waterways', in 5.8% of reviews). So, while the combination between history and atmosphere in reviews does seem to suggest at least some cultural interest, the drilldown analysis explores how in many cases the specific reviews seem to include more hedonic interests (food and drinks, shopping). This part of the sample could therefore only be considered weakly culturally motivated.

A second set of rules takes 'landmarks.cathedral' as antecedent. Reviews focusing on the Ghent cathedrals are more likely to include reference to the 'waterways' (rule 9, 7.3% of reviews) or the 'history' (rule 11, 7.1% of reviews). Furthermore, rule 2 links 'landmarks.cathedral' and 'atmosphere' combined with 'waterways' (5.2% of reviews). Visitors to the Saint Bavo Cathedral and other churches/cathedrals thus seem less likely to also focus on the more commercial aspects of the tourist system. As such, they might be considered more strongly culturally motivated than the previous group.

Finally, rules 7, 13, 14, 15, 16 all combine 'history', 'atmosphere', 'walkability', and 'waterways' in one way or another, with support for these rules in the dataset ranging from 8.3% to 5.8%. These visitors might be more akin to the sightseeing cultural tourists in that they place importance on the atmosphere and general urban layout, without mentioning individual cultural attraction points in any depth.

Looking back at the results from the visitor surveys in Ghent, 33% of respondents had indicated to be motivated for their trip by the local heritage of the city. We can now compare these data to the results from the analysis of review data, both the single-item frequency analysis from Fig. 1, and the item association rules from Table 2. We could see from Fig. 1 that 37.1% of reviews mentioned 'history', thus being relatively comparable in magnitude to the traditional visitor survey. A further analysis of item associations revealed that in 23.1% of cases, 'history' was combined with elements of 'atmosphere'. However, in many cases, this itemset could be extended with codes from 'food and drink', 'shopping', indicating that of the 23.1%, an important section was not just (or purely) culturally motivated but also had a strong hedonic incentive. While the analysis does not allow us to quantify these typological segments exactly, the analysis of item associations can therefore help in better framing the centrality of the cultural travel motive. The results indicate that while Ghent is an important destination for culturally motivated visitors, it is primarily the combination of attraction elements that entices visitation, with tourists rarely being singular in their motives. While important attractions such as the Saint Bavo Cathedral, with the famous altar piece of the van Eyck brothers, and Gravensteen castle are important attractions, they are framed within the wider experience of the historical city centre of Ghent. In this sense, many cultural tourists attracted to Ghent are reminiscent to 'flâneurs', which is likely the case for cultural tourists in European heritage cities in general. This underlines the importance of a strong and qualitative supportive tourist infrastructure around cultural sites.

A significant advantage provided in the use of web scraping of user reviews is the potential richness of the data that can be analysed, which allows for a more detailed categorization of tourist behaviour and experiences as opposed to more traditional questionnaires which are typically limited by predefined question scales and choices. While such depth of experiences can be uncovered via traditional research techniques in the form of interviews, in such cases the number of data points collected would typically be small. Our approach allows for combining the richness of open text—typical in qualitative studies—with the scale of analysis of quantitative studies, while providing such analysis in a cost-effective fashion.

4 Conclusion

Cultural tourism has evolved from a historic market niche to one of the main forms of tourism within the European continent. General estimates have been bandied around, ranging from 40% of total tourist arrivals to 11%, depending on whether or not only primary cultural motives are considered. Exact calculations are, however, difficult, given a lack of clear and generally accepted definition, the variation in cultural tourism typologies, and the challenge in assessing tourist motivations and on-site behaviour.

This paper put forward the use of user-generated content in the form of TripAdvisor reviews as a basis for better understanding quantity and typology of the cultural tourism market, using the city of Ghent, Belgium, for a proof of concept. Besides computational text analysis, which is useful for calculating single item frequencies across large datasets, the addition of association rule mining improves understanding on combinations of items. This allows for a deeper understanding of the tourist experience—at least as far as it has been reviewed by the visitor—across categories and helps to establish whether a visitor was uniquely interested in culture, if cultural attractions were likely combined in a visit and/or whether culture seemed to be more adjacent to another visitor motivation. The analysis on review data for Ghent revealed estimates more or less in line with existing visitor surveys, granting confidence to the proposed methodology. Furthermore, the association rules helped in identifying more diverse visitation patterns within a general motivation, allowing for a better segmentation along strongly and weakly motivated cultural tourists.

Acknowledgements This article is based on research done in the context of the SmartCulTour project that has received funding from the European Union's Horizon 2020 Research and Innovation Programme under grant agreement number 870708. The authors of the article are solely responsible for the information, denominations, and opinions contained in it, which do not necessarily express the point of view of all the project partners and do not commit them.

References

Arel-Bundock, V., Enevoldsen, N., & Yetman, C. J. (2018). Countrycode: An R package to convert country names and country codes. *J Open Source Softw, 3*(28), 848.

Association for Tourism and Leisure Education and Research. Retrieved 10 August, 2021, from http://www.atlas-euro.org/sig_cultural.aspx.

Benoit, K., Watanabe, K., Wang, H., Nulty, P., Obeng, A., Müller, S., & Matsuo, A. (2018). Quanteda: An R package for the quantitative analysis of textual data. *J Open Source Softw, 3*(30), 774.

Braun, V., & Clarke, V. (2006). Using thematic analysis in psychology. *J Qual Res Psycjol, 3*(2), 77–101.

Cohen, E. (1979). A phenomenology of tourist experiences. *J Brit Sociol Assoc, 13*(2), 179–201.

Galí-Espelt, N. (2012). Identifying cultural tourism: A theoretical methodological proposal. *Journal of Heritage Tourism, 7*(1), 45–58.

Gnoth, J., & Matteucci, X. (2014). A phenomenological view of the behavioral tourism research literature. *Int J Cult, Tour Hosp Res, 8*(1), 3–21.

Goh, D. H., & Ang, R. P. (2007). An introduction to association rule mining: An application in counselling and help-seeking behavior of adolescents. *Behavior Research Methods, 39*(2), 259–266.

Hahsler, M., & Grün, B. (2005). Arules – a computational environment for mining association rules and frequent item sets. *J Stat Soft, 14*(15), 1–25.

Hughes, H. (2000). *Arts, entertainment and tourism.* Butterworth-Heinemann.

Lord, G. D. (1999). The power of cultural tourism. Keynote presentation at the Wisconsin Heritage Tourism Conference, Lac du Flambeau, Wisconsin, US.

Matteucci, X., & Von Zumbusch, J. (2020). Theoretical framework for cultural tourism in urban and regional destination. Deliverable D2.1 of the Horizon 2020 Project SmartCulTour (GA Number 870708).

McKercher, B. (2002). Towards a classification of cultural tourists. *International Journal of Tourism Research, 4*, 29–38.

McKercher, B., Ho, P. S., Cros, H. D., & Chow, B. (2002). Activities based segmentation of the cultural tourism market. *Journal of Travel & Tourism Marketing, 12*(1), 23–46.

Neuts, B. (2021). Revisiting bruges: Investigating the importance of tourist crowding perception in the visitor experience through computational text analysis. In: Suzuki, S., Patuelli, R. (eds.) A broad view of regional science. Essays in honor of Peter Nijkamp, pp. 235–258. Springer, Singapore.

Presi, C., Saridakis, C., & Hartmans, S. (2014). User-generated content behaviour of the dissatisfied service customer. *Eur J Marketing, 48*(9/10), 1600–1625.

Richards, G. (2018). Cultural tourism: A review of recent research and trends. *J Hosp Tour Manage, 36*, 12–21.

United Nations World Tourism Organization. (2018). *Tourism and culture synergies.* UNWTO.

Welbers, K., Van Atteveldt, W., & Benoit, K. (2017). Text analysis in R. *Communication Methods and Measures, 11*(4), 245–265.

World Economic Forum. Retrieved 14 June, 2023, from https://www3.weforum.org/docs/WEF_TTCR_2019.pdf.

Vlaanderen, T. (2018). *Kunststedenonderzoek 2018.* Toerisme Vlaanderen.

Xiang, Z., Du, Q., Ma, Y., & Fan, W. (2017). A comparative analysis of major online review platforms: Implications for social media analytics in hospitality and tourism. *Tourism Manage, 58*, 51–65.

SPOT-IT: An Advanced Tool for Dynamic Cultural Tourism Management and Regional Development

Anat Tchetchik, Shilo Shiff, Yaron Michael, Michael Sinclair,
Irit Cohen-Amit, Irit Shmuel, and Micheal Sofer

Abstract Global changes and trends have been greatly influencing the way cultural tourism is defined, operated, and developed. These changes require the creation of new measurement and management tools. Given the diverse nature of cultural tourism, one of the most pertaining obstacles hindering its sustainable development is that the required relevant information for effective decision-making and management is currently not well complied with, organized, and processed. SPOT-IT, which was developed under SPOT, an EU-Horizon2020-funded project, rises to this challenge by offering a new approach to cultural tourism that reflects the tourism patterns of the twenty-first century. It is a decision-supporting platform for the development of cultural tourism sites within a Web-based Resource Centre. This paper describes the purposes of the tool, its conceptualization, its components, and its importance. It concludes with some policy implications.

Keywords Cultural tourism · Tourism development · Web platform · ArcGIS · Decision making

1 Introduction

Before the twenty-first century, the focus of Cultural Tourism (cultural tourism) was limited mostly to cultural values, conservation, and the economic potential of property or landscape. Given global trends and changes, today's cultural tourism is both influenced and at the same time influences, physical changes such as climate change; social and economic changes, including cultural differences and diversity; global

A. Tchetchik (✉) · S. Shiff · Y. Michael · I. Cohen-Amit
Bar-Ilan University, Tel Aviv, Israel
e-mail: anat.tchetchik@biu.ac.Il

M. Sinclair · M. Sofer
The University of Glasgow, Glasgow, Scotland

I. Shmuel
Hadassah Academic College, Jerusalem, Israel

© The Author(s) 2025   203
B. Neuts et al. (eds.), *Advances in Cultural Tourism Research*, Advances in Digital and
Cultural Tourism Management, https://doi.org/10.1007/978-3-031-65537-1_13

crisis (e.g., Covid19), migration, and opportunities for quick and easy movement from place to place; cross-border communication; and globally accessible information. These changes have also had a great impact on the way cultural heritage tourism is defined, its characteristics, and its development (Lexhagen et al., 2022; Richards, 2018). In that vein, the traditional definitions of cultural tourism are becoming obsolete as they fail to capture the multidimensional and dynamic nature of contemporary cultural tourism (Richards, 2021) Rather, they focus on visits to cultural heritage sites, such as museums, historical monuments, and archaeological sites while neglecting the broader spectrum of cultural experiences that tourists seek, such as local festivals, culinary traditions, indigenous communities, and contemporary cultural practices. As a result, new and updated definitions have emerged to reflect the evolving landscape of cultural tourism and its broader impacts (Richards, 2018).

Old definitions also neglected the importance of sustainable practices. It appears that while there is a growing demand for cultural tourism, there is a growing concern about surpassing the carrying capacity and therefore harming cultural heritage sites and cultural landscapes (Kitchen & Marsden, 2009). Social, ethical, and environmental issues became essential (Vučetić, 2018), and sometimes even more important than economic issues, which characterized the tourism industry so far (Macdonald & King, 2018).

The changes that have taken place in the definition and characterization of cultural tourism require the creation of new measurement and management tools that can tackle the numerous issues and considerations that need to be taken into account when planning, marketing, and managing cultural tourism sites, their components, and the relationships between them. However, one of the most pertaining obstacles hindering the shift towards effective development and management of CT is that the required relevant information is currently not well complied with, organized, presented, and processed in a manner that allows for effective decision-making for the development of cultural tourism sites and infrastructure.

The underlying goal of this paper is to address the emerging complexity and multidimensionality of cultural tourism that reflects the tourism and travel patterns of the twenty-first century (Lam et al., 2022). For this purpose, we offer a new approach to cultural tourism development, planning, and marketing. In particular, we aim to fill several research gaps in the research on cultural tourism development. First, there is a lack of systematically organized information required for cultural tourism development. Second, there is no decision-making support platform for the development of cultural tourism which provides a holistic view and integrates economic, social, and environmental considerations. Third, current tools are quite rigid and do not endow power and flexibility to their users (including the decision on which developing criteria are the most important). Fourth, most tools cannot benefit numerous stakeholders, they are either designed for central/regional authorities, or visitors (Aas et al., 2005). Accordingly, we offer a Social Platform on Cultural Tourism (SPOT-IT) which is the first inclusive web-based platform, designed to accommodate the needs of cultural tourism developers, planners, and visitors. The SPOT-IT tool is applied in several case study areas including rural and peri-urban areas.

The SPOT-IT tool is an innovative GIS-based decision-supporting platform for the development of cultural tourism sites and infrastructure within a Web-based Resource Centre. It was designed to help realize the current and future potential of cultural tourism. It provides extensive and diversified information (represented visually and geo-referenced) regarding the development of cultural tourism in a given area and it integrates several features based on machine learning methods and automatic procedures. In line with new definition and approaches for cultural tourism (Cros & McKercher, 2020) this platform integrates social considerations (e.g., it identifies potential social conflicts and empower local communities), environmental considerations (e.g., by pointing to vulnerable landscape and ecosystems), and economic considerations (e.g., by providing annual visitors prediction algorithm) in a unified framework, which was so far lacking in existing IT-tools. The tool is designed for various cultural tourism stakeholders, with a special focus on remote and peripheral areas that can benefit tourism as a mechanism for local and regional development (Salvatore et al., 2018). It was developed by a group of researchers and designers from Bar-Ilan University (Israel) and incorporates inputs from Israel and all 14 European teams that contributed with empirical data from their case studies and tested the tool with their local and regional stakeholders. The tool enables the capturing of multiple information layers relating to cultural tourism development and management (including environmental, economic, and social indicators) at a high-resolution level and accuracy while leveraging technological advancement in GIS and machine learning, and involving multiple stakeholders. The tool can help long-term planning that includes spatial elements, infrastructure, climate forecasts, zoning, and other considerations. It was developed as a pilot for a case study region in Israel. Below we describe the purposes of the tool, its conceptualization, its components, and its importance. We conclude with a description of the application of the tool in the Israel case study and a short summary.

2 The SPOT-IT Goals

The over-arching goal of the SPOT-IT innovative tool is to provide a decision-support mechanism for the development of CHT attractions/sites.

The sub-goals of the tool are:

1. To enable the sustainable development of CT which takes into account the interest of multiple stakeholders (i.e., entrepreneurs, officials in local authorities and supra-regional bodies, tourists, residents, ethnic and cultural minorities, etc.) (Esfehani & Albrecht, 2018).
2. To enable localities interested in developing cultural tourism to be able to systematically assess their tourism potential and identify gaps and barriers.
3. To help design strategies for establishing, promoting, and marketing new and existing attractions.

4. To enable sponsors, local authorities, and entrepreneurs to evaluate the development potential of a given cultural heritage asset.
5. To enable communities to be incorporated into the development of a chosen project.

3   SPOT-IT Concept and Design

The first step was to develop the concept of the innovative tool (SPOT-IT) as a multi-criteria decision-supporting mechanism by identifying its main objectives, the stakeholders it is expected to serve, data availability, and, finally, based on these inputs, to design the tool's concept, its components and how they will interact with each other.

The tool is an innovative GIS-based website that helps realize the current and future potential of cultural heritage tourism, and as such it provides a decision support mechanism for the development of cultural tourism sites and infrastructure. The tool was designed to provide extensive and diversified information (represented visually and geo-referenced) regarding the development of cultural tourism in a given area. The tool is designed to allow several sources of flexibility including the choice of data layers to be used.

Since effective decision-making regarding the development of any tourism market requires various information on multiple aspects that have a spatial and geographical context, at the heart of the tool are the multiple data layers, their integration, and their spatial representation. The tool delivers in one place, exhaustive and diversified social, economic, and environmental information (data layers, which are visually, and geo-references represented). By bridging multiple sources of information and knowledge in a single GIS-based platform, the tool was designed to contribute to a better decision-making process regarding new or existing CT initiatives, better destination management, and marketing and to promote integration and intra-regional joint planning.

3.1   The First Stage

The first stage was to decide which data layers and features to include in the tool. These data can be categorized into two types of input data:

(1) Primary data, i.e., data that was collected directly from main sources through interviews with experts, and officials. Local residents' knowledge and experience were collected via surveys.
(2) Secondary data, i.e., censuses, information collected by government departments and other official organizations, online consumer reviews, or data that was collected for other research purposes.

Based on the literature and experts' opinions, it was decided which data layers are relevant to the development of CT and can support initiatives for CT development and management. The selection of the layers can be modified and extended based on the users' needs and availability of information and data. The selected variables include:

1. Land use data—distinguishes between several land use categories including Residential; Services; Industrial; Transportation; Industrial and Commercial Complexes and Recreational. This layer enables the end-user to identify geographical locations (pixels) that can be suitable for cultural tourism development.

2. Distance from the nearest metropolitan area—distance surface map showing the distance from each pixel to the nearest metropolis. Due to the limited area of the Israeli case study, this layer has not been included in the Israeli version.

3. Transport accessibility—A map indicating locations of intercity bus routes and stations, train stations, and exits on the highway. (In the Israeli case study area there is only one highway and one railroad connecting the region to the country's center).

4. Cultural tourism sites in the region—distinguished by each site's theme. This layer can identify agglomeration or clusters of cultural sites, the potential for generating complementarities, and compatibilities.

5. Cultural tourism potential (cultural stock)—this refers to cultural points of interest which have not been developed, categorized by three levels of interest: 1. The local visitors; 2. The National/regional visitors; 3. the international visitors. This layer is based on CT experts' opinions.

3.2 The Second Stage

The second stage was designed so it was possible to integrate these data into one user-friendly platform to facilitate decision-making. Figure 1 illustrates this integration via a logical block scheme of the SPOT-IT tool.

1. Complementarity tourism infrastructure (hotels, restaurants, other touristic attractions)—in the case study area. This layer can help identify tourism 'hot spots' and highlight available facilities activities and visitor attractions in the area.

2. Potential social conflicts– mapping locations of potential conflicts including conflicts between new and old comers, ultra-orthodox and secular populations, socio-economic classes, or conflicts over the use of natural resources. These data were derived from stakeholder and expert opinions.

3. Environmental vulnerability—mapping locations in which vulnerable/fragile ecosystems, important habitats, endangered species, and ecological corridors exist. These data were retrieved from Israel's National Terrestrial Biodiversity Assessment Program and the Open Landscape Institute (OLI) of Israel. These

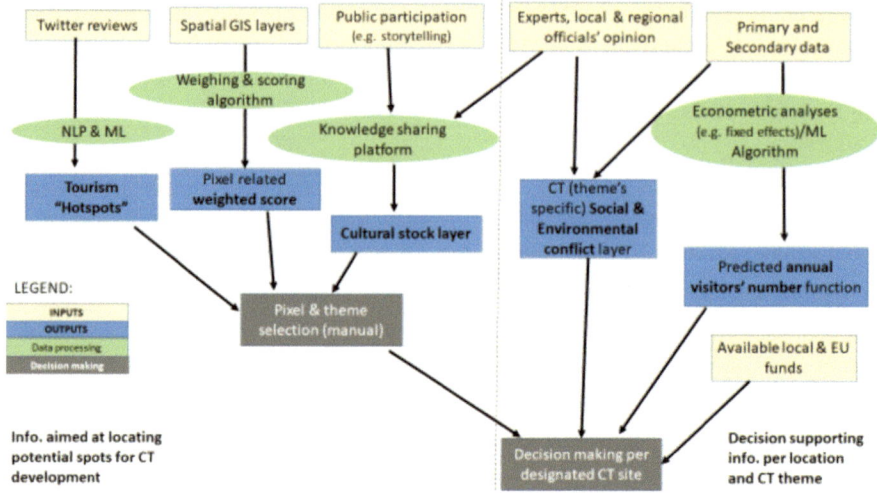

Fig. 1 Logical block scheme of the spot-it tool

layers reflect the environmental carrying capacity of the case study area indicating the ecological fragility and vulnerability in terms of wildlife, biodiversity, and landscape.

4. Microclimate conditions—several interrelated factors that characterize the local microclimate are Temperature, solar radiation, wind distribution, wind speed, and relative humidity. These conditions, jointly, are responsible for thermal comfort. A mapping of these conditions was done such that each pixel's thermal comfort was ranked compared to the optimal thermal comfort conditions in Israel (The data for this layer was received from the Israel Meteorological Services).

3.3 The Third Stage

In the third stage in addition to the multiple data layers, several features were designed to facilitate decision-making. These features include:

(3) Suitability analysis ("layer by layer" summation) component that allows the user to define the desired criteria for initiating, developing, and visiting cultural tourism sites, based on the location's peculiar attributes. In particular, layers were ranked on a scale (1–5 or 1–3) where the lowest level indicates the least favorable conditions for cultural tourism development and the highest level indicates the most favorable conditions. For example, for the micro-climate layer, a score of 1 is endowed to pixels with a 'very hot' categorization. This component allows the creation of a map where each pixel is characterized by a (layer-by-layer) summation of these scales. Pixels with the highest total score

are presumed to have favorable conditions across all combined layers and vice versa.

(4) Visitors' prediction algorithm that allows to receive an estimate of the economic performance of cultural tourism sites. In particular, the tool is equipped with an algorithm that returns the predicted number of annual visitors for a potential cultural tourism site at a chosen geographical point (pixel) in the case-study area. The function is based on the features of the chosen location (e.g., population density, distance from nature reserves within a certain radius) as well as characteristics of the designated tourism site as defined by the user. The annual number of visitors is a good proxy for a site's prospected revenue. The function that returns the expected annual visitors was estimated on Israeli market-based data collected in 2015 and 2018 of visitors' attractions in the rural space. The function was drawn from an adapted version of the rural attraction's equilibrium model (demand and pricing equations) developed by Hatan et al. (2021)

(5) User-Generated Content: two different layers based on online consumers' contributions were added to the tool. These layers were created by employing online reviews and images retrieved from social media and tourism websites in 2019 (before the outbreak of Covid-19, (Sinclair et al., 2020) Sinclair et al., 2020). Images were analyzed via a machine learning algorithm. Machine tags were attached to each of the images. Based on these results we performed sentiment analysis on the content to assign the photograph as positive/neutral/negative. The texts were analyzed via big data methods to create a landscape characterization layer. The sentiment analysis layer may help realize the general disposition towards a specific location. An interesting insight, for example, that was derived from the sentiment map, is the incongruence between the high ranking on Google and TripAdvisor reviews and the sometimes-unsatisfied sentiment on the image sentiments analyses as reflected in Fig. 2. While Gan-Guru Zoo and nearby Gan Ha'shlosha National Park have both high rankings on Google and TripAdvisor reviews (4.5 stars), Gan-Guru has many images with a negative attitude, whereas nearby Gan Ha'shlosha has almost only positive images.

(6) Community Collaboration app is a web\mobile app intended for the general public and the local community, in particular. It enables community members including minorities to propose potential cultural tourism sites or reflect on existing sites and actively participate in the process of cultural tourism development. The CT sites proposed by the community are automatically added to the decision-supporting tool's map. The intention is to contribute to CT 'from below' by recognizing place identity through the involvement and engagement of local communities, minorities, and organizations in protecting and presenting their own cultural heritage.

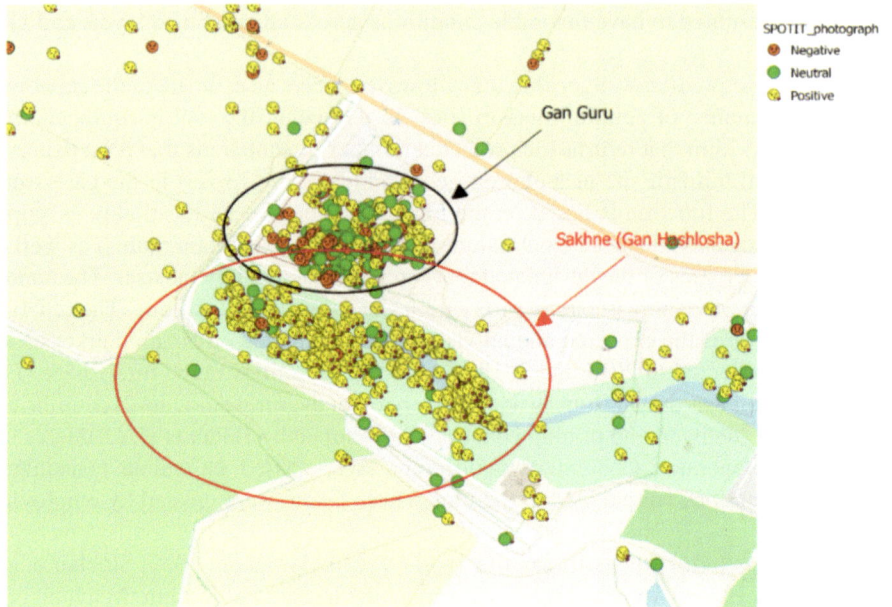

Fig. 2 An example of the sentiment analysis layer in Emek Ha'Maayanot

3.4 The Last Stage: Testing the Tool and Dissemination.

A prototype of the tool has been developed and tested on an ArcGIS Server that was deployed on the Microsoft Azure: Cloud Computing Services. In 2022, the beta version of SPOT-IT was designed and launched for testing by Consortium members and experts. This process was carried out as a feedback loop mechanism in which the teams provided continuous feedback, reported on problems and faults, suggested ways to improve the tool, and communicated their case study's specific needs and requirements. The last stage was fine-tuning and re-circulating the tool among the partners for final comments.

A dissemination process of the tool among the officials of the case study regional council and municipality was initiated with the intention that the tool will be employed to its full potential and will be updated regularly (see for details Sect. 4).

After the project ends, the responsibility for the operation of the tool, including its maintenance, and regular updates, should be granted to tourism officials at the regional level. Procedures for regular and ongoing updates of the tool should be established. Such updates include data regarding new tourism sites or facilities (or the closure of existing ones), public or private. Updates should also include data on new infrastructure (e.g., transportation), socio-demographic and economic data from the Central Bureau of Statistics, zoning updates from National, and regional planning authorities, climatic data from the Meteorological services, and so on. The entities responsible for the updates and maintenance of the tool should ensure that it is accessible to all stakeholders.

4　The Potential Benefits and Contribution of the SPOT-IT Tool

As mentioned earlier, SPOT-IT encourages a range of stakeholders to initiate CT activities from the personal/business level (micro) up to the regional and national levels (macro). The tool can be used at the supra-regional level (district, national, global) by developing new attractions and pulling tourist, human and economic capital to those less developed areas. The development momentum can potentially have impacts on a large scale, economically, socially, and image-wise. Its main beneficiaries include, among others, tourism entrepreneurs and sponsors, tourism officials, planning authorities, local and regional municipal authorities, and residents (including ethnic and cultural minorities). The tool can support the evaluation of developing cultural heritage sites by allowing preliminary examination of the area's carrying capacity, accessibility, landscape characteristics and availability of other complementary tourism services (Tieskens et al., 2018). The tool can help in marketing the area and the cultural tourism sites in it, by its ability to identify unique special propositions as well as clusters of compatible cultural assets, that may attract tourists to the region.

Potential local and international visitors can also benefit from SPOT-IT as an inclusive unified platform for trip planning, which includes the required information to optimize the experience. The tool enriches the visit experience; it encourages the pre-planning of thematic tours. For example, a visit to several heritage sites related to a certain historical event, or a visit following an adventure or plot described in a book. Updated information regarding opportunities for active travel (walking, cycling) can motivate visitors to visit the area thus reducing the negative impact of tourism whilst spreading the economic benefit. Future extensions and updated versions of the tool can include options for booking sites, communicating with site operators and other visitors, booking tickets for shows and festivals, leaving feedback, etc. Finally, the tool can benefit and inspire tourism scholars in universities and colleges.

4.1　Applying the SPOT-IT in the Israel Case-Study Area

For the Israeli case study area, we chose the Emek HaMayanot Valley which is part of the Jordan River Valley in the north of Israel (Fig. 3 illustrates the case study region). It consists of two municipalities: The town of Beit She'an and the regional council Emek Ha'Maayanot which comprises 24 rural settlements, most of which are kibbutz-type settlements (Amit-Cohen, 2012). The rationale for choosing Beit

She'an Valley as our case study is that (1) it is a peripheral region, far from the core of the country and the center of economic activities. The area, and in particular the town of Beit She'an, suffers from low socio-economic status and is in a dearth of economic development. (2) the region is a well-known global corridor for seasonal bird migration; therefore, it has a potential for cultural tourism development which should be responsible (Chan et al., 2006). (3) since the rural and the urban spaces developed apart, there is some degree of alienation between the rural and the urban municipalities (Sofer et al., 2021). These features all together turn the case study area into a suitable choice for the purposes and targets of the SPOT-IT.

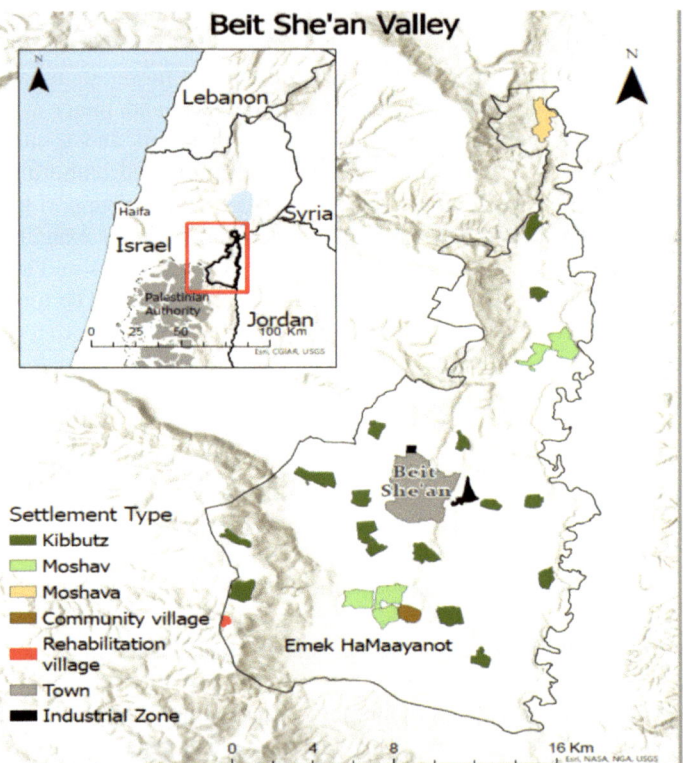

Fig. 3 A map of the Israeli case study region

4.2 Challenges of the Cultural Tourism in the Case Study Area

One of the most pertaining issues is the lack of consistently collected, tourism related data (e.g., visitors' attractions, complementary services, infrastructure, micro-climate, etc.). The lack of knowledge-based destination planning platform is reflected in the inability to design long-term tourism planning and marketing strategies. This is manifested in the sporadic nature of local initiatives which are usually not reaching maturity. In fact, most of the tourist attractions in the area are run by government bodies (e.g., the Israel National Parks and Natural Reserves) mostly managed by non-residents of the area. In addition, there is a lack of cooperation and trust between the regional council and the town. This is even though they offer complementary tourism sites (natural, water, and wildlife vs. cultural and historic sites). These complementarities can be used for the benefit of both municipalities. Finally, tourism in the case study area is mostly domestic tourism. In order to penetrate the international market, there is a need in massive tourism development which levers on cultural local assets and resources while meeting international tourism standards.

4.3 How the Tool Accommodates These Challenges

The tool offers a platform, currently not existing, that enables to plan and design of prosperous and sustainable cultural tourism, which integrates into the life of local landscapes and communities. The tool holds a holistic view of the area, which crosses the boundaries between the regional council and the town. It thus allows a spatial 'view from above' of the entire area and help identify deficiencies of facilities and infrastructure. In particular, each type of cultural tourism being developed has its infrastructure requirements. The tool can help in this process by providing visualized spatial information on the already existing infrastructure, as well as required ones.

It can promote collaboration between the regional council and the town by providing a common platform for tourism managers. This platform can be used for designing a balanced bundle of attractions and exploiting potential synergies and external economics. For example, given the temperature rise in the area, which is characterized by extremely hot summers, indoor activities need to be developed in new and existing sites. Since the regional council hosts numerous springs, indoor facilities and the development of 'night tourism' are critical in Beit She'an town. Via its potential social and environmental conflict layers, the tool can facilitate trust-building between the two municipalities and involve multiple stakeholders. Its public participation platform can accommodate feedback and recommendations related to the current local, and regional, development.

Finally, acknowledging the diverse range of experiences sought by modern cultural tourism travelers, so far overlooked by tourism designers, this platform integrates multiple layers of information that are required for a compatible and diversified tourism experience.

5 Summary

In this paper we have presented the SPOT-IT tool designed to accommodate contemporary cultural tourism planning needs. We have outlined the motivation for establishing the tool, the research gaps it addresses, its concepts, rationale and potential benefits. The tool levers on state-of-the-art knowledge in ArcGIS and machine learning methods as well as additional features which allow prediction and better-informed decision-making. The tool can promote structured idea exchange (thinking outside the box thinking) between people involved in the cultural tourism industries and local administrations. The tool was applied to 15 case studies of which 14 are located in European countries, and one is located in Israel. The paper addresses and emphasizes the suitability of the tool to the Israeli case study region, i.e., the Valley of Springs. While the tool was demonstrated on a regional case study, it is very well suited to accommodate different geographic scales, from the very local to the supra-regional. The relatively wide access to the tool may lead to cross-ministries, cross-municipalities, and cross-regional initiatives, for joint, synergetic, cultural tourism projects.

It should be noted however that while the conceptualization of the tool is universal, its specifications should be place dependent. Therefore, it is recommended to develop the tool for each location (e.g., city or regional councils and other urban and rural municipalities) based on its needs and specific characteristics.

Acknowledgements This project has received funding from the European Union's H2020 programme for research and innovation under grant agreement no. 870644.

References

Richards, G. (2018). Cultural tourism: A review of recent research and trends. *Journal of Hospitality and Tourism Management, 36*, 12–21.

Lexhagen, M., Ziakas, V., & Lundberg, C. (2022). Popular Culture Tourism: Conceptual Foundations and State of Play. *Journal of Travel Research*, 004728752211140903.

Richards, G. (2021). Rethinking cultural tourism. Edward Elgar Publishing.

Kitchen, L., & Marsden, T. (2009). Creating sustainable rural development through stimulating the Eco-economy: Beyond the Eco-economic paradox? *Sociologia Ruralis, 49*, 273–294.

Vučetić, A. Š. (2018). Importance of environmental indicators of sustainable development in the transitional selective tourism destination. *International Journal of Tourism Research, 20*(3), 317–325.

Macdonald, E., & King, E. G. (2018). Novel ecosystems: A bridging concept for the consilience of cultural landscape conservation and ecological restoration. *Landscape and Urban Planning, 177*, 148–159.

Lam, J. M., Makhbul, Z. K. M., Aziz, N. A., & Ahmat, M. A. H. (2022). Incorporating multidimensional images into cultural heritage destination: does it help to explain and analyse better?. Journal of Cultural Heritage Management and Sustainable Development.

Aas, C., Ladkin, A., & Fletcher, J. (2005). Stakeholder collaboration and heritage management. *Annals of Tourism Research, 32*(1), 28–48.

Du Cros, H., & McKercher, B. (2020). *Cultural tourism.* Routledge.

Salvatore, R., Chiodo, E., & Fantini, A. (2018). Tourism transition in peripheral rural areas: Theories, issues, and strategies. *Annals of Tourism Research, 68*, 41–51.

Esfehani, M. H., & Albrecht, J. N. (2018). Roles of intangible cultural heritage in tourism in natural protected areas. *Journal of Heritage Tourism, 13*(1), 15–29.

Hatan, S., Fleischer, A., & Tchetchik, A. (2021). Economic valuation of cultural ecosystem services: The case of landscape aesthetics in the agritourism market. *Ecological Economics, 184*, 107005. https://doi.org/10.1016/j.ecolecon.2021.107005

Sinclair, M., Mayer, M., Woltering, M., & Ghermandi, A. (2020). Using social media to estimate visitor provenance and patterns of recreation in Germany's national parks. *Journal of Environmental Management, 263*, 110418.

Tieskens, K. F., Van Zanten, B. T., Schulp, C. J., & Verburg, P. H. (2018). Aesthetic appreciation of the cultural landscape through social media: An analysis of revealed preference in the Dutch river landscape. *Landscape and Urban Planning, 177*, 128–137.

Amit-Cohen, I. (2012). Cultural tourism in the Kibbutz: Values, assets, and attitudes. *Horizons in Geography, 79–80*, 210–225.

Chan, J., To, H.-P., & Chan, E. (2006). Reconsidering social cohesion: Developing a definition and analytical framework for empirical research. *Social Indicators Research, 75*, 273–302.

Sofer, M., Cohen, N., Applebaum, L., Amit-Cohen, I., Shaul, Y, and Shmuel, I. (2021) Changing Urban-Rural Relations in Israel's Periphery, in Banski, J. (ed.) Routledge Handbook of Small Towns, Routledge. pp. 203–217. https://doi.org/10.4324/9781003094203

Redefining Cultural Tourism Leadership: Innovative Approach and Tool

João Martins⊙, Pedro Pereira⊙, Shabnam Pasandideh⊙,
Kashyap Raiyani⊙, Tarmo Kalvet⊙, Mikel Zubiaga De la cal⊙,
and Alessandra Gandini⊙

Abstract The paper discusses the intersection of Cultural Tourism and topics that emerged during the IMPACTOUR project's lifespan. It showcases innovative approaches to managing Cultural Tourism and emphasizes essential trends related to tools and data. The paper also introduces the IMPACTOUR methodology and tool, which enhances the crucial role of Cultural Tourism stakeholders and offers a forward-looking perspective.

Keywords Cultural tourism · Data · Tools · Evaluation · Assessment

1   Introduction

The travel and tourism sector plays a significant role in the global economy, contributing $2.8 trillion to the GDP in 2018 and generating $8.8 trillion including its indirect and induced impacts. It was also the fastest-growing sector in the world in 2018, expanding by 3.9% (World Travel Tourism Council (WTTC) 2019). Europe accounts for a significant portion of the global tourism (see Fig. 1), with Southern Mediterranean destinations making up 21% of the global international tourist arrivals and 15% of international tourism receipts. The top destinations in Europe include France, Spain, Italy, Germany, and the UK. On average, tourism directly contributes 4.4% of GDP and 6.9% of employment, although there are considerable differences among countries.

J. Martins (✉) · P. Pereira · S. Pasandideh · K. Raiyani
NOVA School of Science and Technology, UNINOVA-CTS and LASI, Universidade NOVA de Lisboa, 2829-516 Caparica, Portugal
e-mail: jf.martins@fct.unl.pt

T. Kalvet
Institute of Baltic Studies, Lai 30, 51005 Tartu, Estonia and Department of Business Administration, Tallinn University of Technology 5, 19086 Tallinn, Estonia

M. Z. De la cal · A. Gandini
TECNALIA, Basque Research and Technology Alliance (BRTA), Parque Científico y Tecnológico de Bizkaia, Astondo Bidea, Edificio 700, E-48160 Derio, Spain

B. Neuts et al. (eds.), *Advances in Cultural Tourism Research*, Advances in Digital and Cultural Tourism Management, https://doi.org/10.1007/978-3-031-65537-1_14

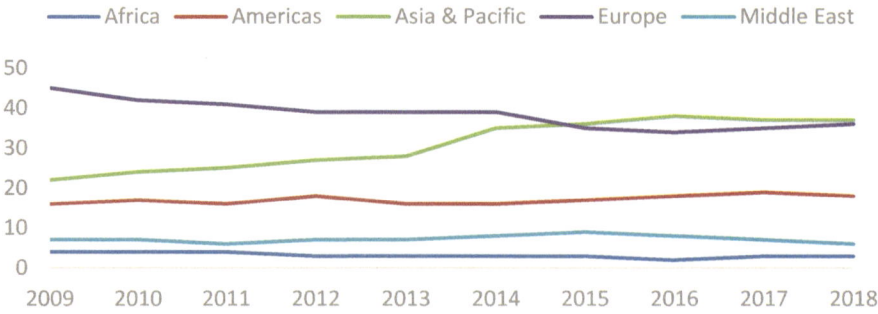

Fig. 1 International tourism expenditure (share %)

Cultural tourism, as a sub-sector of tourism, has been defined as a type of tourism where the visitor's main motivation is to learn and experience the cultural attractions and products in a destination. It has developed towards the mass market and comprises several distinct themes such as historic and cultural heritage, arts, gastronomy, film and music, and tourism based on creative industries. The size of the cultural tourism market is estimated to account for 40% of all international tourism arrivals and is expected to further grow in the coming years (OECD, 2009).

Cultural tourism has the potential to drive growth, jobs, economic development and to substantially reduce seasonality. Cultural tourists are also known to spend more than other tourists, making cultural tourism a significant source of revenue for destinations. However, the economic contribution of cultural tourism can be impacted by factors such as inadequate quality of cultural tourism products and suboptimal policy for pricing cultural tourism products. The demographic, socio-economic, and behavioural characteristics of visitors who travel for cultural tourism are important parameters to consider for the analysis of tourism flows and the management of cultural heritage sites, destinations, and events.

Cultural tourism holds great potential for economic development and job creation, but its impact must be carefully monitored and assessed to inform policy decisions that will best utilize its economic potential. The Cultural Tourism ecosystem must be then prepared to catch up with the economic recovery, supported by three fundamental pillars, as addressed on the IMPACTOUR Re-Discover Europe Workshop: data, people and technology 3.

In order to identify recent key trends related to policy monitoring and evaluation, as well as the use of data and tools in the fields of tourism and cultural tourism, a research process was conducted. Academic sources were analyzed using specific key terms such as " + tourism + impact assessment + evaluation + data" and "cultural tourism." Additionally, policy-relevant sources were identified by employing similar terms and exploring the websites of prominent international organizations such as the European Commission, Eurostat, OECD, and UN/UNWTO.

2   Towards a New Way of Leading Cultural Tourism

Data plays a crucial role in the development and success of cultural tourism for several reasons:

- **Understanding Tourist Demands**: Data helps in understanding the preferences, behaviours and expectations of tourists who are interested in cultural tourism. This information can be used to tailor products and services that meet the needs of these tourists, which can help to attract and retain them.
- **Destination Planning and Development**: Data can be used to identify cultural tourism resources, such as museums, monuments, festivals, and cultural events, and determine their popularity, attendance, and potential for future development. This information can be used to guide destination planning and development, to ensure that resources are being used effectively and efficiently.
- **Market Segmentation**: Data can be used to identify different market segments within the cultural tourism sector, such as heritage tourists, cultural travellers, and adventure tourists. This information can be used to target marketing and promotional efforts more effectively, and to provide tailored products and services that meet the needs of each segment.
- **Evaluation and Assessment**: Data can be used to measure the impact of cultural tourism on local economies and communities, and to evaluate the effectiveness of cultural tourism development strategies. This information can be used to make informed decisions about the future development of cultural tourism, to ensure that it continues to contribute positively to local communities.

2.1   Key Trends Regarding Data and Tools

There are three key trends in the field of data analysis and their applications in public policy.

The first trend is big data, which refers to extremely large data sets that can be analysed computationally to reveal patterns, trends, and associations (Miah et al., 2017). The characteristics of big data include variety, volume, and velocity. Additional characteristics such as volatility, veracity, and value have also been emphasized by some authors (Grover & Kar, 2017). The processing of big data poses several challenges, but it also offers extensive benefits, including social and economic value. The use of big data for public policy is still in its early stages, but it is seen as of strategic importance for the European statistical system.

The second trend described is the rapid development of intelligence and analytical tools, including geoinformation and GIS tools, which are particularly important for cultural tourism assessment. Stakeholders in the tourism sector are increasingly looking for user-friendly solutions for data analysis, with Tableau and Microsoft being leading solutions in this field. Simple visualization applications built on open data access to public statistical data are also making a significant impact, such as the Harvard Growth Lab's Atlas of Economic Complexity (The Atlas of Economic Complexity, 2020).

The third trend is the inclusion of data science tools, particularly predictive analytics, into platforms. Artificial intelligence is seen as having a significant impact on public policies and services, with the potential to free up time for public servants and improve the speed and quality of public services. However, there are also extensive challenges to overcome in this field (Berryhill et al., 2019).

2.2 Key Trends Regarding Data and Tools in Cultural Tourism

The tourism industry is heavily reliant on information and is influenced by current trends in data analytics. The increasing use of Information and Communication Technologies (ICTs) and big data analytics is becoming increasingly important as organizations use their information assets to gain a competitive advantage. The use of big data analytics has been shown to improve the understanding of the consumer market and support strategic decision-making. This has led to the concept of "smart tourism," where advanced technologies and data collection from physical infrastructure, social connections, and human sources are used to transform data into improved experiences and business value-propositions (Xiang et al., 2017).

Smart tourism is based on the concept of "smart destinations", where tourism destinations use ICTs to improve the physical tourism infrastructure. Data generated from smart tourism can support tourism planning and governance, with tourists seen as co-creators of valuable data. The shift in tourism statistics is moving from traditional surveys to big data sources, with big data expected to eventually become the main source of information for tourism statistics.

The benefits of using big data for tourism statistics include the immense volume of information, real-time synchronisation, and granularity. However, there are also challenges, such as potential problems with the alignment of concepts and definitions and issues around objectivity, independence, and trust by users. Potential big data sources for tourism include social media, travel reviews, and location-based data. The potential of open data is also becoming increasingly important, with open data seen as a means of enhancing tourist experiences.

2.3 Emerging Tools for Cultural Tourism Impact Assessment

2.3.1 Mobile Positioning Data

Information and communication technology have enabled the collection of data on tourists and their behaviour through the widespread use of mobile phones. Mobile phones, especially smartphones, have various sensors that can be used to gather information, but most studies are limited in time and space. The main source of data is **mobile positioning data** (MPD) which is collected automatically by mobile network operators and includes the time and location of mobile phone events. Mobile positioning data can be obtained through passive means, which is the majority of mobile phone tracking studies in tourism research. Passive MPD is valuable in analysing human mobility in time, space, and frequency of trips and can be used to describe different forms of temporary mobility including tourism (Ahas et al., 2007).

Despite its potential advantages over traditional data sets, mobile positioning data also has several limitations, including differences in phone use patterns, lack of qualitative information, and difficulties in access to data due to international regulations and network operators' reluctance to provide the data for privacy and confidentiality reasons.

2.3.2   World Wide Web Data

Online big data sources (**World Wide Web Data**) have surfaced in the recent years as a source with a lot of promise for tourism research and evaluation. Whereas satellite imagery or mobile phone data are relatively well-defined as data sources, big data generated from Internet users' online activities constitute more of a mixed basket, including data from various social media sites, online searches, website traffic, online booking and review sites, and so on. A general common denominator of such data is that they are disseminated throughout the Internet. Further, most data collected comes from text messages, images, video or searches voluntarily submitted by persons. Against this background, the following section explores which kind of online data could be collected, analysed and processed into (statistical) information that will be useful for tourism policy purposes.

Geotagged data from social networks (**Social Media Data**) such as Twitter, Foursquare, Flickr, and Instagram have become a valuable source of information on human movement over the past decade (Ahas et al., 2007). Studies in tourism have utilized this data to estimate the number of inbound tourists and profile travellers based on their country of residence, interests, and other tourist attractions visited. Previous studies have successfully used Flickr photo data to quantify visits to tourist sites, predict tourism demand, and extract trend and seasonal patterns. The analysis of textual metadata on Flickr photos can also give valuable information on tourist interests and activities. In addition, Twitter messages with photo attachments, spatial coordinates, hashtags, and social links have also been used to assess users' mobility patterns, trip purposes, and engagement with specific tourism sites. The analysis of Twitter data has shown the potential to assess spatiotemporal fluctuations in mobility, identify popular times for visiting sites, and plan potential attractions.

Tourists are increasingly using online sources, such as search engines and websites, to plan their trips. Big data from online searches (**Web Traffic and Search Data**) is used to measure and forecast tourism arrivals (Gunter & Önder, 2016). The World Economic Forum's Travel and Tourism Competitiveness Index includes a "digital demand" indicator that measures tourists' interest in a country's cultural resources based on the number of related online searches. In addition to search engines, website traffic can also be used for forecasting tourist demand. Previous studies have used website traffic data on Google Analytics for predicting tourism arrivals and Google Trends to predict numbers of visitors to specific tourist attractions such as museums. Similarly, the potential of big data from Wikipedia page views is being actively explored as a source of data on tourism flows.

The growth in **online travel reviews** (OTR) is significant in the field of tourism and hospitality (Marine-Roig & Anton Clavé, 2015). These user-generated data from OTRs are used to study the image of tourism destinations. For example, Roig and Clavé analysed more than 100,000 travel blog posts and online travel reviews to study the image of Barcelona and found recurring problems and discrepancies between the city's branding and visitors' perceptions (Marine-Roig & Anton Clavé, 2015). Another study by Tilly and colleagues supports the use of online travel reviews as a source of macro-level information on the spatio-temporal distribution of tourism and found that the information quality has greatly improved over time and is highly correlated with official statistical sources (Tilly et al., 2015).

2.3.3   Data on Sharing and Collaborative Economy

The collaborative economy has greatly impacted cultural tourism, with the sharing and collaborative economy being used interchangeably. The collaborative economy involves service providers who share assets, resources, time, and/or skills, users of these services, and intermediaries that connect providers with users. The growth of the collaborative economy has been notable in transportation and accommodation with a projected 31% annual growth rate for the global peer-to-peer accommodation economy between 2013 and 2025. Despite the impact of the collaborative economy, comprehensive data on its effect on tourism is limited and nuanced understandings of it and its relationship with tourism remains a challenge. It is seen as a potential contributor to the Sustainable Development Goals (SDG), but critical questions have been raised about whether it is in the public interest and its regulation (O'Rourke & Lollo, 2015). Data from collaborative platforms like Airbnb and Tripadvisor can be a useful source of information on occupancy rates, average prices per night, customer ratings, and more, but access to this data may be limited. Third-party companies like AirDNA collect data from public websites to estimate Airbnb activities. Other collaborative economy practices like car sharing or short-term car rental services have potential to provide useful data on tourist mobility, but accessing proprietary data may be difficult.

2.3.4   Passenger Data

Passenger data is information about individuals' movements to, from, and within a geographic location. There are big data sources for analysing passenger traffic flows, including tourist flows, such as road sensors, taxi GPS logs, online traffic and navigation services, and pedestrian monitoring systems. An example of a pedestrian monitoring system is the Smart Heritage City project in which cameras were used to record the regular patterns of tourist movement and occupancy levels of sites in the Historic City of Ávila (Zubiaga et al., 2019). The gathered data was used to provide city managers with 2-D and 3-D visualizations to identify overcrowded sites and to develop smartphone applications for tourists. However, a common difficulty is that it is often difficult to distinguish between local and tourist traffic. To overcome this, data from road sensors can be complemented with computer vision from traffic control cameras and CCTV surveillance cameras in parking lots to analyse license plates and the size and type of vehicles. Other data sources, such as aviation data and public travel data sources, may also be relevant in analysing passenger traffic connections.

3   Evaluation and Assessment

In the previous section, a wide range of emerging tools were identified for assessing the impact of cultural tourism, providing a general overview of the various possibilities available. However, several limitations were identified in Kalvet et al., (2020a), which were further examined during the IMPACTOUR pilots. The findings indicated that while a number of the innovative data sources and tools have the potential to be useful for evaluating the cultural, social, economic, and environmental impacts of cultural tourism, certain data sets are not readily available at the regional level. Additionally, some of the tools require advanced data science expertise that is not currently available, while others are more applicable to the tourism sector as a whole rather than specifically to cultural tourism (as discussed in Zubiaga et al., 2022b).

Evaluation and Assessment is important in cultural tourism for several reasons:

- To understand the impact of cultural tourism on the host community: Cultural tourism can bring economic benefits to a community, but it can also have negative impacts such as overcrowding and strain on local resources. Assessment helps to understand the positive and negative effects of cultural tourism and identify ways to mitigate any negative impacts.
- To monitor and evaluate the effectiveness of cultural tourism initiatives: By monitoring and evaluating the results of cultural tourism initiatives, such as the development of new attractions or the implementation of cultural heritage preservation programs, it is possible to assess their effectiveness and identify areas for improvement.
- To plan for sustainable cultural tourism development: Assessment helps in developing sustainable cultural tourism initiatives by taking into account the capacities and needs of the host community, as well as the potential impact on the environment and cultural heritage.

- To allocate resources efficiently: Assessment provides information on the demand for cultural tourism and the most popular destinations, allowing for the efficient allocation of resources and the development of targeted marketing and tourism development initiatives.
- To ensure the preservation of cultural heritage: Cultural heritage is an important aspect of cultural tourism, and assessment helps to ensure that cultural heritage is being conserved and managed in a sustainable manner. This is important for preserving cultural heritage for future generations and maintaining its authenticity for tourists.

3.1   The IMPACTOUR Methodology and Tool

Any assessment methodology needs a list of indicators to help stakeholders and destination managers measuring the impact that cultural tourism has or may have on their local sites. Establishing a set of useful, usable and understandable set of criteria and indicators following a clear metrics system, will be essential to compare different cases in similar contexts with the same form of cultural tourism. Several world-wide tourism institutions consider distinct analysis impact domains in their indicator systems, as presented in Table 1.

Dealing with the particular field of Cultural Tourism the IMPACTOUR project proposed a modified set of domain indicators to tackle the Cultural Tourism filed:

- **Characterisation indicators**: Embrace the overall site context indicators that will help understand the site. Those related to comparison criteria, which will help us to discover the relevant issues in each site. General management indicators are also part of this first characterization list of indicators.
- **Resilience indicators**: Related to tourism management when destinations face or may face a crisis (whoever or whatever the source of the crisis is) that produces an adverse change in the circumstances of the site, and therefore directly impacts on the cultural tourism trends; how these crises are measured and how the site's resilience can be measured via indicators.
- **Impact indicators**: Indicators per impact domain. They help understand the need for measuring one or more aspects. We will define the list of impact indicators to be measured in the next steps of the project (the comparative assessment with pilots). Also, inter-relations between indicator Domains are meaningful. The four domains are:
- Cultural domain;
- Social domain;
- Economic domain;
- Environmental domain.

The IMPACTOUR Methodology embodies step-based guidance in the decision-making process that tourism destinations deal with in the selection of the most suitable development Strategies for CT in their site. It was conceived as an operational and

Table 1 Summary of how existing indicator systems tackle the different domains (O'Rourke & Lollo, 2015)

Source	Analysis domains							
	Characterization (or management)	Resilience	Environment	Economic	Socio-economic	Social & cultural (together)	Cultural (separated to social)
UNWTO	X	X	X	X		X	
ETIS	X		X	X		X	
SIROCCO	X		X	X		X	
CO-EVOLVE	X		X	X		X	
MITOMED +		X	X	X		X	
GSTC D-C	X		X		X		X
IMPACTOUR	X	X	X	X	X		X

Fig. 2 Step-based approach of the IMPACTOUR Methodology (Gössling & Michael Hall, 2019)

user-oriented step-by step method to ensure replication beyond the IMPACTOUR Community (see Fig. 2).

Understanding the generic context of the Cultural Tourism sites (urban, rural, natural or itinerary) plus their main Strategic Objectives when facing any transition in Cultural Tourism management, IMPACTOUR Tool will provide them with a set of Strategies and Actions that they can follow.

The IMPACTOUR Tool provides a set of decision support tools for Cultural Tourism stakeholders and pilot and site managers. Users can input and visualize their data, access the Decision Support System and follow the impact of their Actions through the KPIs Graphic Representation or using the Visual analytics Tool (see Fig. 3).

Each user must categorize its own site (urban, rural, natural or itinerary) and also indicate the main type of local cultural activity along with the cultural activity impact. After selecting, and prioritizing, a set of objectives for its site (cultural, social, economic, environmental), the user will be presented with a list of strategies more suitable to his site. After the user chooses the most suitable ones, the IMPACTOUR Tool will display a set of Actions that can be pursued in order to achieve the previously chosen strategies and objectives.

To explore the impact of the adopted Strategies and Actions, evaluating how those Actions are having a positive or negative impact on the performance of sustainable

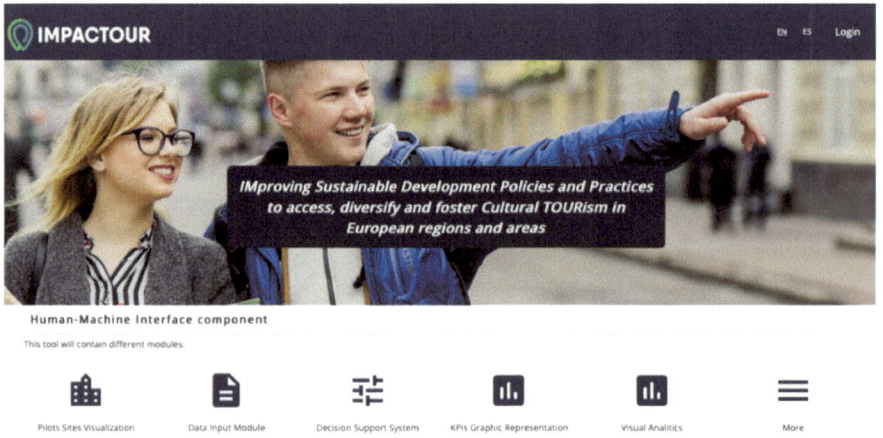

Fig. 3 IMPACTOUR Tool front web page

CT development is mandatory. For that a complete set of Key Performance Indicators (KPIs) was developed and adopted (going beyond the usual indicator systems) comprising **12 Characterization Indicators, 4 Resilience Indicators, 8 Social Indicators, 7 Cultural Indicators, 5 Environmental Indicators, and 10 Economic Indicators**. The complete list of IMPACTOUR Indicators can be found in Gandini et al. (2021).

To compute these Key Performance Indicators data is needed. Good quality data is actually needed to access the impact of the adopted Actions and Strategies in Cultural Tourism development. No accurate assessment can be made without data. In order to compute the 41 IMPACTOUR Key Performance Indicators 110 data elements are needed.

4 The Role of Stakeholders

Stakeholders (Tourists/Travelers, Local communities, National/Regional/Local government, Tour operators, Government agencies, Non-governmental organizations, Museums, galleries, and heritage sites, Local businesses, Tourist guides, Transport providers, Mobile Phone Operators, or Academics and researchers) are important in cultural tourism data gathering process because they have access to primary information, thus they can provide support and collaboration while managing and operating Decision Support System's tools, contributing to the sustainability of the local Cultural Tourism.

Stakeholders can gather cultural tourism data (either manual or automatically) using a variety of ways, including:

- Surveys and Interviews, providing valuable insights into the needs and expectations of visitors.
- Cultural Asset Mapping, identifying, mapping and characterising local cultural assets.
- Tourism Statistics and Data related to tourism in the destination, such as the number of visitors, their spending habits, and their satisfaction levels.

In order to successful use Cultural Tourism Decision Support System's tools, it is important to gather data about the interests, needs, and preferences of visitors as well as the cultural resources available at the destination. Stakeholders can contribute to this data gathering process in a number of ways:

- Providing insights about cultural resources: Stakeholders such as local residents, cultural institutions, municipalities, or historical societies have valuable knowledge about the cultural resources available at the destination. They can provide insights about the history, traditions, and cultural events that visitors may find interesting.
- Collecting data about visitor preferences: Stakeholders such as tourism businesses, tour operators, or even mobile phone operators can collect data about visitor

preferences through surveys, focus groups, and other forms of market research or data gathering.

- Monitoring visitor behaviour: Stakeholders such as tourism businesses and attractions can use data from visitor behaviour, such as ticket sales and visitor numbers, to understand which cultural tourism experiences are most popular and adjust their offerings accordingly.

Stakeholders play a critical role in data gathering for cultural tourism initiatives, and their input and insights can help to ensure that cultural tourism experiences are engaging, informative, and enjoyable for visitors. IMPACTOUR project gathered a large number of stakeholders grouped around 30 Pilots, with distinct characteristics spread around Europe (https://www.impactour.eu/).

The involvement of stakeholders in the IMPACTOUR data gathering information process was essential to access relevant data sources, maximise the quality of gathered information and identifying the best practices and roles that involved actors play in the development of cultural tourism strategies. However, in order to be effective and motivated, their commitment must include a human dimension highly related to the governance of the projects they are involved.

5 The Future Vision

Digital transformation is the basis for a new diversity paradigm, where new offers and markets will come into place. Cultural Tourism new markets and new tourist profiles will undoubtedly consider new indicators where quality outperforms quantity. Often forgotten, accessibility issues will provide huge benefits for the Cultural Tourism ecosystem.

In Europe, culture plays a vital role in sustainable development as it is both a driver and an enabler of it. The region's cultural richness is particularly significant for global and local ecosystems, making it an invaluable resource for sustainable development in education, the economy, and tourism. As local communities are the primary beneficiaries of sustainable Cultural Tourism, it is of utmost important to develop their sense of natural and cultural pride, being themselves, not copying others.

The effective use of data is essential for enhancing the quality of information and communication among stakeholders in the Cultural Tourism ecosystem (Kalvet et al., 2020b). Leveraging "smart" data has become a crucial element in the transition towards a collaborative economy framework. Adopting a multisectoral and interdisciplinary approach that engages local communities, tourism providers, visitors, and digital platform intermediaries is critical. This approach enables decision-making that is backed by recorded evidence and analysis of best practices, as envisaged by the IMPACTOUR methodology and tool.

Local communities, SMEs, cooperatives, and CCIs are critical to promoting people-centric innovation and entrepreneurship in Cultural Tourism. By engaging people from all walks of life, they can reach new markets and create strong emotional bonds based on local cultural roots. The new generation of entrepreneurs should adopt lifelong learning strategies and have access to cutting-edge technologies and deep knowledge. By engaging with and respecting local communities, we can promote social inclusion and cohesion, leading to a shared identity and unity.

Acknowledgements This work has been supported by the project IMPACTOUR, "IMproving Sustainable Development Policies and Practices to access, diversify and foster Cultural TOURism in European regions and areas" which has received funding from the European Union's Horizon 2020 research and innovation programme under grant agreement No 870747 and from TEXTOUR, "Social Innovation and TEchnologies for sustainable growth through participative cultural TOURism" which has received funding from the European Union's Horizon 2020 research and innovation programme under grant agreement No 101004687. Additional support was granted by national funds through FCT Fundação para a Ciência e a Tecnologia with reference UIDB/00066/2020 and UIDP/00066/2020.

References

World Travel & Tourism Council (WTTC). (2019). Travel & Tourism. Economic Impact 2019. Retrieved 22 February, 2023, from https://wttc.org/Research/Economic-Impact.

OECD. (2009). The Impact of Culture on Tourism, Paris. Retrieved 22 February, 2023, from https://www.oecd.org/cfe/tourism/theimpactofcultureontourism.htm.

Consensus Declaration. (2021, 9 May). IMPACTOUR ReDiscover Europe Workshop. Retrieved 22 February, 2023, from https://www.impactour.eu/pages/consensus-declaration-rediscover-eur ope-workshop.

Miah, S. J., Vu, H. Q., Gammack, J., & McGrath, M. (2017, September). A big data analytics method for tourist behaviour analysis. *Information and Management, 54*(6), 771–785. https://doi.org/10.1016/j.im.2016.11.011.

Grover, P., & Kar, A. K. (2017). Big data analytics: A review on theoretical contributions and tools used in literature. *Global Journal of Flexible Systems Management, 18*(3), 203–229. https://doi.org/10.1007/s40171-017-0159-3

The Growth Lab at Harvard University. (2020). The Atlas of Economic Complexity. Retrieved 13 July, 2020, from https://atlas.cid.harvard.edu/.

Berryhill, J., Heang, K. K., Clogher, R., & McBride, Hello, K. (2019). World: Artificial intelligence and its use in the public sector. OECD Working Papers on Public Governance, No. 36. Paris: OECD Publishing.

Xiang, Z., & Fesenmaier, D. R. (2017). Big data analytics, tourism design and smart tourism. In Z. Xiang & D. Fesenmaier (Eds.), *Analytics in smart tourism design, tourism on the verge* (pp. 299–307). Springer.

Ahas, R., Aasa, A., Roose, A., Mark, Ü., & Silm, S. (2007). Evaluating passive mobile positioning data for tourism surveys: An Estonian case study. *Tourism Management, 29*(3), 469–486. https://doi.org/10.1016/j.tourman.2007.05.014.

Zheng, Y. T., Zha, Z. J., & Chua, T. S. (2012). Mining travel patterns from geotagged photos. *ACM Transactions on Intelligent Systems and Technology, 3*(3), 1–18. https://doi.org/10.1145/2168752.2168770.

Gunter, U., & Önder, I. (2016). Forecasting city arrivals with Google Analytics. *Annals of Tourism Research, 61*, 199–212. https://doi.org/10.1016/j.annals.2016.10.007.

Signorelli, S., Reis, F., & Biffignandi, S. (2020). What attracts tourists while planning for a journey? An analysis of three cities through Wikipedia page views. *Global Forum on Tourism Statistics, Venice*. Retrieved 13 July, 2020, from https://www.researchgate.net/publication/310605164.

Marine-Roig, E., & Anton Clavé, S. (2015). Tourism analytics with massive user- generated content: A case study of Barcelona. *Journal of Destination Marketing and Management, 4*(3), 162–172. https://doi.org/10.1016/j.jdmm.2015.06.004.

Tilly, R., Fischbach, K., & Schoder, D. (2015). Mineable or messy? Assessing the quality of macro-level tourism information derived from social media. *Electronic Markets, 25*(3), 227–241. https://doi.org/10.1007/s12525-015-0181-2.

O'Rourke, D., & Lollo, N. (2015). Transforming consumption: From decoupling, to behavior change, to system changes for sustainable consumption. *Annual Review of Environment and Resources, 40*(1), 233–259. https://doi.org/10.1146/annurev-environ-102014-021224

Gössling, S., & Michael Hall, C. (2019). Sharing versus collaborative economy: how to align ICT developments and the SDGs in tourism? *Journal of Sustainable Tourism, 27*(1), 74–96. https://doi.org/10.1080/09669582.2018.1560455.

Zubiaga, M., Izkara, J. L., Gandini, A., Alonso, I., & Saralegui, U. (2019). Towards smarter management of overtourism in historic centres through visitor-flow monitoring. *Sustainability, 11*(24), 7254. https://doi.org/10.3390/SU11247254.

Alessandra Gandini, Elena Usobiaga, Mikel Zubiaga, Amaia Sopelana. (2021). List of criteria and indicators to carry out the comparative assessment. IMPACTOUR Deliverable 2.1. Retrieved February, 2023, from https://www.impactour.eu/.

Zubiaga, M., Gandini, A., & Sopelana, A. (2022a). Sustainable cultural tourism methodology and validation. *Impactour Deliverable, 4*, 4.

Kalvet, T., Olesk, M., Tiits, M., & Raun, J. (2020a). Identification of tools for cultural tourism impact assessment. *Impactour Deliverable, 1*, 3.

Zubiaga, M., Gandini, A., & Sopelana, A. (2022b). IMPACTOUR key performance indicators. *Impactour Deliverable, 4*, 2.

Kalvet, T., Olesk, M., Tiits, M., & Raun, J. (2020b). Innovative tools for tourism and cultural tourism impact assessment. *Sustainability, 12*(18), 7470. https://doi.org/10.3390/su12187470